States United

The Tariffs of 1894 and 1897 on Imports into the United States,

and customs administrative act of June 10, 1890, with amendments to sections 7

and 11. Indexed.

States United

The Tariffs of 1894 and 1897 on Imports into the United States,
and customs administrative act of June 10, 1890, with amendments to sections 7 and 11.
Indexed.

ISBN/EAN: 9783337256333

Printed in Europe, USA, Canada, Australia, Japan

Cover: Foto ©Suzi / pixelio.de

More available books at **www.hansebooks.com**

THE TARIFFS OF 1894 AND 1897

ON

IMPORTS INTO THE UNITED STATES,

AND

CUSTOMS ADMINISTRATIVE ACT OF JUNE 10, 1890, WITH AMENDMENTS TO SECTIONS 7 AND 11.

INDEXED.

WASHINGTON:

GOVERNMENT PRINTING OFFICE.

1897.

THE TARIFFS OF 1894 AND 1897

ON

IMPORTS INTO THE UNITED STATES,

AND

CUSTOMS ADMINISTRATIVE ACT OF JUNE 10, 1890, WITH AMENDMENTS TO SECTIONS 7 AND 11,

INDEXED.

WASHINGTON:

GOVERNMENT PRINTING OFFICE.

1897.

TREASURY DEPARTMENT,
Document No. 1953.
Office of Secretary, Division of Customs.

THE TARIFF

ON

IMPORTS INTO THE UNITED STATES

AND THE

FREE LIST

AS

CONTAINED IN ACT OF AUGUST 28, 1894.

SCHEDULES.

5

An Act To reduce taxation, to provide revenue for the Government, and for other purposes.

Be it enacted by the Senate and House of Representatives of the United States of America in Congress assembled, That on and after the first day of August, eighteen hundred and ninety-four, unless otherwise specially provided for in this Act, there shall be levied, collected, and paid upon all articles imported from foreign countries or withdrawn for consumption, and mentioned in the schedules herein contained, the rates of duty which are, by the schedules and paragraphs, respectively prescribed, namely:

SCHEDULE A.—CHEMICALS, OILS, AND PAINTS.

ACIDS.—

1. Acetic or pyroligneous acid, twenty per centum ad valorem.
2. Boracic acid, three cents per pound.
3. Chromic acid, four cents per pound.
4. Citric acid, twenty-five per centum ad valorem.
5. Tannic acid or tannin, sixty cents per pound.
6. Tartaric acid, twenty per centum ad valorem.
7. Alcoholic perfumery, including cologne water and other toilet waters, and alcoholic compounds not specially provided for in this Act, two dollars per gallon and fifty per centum ad valorem.
8. Alumina, alum, alum cake, patent alum, sulphate of alumina, and aluminous cake, and alum in crystals or ground, four-tenths of one cent per pound.
8½. Ammonia, carbonate of, twenty per centum ad valorem; muriate of, or sal ammoniac, ten per centum ad valorem; sulphate of, twenty per centum ad valorem.
9. Blacking of all kinds, twenty per centum ad valorem. Bone char suitable for use in decolorizing sugars, twenty per centum ad valorem.
10. Borax, crude, or borate of soda, two cents per pound; borate of lime, one and one-half cents per pound. Refined borax, two cents per pound.
10½. Camphor, refined, ten per centum ad valorem.
11. Chalk, prepared, precipitated, French, red, and all other chalk preparations not specially provided for in this Act, twenty per centum ad valorem.
12. Chloral hydrate, twenty-five per centum ad valorem.
13. Chloroform, twenty-five cents per pound.

COAL-TAR PREPARATIONS.—

14. All coal-tar colors or dyes, by whatever name known, and not specially provided for in this Act, twenty-five per centum ad valorem.
14½. Cobalt, oxide of, twenty-five cents per pound.
15. Collodion and all compounds of pyroxyline, by whatever name known, forty cents per pound; rolled or in sheets, but not made up

into articles, fifty cents per pound; if in finished or partly finished articles, forty-five per centum ad valorem.

16. Coloring for brandy, wine, beer, or other liquors, fifty per centum ad valorem.

16½. Drugs, such as barks, beans, berries, balsams, buds, bulbs, bulbous roots, excrescences, fruits, flowers, dried fibers, dried insects, grains, gums and gum resin, herbs, leaves, lichens, mosses, nuts, roots and stems, spices, vegetables, seeds (aromatic, not garden seeds), seeds of morbid growth, weeds, and woods used expressly for dyeing; any of the foregoing which are not edible, but which are advanced in value or condition by refining or grinding, or by other process of manufacture, and not specially provided for in this Act, ten per centum ad valorem.

17. Ethers, sulphuric, forty cents per pound; spirits of nitrous ether, twenty-five cents per pound; fruit ethers, oils, or essences, two dollars per pound; ether of all kinds not specially provided for in this Act, one dollar per pound.

18. Extracts and decoctions of logwood and other dyewoods, extract of sumac, and extracts of barks, such as are commonly used for dyeing or tanning, not specially provided for in this Act, and extracts of hemlock bark, ten per centum ad valorem.

19. Gelatine, glue, isinglass or fish glue, and prepared fish bladders or fish sounds, twenty-five per centum ad valorem.

20. Glycerine, crude, not purified, one cent per pound; refined, three cents per pound.

21. Ink and ink powders, printers' ink, and all other ink not specially provided for in this Act, twenty-five per centum ad valorem.

22. Iodoform, one dollar per pound.

23. Licorice, extracts of, in paste, rolls, or other forms, five cents per pound.

24. Magnesia, carbonate of, medicinal, three cents per pound; calcined, seven cents per pound; sulphate of, or Epsom salts, one-fifth of one cent per pound.

25. Morphia, or morphine, and all salts thereof, fifty cents per ounce.

OILS.—

26. Alizarine assistant, or soluble oil, or oleate of soda, or Turkey red oil, thirty per centum ad valorem.

27. Castor oil, thirty-five cents per gallon.

28. Cod-liver oil, twenty per centum ad valorem.

29. Flaxseed or linseed and poppy-seed oil, raw, boiled, or oxidized, twenty cents per gallon of seven and one-half pounds weight.

30. Fusel oil, or amylic alcohol, ten per centum ad valorem.

31. Hemp-seed oil and rape-seed oil, ten cents per gallon.

32. Olive oil, fit for salad purposes, thirty-five cents per gallon.

33. Peppermint oil, twenty-five per centum ad valorem.

34. Seal, herring, whale, and other fish oil not specially provided for in this Act, twenty-five per centum ad valorem.

35. Opium, aqueous extract of, for medicinal uses, and tincture of, as laudanum, and all other liquid preparations of opium, not specially provided for in this Act, twenty per centum ad valorem.

36. Opium containing less than nine per centum of morphia, and opium prepared for smoking, six dollars per pound; but opium prepared for smoking and other preparations of opium deposited in bonded warehouse shall not be removed therefrom without payment of duties, and such duties shall not be refunded.

PAINTS, COLORS, AND VARNISHES.—

37. Baryta, sulphate of, or barytes, manufactured, three dollars per ton.

38. Blues, such as Berlin, Prussian, Chinese, and all others, containing ferrocyanide of iron, dry or ground in or mixed with oil, six cents per pound; and in pulp or mixed with water, six cents per pound on the material contained therein when dry.

39. Blanc-fixe, or artificial sulphate of barytes and satin white, or artificial sulphate of lime, twenty-five per centum ad valorem.

40. Black, made from bone, ivory, or vegetable, under whatever name known, including bone black and lampblack, dry or ground in oil or water, twenty per centum ad valorem.

41. Chrome yellow, chrome green, and all other chromium colors in which lead and bichromate of potash or soda are component parts, dry or ground in or mixed with oil, or in pulp or mixed with water, three cents per pound on the material contained therein when dry.

42. Ocher and ochery earths, sienna and sienna earths, umber and umber earths, ground in oil, one and one-fourth of one cent per pound.

43. Ultramarine blue, whether dry, in pulp, or mixed with water, and wash blue containing ultramarine, three cents per pound.

44. Varnishes, including so-called gold size or japan, twenty-five per centum ad valorem; and on spirit, varnishes for the alcohol contained therein, one dollar and thirty-two cents per gallon additional.

45. Vermilion red, and other colors containing quicksilver, dry or ground in oil or water, twenty per centum ad valorem; vermilion red, not containing quicksilver but made of lead or containing lead, six cents per pound.

46. Whiting and Paris white, dry, one-fourth of one cent per pound; ground in oil, or putty, one-half of one cent per pound.

47. Zinc, oxide of, and white paint or pigment containing zinc, dry or ground in oil, one cent per pound.

48. All other paints, colors, and pigments, whether dry or mixed, or ground in water or oil, or other solutions, including all colors in tubes, lakes, crayons, smalts, and frostings, and not specially provided for in this Act, twenty-five per centum ad valorem.

LEAD PRODUCTS.—

49. Acetate of lead, white, two and three-quarters cents per pound; brown, one and three-quarters cents per pound; litharge, one and one-half cents per pound.

50. Nitrate of lead, one and one-half cents per pound.

51. Orange mineral, one and three-quarters cents per pound; red lead, one and one-half cents per pound.

52. White lead, and white paint and pigment containing lead, dry or in pulp, or ground or mixed with oil, one and one-half cents per pound.

53. Phosphorus, fifteen cents per pound.

POTASH.—

54. Bichromate and chromate of, twenty-five per centum ad valorem.

55. Hydriodate, iodide, and iodate of, twenty-five cents per pound.

56. Nitrate of, or saltpeter, refined, one-half of one cent per pound.

57. Prussiate of, red, or yellow, twenty-five per centum ad valorem.

PREPARATIONS.—

58. All medicinal preparations, including medicinal coal-tar preparations and medicinal proprietary preparations, of which alcohol is a component part, or in the preparation of which alcohol is used, not specially provided for in this Act, fifty cents per pound: *Provided*, That no such preparation shall pay less than twenty-five per centum ad valorem.

59. All medicinal preparations, not specially provided for in this Act, twenty-five per centum ad valorem.

59½. Paris green and London purple, twelve and one-half per centum ad valorem.

60. Products or preparations known as alkalies, alkaloids, distilled oils, essential oils, expressed oils, rendered oils, and all combinations of the foregoing, and all chemical compounds and salts, not specially provided for in this Act, twenty-five per centum ad valorem.

61. Preparations used as applications to the hair, mouth, teeth, or skin, such as cosmetics, dentifrices, pastes, pomades, powders, and all toilet preparations, and articles of perfumery, not specially provided for in this Act, forty per centum ad valorem.

62. Santonine, and all salts thereof containing eighty per centum or over of santonine, one dollar per pound.

SOAP.—

63. Castile soap, twenty per centum ad valorem; fancy, perfumed, and all descriptions of toilet and medicinal or medicated soap, thirty-five per centum ad valorem; all other soaps, not specially provided for in this Act, ten per centum ad valorem.

SODA.—

64. Bicarbonate of soda or supercarbonate of soda or saleratus, one-half cent per pound.

65. Hydrate of, or caustic soda, one-half of one cent per pound.

66. Bichromate and chromate of, twenty-five per centum ad valorem.

67. Sal soda, or soda crystals, one-eighth of one cent per pound; soda ash, one-fourth of one cent per pound.

68. Silicate of soda, or other alkaline silicate, three-eighths of one cent per pound.

69. Sponges, sea moss or Iceland moss, ten per centum ad valorem.

70. Strychnia, or strychnine, and all salts thereof, thirty cents per ounce.

71. Sulphur, refined, sublimed, or flowers of, twenty per centum ad valorem.

72. Sumac, ground, ten per centum ad valorem.

73. Tartar, cream of, and patent tartar, twenty per centum ad valorem.

74. Tartars and lees crystals, partly refined, twenty per centum ad valorem.

75. Tartrate of soda and potassa, or Rochelle salts, two cents per pound.

SCHEDULE B.—EARTHS, EARTHENWARE, AND GLASSWARE.

BRICK AND TILE:

76. Brick, not glazed, enameled, ornamented, or decorated in any manner, twenty-five per centum ad valorem; glazed, enameled, ornamented, or decorated, thirty per centum ad valorem.

77. Magnesic fire-brick, one dollar per ton.
78. Tiles, plain, not glazed, ornamented, painted, enameled, vitrified, or decorated, twenty-five per centum ad valorem; ornamented, glazed, painted, enameled, vitrified, or decorated, and encaustic, forty per centum ad valorem.

CEMENT, LIME, AND PLASTER:
79. Roman, Portland, and other hydraulic cement, in barrels, sacks, or other packages, eight cents per one hundred pounds, including weight of barrel or package; in bulk, seven cents per one hundred pounds; other cement, ten per centum ad valorem.
80. Lime, five cents per one hundred pounds, including weight of barrel or package.
81. Plaster of Paris, or gypsum, ground, one dollar per ton; calcined, one dollar and twenty-five cents per ton.

CLAYS OR EARTHS:
82. Clays or earths, unwrought or unmanufactured, not specially provided for in this Act, one dollar per ton; wrought or manufactured, not specially provided for in this Act, two dollars per ton; china clay or kaolin, two dollars per ton.

EARTHENWARE AND CHINA:
83. Common yellow and brown earthenware, plain or embossed, common stoneware, and crucibles, not decorated in any manner, twenty per centum ad valorem.
84. China, porcelain, parian, bisque, earthen, stone and crockery ware, including placques, ornaments, toys, charms, vases, and statuettes, white, not changed in condition by superadded ornamentation or decoration, thirty per centum ad valorem.
85. China, porcelain, parian, bisque, earthen, stone, and crockery ware, including plaques, ornaments, toys, charms, vases, and statuettes, painted, tinted, enameled, printed, gilded, or otherwise decorated in any manner, thirty-five per centum ad valorem.
86. All articles composed of earthen or mineral substances, including lava tips for burners, not specially provided for in this Act, if decorated in any manner, forty per centum ad valorem; if not decorated, thirty per centum ad valorem.
87. Gas retorts, twenty per centum ad valorem.

GLASS AND GLASSWARE:
88. Green and colored, molded, or pressed, and flint and lime glass bottles holding more than one pint, and demijohns and carboys, covered or uncovered, whether filled or unfilled and whether their contents be dutiable or free, and other molded or pressed green and colored and flint or lime bottle glassware, not specially provided for in this Act, three-fourths of one cent per pound; and vials, holding not more than one pint and not less than one-quarter of a pint, one and one-eighth cents per pound; if holding less than one-fourth of a pint, forty cents per gross; all other plain green and colored, molded or pressed, and flint lime and glassware, forty per centum ad valorem.
89. All articles of glass, cut, engraved, painted, colored, printed, stained, decorated, silvered, or gilded, not including plate glass silvered, or looking-glass plates, forty per centum ad valorem.

90. All glass bottles, decanters, or other vessels or articles of glass, when cut, engraved, painted, colored, printed, stained, etched, or otherwise ornamented or decorated, except such as have ground necks and stoppers only, not specially provided for in this Act, including porcelain or opal glassware, forty per centum ad valorem: *Provided*, That if such articles shall be imported filled, the same shall pay duty, in addition to any duty chargeable upon the contents as if not filled, unless otherwise specially provided for in this Act.

91. Unpolished cylinder, crown and common window glass, not exceeding ten by fifteen inches square, one cent per pound; above that, and not exceeding sixteen by twenty-four inches square, one and one-fourth cents per pound; above that, and not exceeding twenty-four by thirty inches square, one and three-fourths cents per pound; above that, and not exceeding twenty-four by thirty-six inches square, two cents per pound; all above that, two and one-eighth cents per pound: *Provided*, That unpolished cylinder, crown and common window glass, imported in boxes, shall be packed fifty square feet per box as nearly as sizes will permit, and the duty shall be computed thereon according to the actual weight of glass.

92. Cylinder and crown glass, polished, not exceeding sixteen by twenty-four inches square, two and one-half cents per square foot; above that, and not exceeding twenty-four by thirty inches square, four cents per square foot; above that, and not exceeding twenty-four by sixty inches square, fifteen cents per square foot; above that, twenty cents per square foot.

93. Fluted, rolled, or rough plate glass, not including crown, cylinder, or common window glass, not exceeding sixteen by twenty-four inches square, three-fourths of one cent per square foot; above that, and not exceeding twenty-four by thirty inches square, one cent per square foot; all above that, one and one-half cents per square foot; and all fluted, rolled, or rough plate glass, weighing over one hundred pounds per one hundred square feet, shall pay an additional duty on the excess at the same rates herein imposed: *Provided*, That all of the above plate glass when ground, smoothed, or otherwise obscured, shall be subject to the same rate of duty as cast polished plate glass unsilvered.

94. Cast polished plate glass, finished or unfinished and unsilvered, not exceeding sixteen by twenty-four inches square, five cents per square foot; above that, and not exceeding twenty-four by thirty inches square, eight cents per square foot; above that, and not exceeding twenty-four by sixty inches square, twenty-two and one-half cents per square foot; all above that, thirty-five cents per square foot.

95. Cast polished plate glass, silvered, and looking-glass plates, exceeding in size one hundred and forty-four square inches, and not exceeding sixteen by twenty-four inches square, six cents per square foot; above that, and not exceeding twenty-four by thirty inches square, ten cents per square foot; above that, and not exceeding twenty-four by sixty inches square, twenty-three cents per square foot; all above that, thirty-eight cents per square foot.

96. But no looking-glass plates or plate glass, silvered, when framed, shall pay a less rate of duty than that imposed upon similar

glass of like description not framed, but shall pay in addition thereto upon such frames the rate of duty applicable thereto when imported separate.

97. Cast polished plate glass, silvered or unsilvered, and cylinder, crown, or common window glass, when bent, ground, obscured, frosted, sanded, enameled, beveled, etched, embossed, engraved, flashed, stained, colored, painted, or otherwise ornamented or decorated, shall be subject to a duty of ten per centum ad valorem in addition to the rates otherwise chargeable thereon.

98. Spectacles, eyeglasses, goggles, opera glasses, and other optical instruments and frames for the same, forty per centum ad valorem.

99. Glass beads, loose, strung, or carded, ten per centum ad valorem.

100. Lenses of glass or pebble, wholly or partly manufactured, thirty-five per centum ad valorem.

101. Fusible enamel, and glass slides for magic lanterns, twenty-five per centum ad valorem.

102. All stained or painted glass windows, or parts thereof, and all mirrors not exceeding in size one hundred and forty-four square inches, with or without frames or cases, and all manufactures of glass, or of which glass is the component of chief value, not specially provided for in this Act, thirty-five per centum ad valorem.

MARBLE AND STONE, AND MANUFACTURES OF:

103. Marble of all kinds in block, rough or squared only, fifty cents per cubic foot.

104. Marble, sawed, dressed or otherwise, including marble slabs, mosaic cubes, and marble paving tiles, eighty-five cents per cubic foot (no slab to be computed at less than one inch in thickness).

105. Manufactures of marble, onyx, or alabaster not specially provided for in this Act, forty-five per centum ad valorem.

STONE:

105½. Freestone, granite, sandstone, limestone and other building or monumental stone, except marble, unmanufactured, or undressed, not specially provided for in this Act, seven cents per cubic foot.

106. Freestone, granite, sandstone, limestone, and other building or monumental stone, except marble, not specially provided for in this Act, hewn, dressed, or polished, thirty per centum ad valorem.

107. Grindstones, finished or unfinished, ten per centum ad valorem.

SLATE:

108. Slates, slate chimney pieces, mantels, slabs for tables, and all other manufactures of slate not specially provided for in this Act, twenty per centum ad valorem.

109. Roofing slates, twenty per centum ad valorem.

14

SCHEDULE C.—METALS AND MANUFACTURES OF.

IRON AND STEEL.

109½. Iron ore, including manganiferous iron ore, also the dross or residuum from burnt pyrites, forty cents per ton.

110. Iron in pigs, iron kentledge, spiegeleisen, ferro-manganese, ferro-silicon, wrought and cast scrap iron, and scrap steel, four dollars per ton; but nothing shall be deemed scrap iron or scrap steel except waste or refuse iron or steel fit only to be remanufactured.

111. Round iron, in coils or rods, less than seven-sixteenths of one inch in diameter, and bars or shapes of rolled iron, not specially provided for in this Act, eight-tenths of one cent per pound: *Provided*, That all iron in slabs, blooms, loops, or other forms less finished than iron in bars, and more advanced than pig iron, except castings, shall be subject to a duty of five-tenths of one cent per pound: *Provided further*, That all iron bars, blooms, billets, or sizes or shapes of any kind, in the manufacture of which charcoal is used as fuel, shall be subject to a duty of twelve dollars per ton.

112. Bar iron, rolled or hammered, comprising flats not less than one inch wide nor less than three-eighths of one inch thick, six-tenths of one cent per pound; round iron not less than three-fourths of one inch in diameter, and square iron not less than three-fourths of one inch square, six-tenths of one cent per pound; flats less than one inch wide, or less than three-eighths of one inch thick; round iron less than three-fourths of one inch and not less than seven-sixteenths of one inch in diameter; and square iron less than three-fourths of one inch square, six-tenths of one cent per pound.

113. Beams, girders, joists, angles, channels, car-truck channels, T T, columns and posts or parts or sections of columns and posts, deck and bulb beams, and building forms together with all other structural shapes of iron or steel, whether plain or punched, or fitted for use, six-tenths of one cent per pound.

114. Boiler or other plate iron or steel, except saw plates hereinafter provided for, not thinner than number ten wire gauge, sheared or unsheared, and skelp iron or steel sheared or rolled in grooves, valued at one cent per pound or less, five-tenths of one cent per pound; valued above one cent and not above one and one-half cents, six-tenths of one cent per pound; valued above one and one-half cents and not above four cents per pound, thirty per centum ad valorem; valued at over four cents per pound, twenty-five per centum ad valorem: *Provided*, That all plate iron or steel thinner than number ten wire gauge shall pay duty as iron or steel sheets.

115. Forgings of iron or steel, or forged iron or steel combined, of whatever shape, or in whatever stage of manufacture, not specially provided for in this Act, one and one-half cents per pound: *Provided*, That no forgings of iron or steel, or forgings of iron and steel combined, by whatever process made, shall pay a less rate of duty than thirty-five per centum ad valorem.

116. Hoop, band, or scroll iron or steel, except as otherwise provided for in this Act, thirty per centum ad valorem.

117. Railway bars, made of iron or steel, and railway bars made in part of steel, T rails, and punched iron or steel flat rails, seven-twentieths of one cent per pound.

118. Sheets of iron or steel, common or black, including all iron or

steel commercially known as common or black taggers iron or steel, and skelp iron or steel, valued at three cents per pound or less, thinner than number ten and not thinner than number twenty wire gauge, seven-tenths of one cent per pound; thinner than number twenty wire gauge and not thinner than number twenty-five wire gauge, eight-tenths cent per pound; thinner than number twenty-five wire gauge, one and one-tenth cents per pound; corrugated or crimped, one and one-tenth cents per pound: *Provided*, That all common or black sheet iron or sheet steel not thinner than number ten wire gauge shall pay duty as plate iron or plate steel.

119. All iron or steel sheets or plates, and all hoop, band or scroll iron or steel, excepting what are known commercially as tin plates, terne plates, and taggers tin, and hereinafter provided for, when galvanized or coated with zinc or spelter, or other metals, or any alloy of those metals, shall pay one-fourth of one cent per pound more duty than the rates imposed by the preceding paragraph upon the corresponding gauges or forms of common or black sheet or taggers iron or steel.

120. Sheet iron or sheet steel, polished, planished, or glanced, by whatever name designated, one and three-fourths cents per pound: *Provided*, That plate or sheet or taggers iron or steel, by whatever name designated, other than the polished, planished, or glanced herein provided for, which has been pickled or cleaned by acid, or by any other material or process, or which is cold-rolled, smoothed only, not polished, shall pay one-eighth of one cent per pound more duty than the corresponding gauges of common or black sheet or taggers iron or steel.

121. Sheets or plates of iron or steel, or taggers iron or steel, coated with tin or lead, or with a mixture of which these metals, or either of them, is a component part, by the dipping or any other process, and commercially known as tin plates, terne plates, and taggers tin, one and one-fifth cents per pound: *Provided*, That the reduction of duty herein provided for shall take effect on and after October first, eighteen hundred and ninety-four. No article not specially provided for in this Act, wholly or partly manufactured from tin plate, terne plate, or the sheet, or plate iron or steel herein provided for, or of which such tin plate, terne plate, sheet, or plate iron or steel shall be the material of chief value, shall pay a lower rate of duty than that imposed on the tin plate, terne plate, or sheet, or plate iron or steel from which it is made, or of which it shall be the component thereof of chief value.

122. Steel ingots, cogged ingots, blooms, and slabs, by whatever process made; die blocks or blanks; billets and bars and tapered or beveled bars; steamer, crank, and other shafts; shafting; wrist or crank pins; connecting rods and piston rods; pressed, sheared, or stamped shapes; saw plates, wholly or partially manufactured; hammer molds or swaged steel; gun-barrel molds not in bars; alloys used as substitutes for steel in the manufacture of tools; all descriptions and shapes of dry sand, loam, or iron-molded steel castings; sheets and plates not specially provided for in this Act; and steel in all forms and shapes not specially provided for in this Act, all of the above valued at one cent per pound or less, three-tenths of one cent per pound; valued above one cent and not above one and four-tenths cents per pound, four-tenths of one cent per pound; valued above one and four-tenths cents and not above one and eight-tenths cents per pound, six-tenths of one cent per pound; valued above one and eight-tenths cents and not above two and two-tenths cents per pound, seven-tenths of one cent per pound; valued above two and two-tenths cents

and not above three cents per pound, nine-tenths of one cent per pound; valued above three cents per pound and not above four cents per pound, one and two-tenths cents per pound; valued above four cents and not above seven cents per pound, one and three-tenths cents per pound; valued above seven cents and not above ten cents per pound, one and nine-tenths cents per pound; valued above ten cents and not above thirteen cents per pound, two and four-tenths cents per pound; valued above thirteen cents and not above sixteen cents per pound, two and eight-tenths cents per pound; valued above sixteen cents per pound, four and seven-tenths cents per pound.

WIRE:

123. Wire rods: Rivet, screw, fence, and other iron or steel wire rods, whether round, oval, flat, or square, or in any other shape, and nail rods, in coils or otherwise, valued at four cents or less per pound, four-tenths cent per pound; valued over four cents per pound, three-fourths cent per pound: *Provided*, That all round iron or steel rods smaller than number six wire gauge shall be classed and dutiable as wire.

124. Wire: Round iron or steel wire, all sizes not smaller than thirteen wire gauge, one and one-fourth cents per pound; smaller than thirteen wire gauge, and not smaller than sixteen wire gauge, one and one-half cents per pound; smaller than sixteen wire gauge, two cents per pound; all other iron or steel wire and wire or strip steel, commonly known as crinoline wire, corset wire, drill rods, needle wire, piano wire, clock and watch wires, and all steel wires, whether polished or unpolished, in coils or straightened, and cut to lengths, drawn cold through dies, and hat wire, flat steel wire, or sheet steel in strips, uncovered or covered with cotton, silk, or other material, or metal, and all the foregoing manufactures of iron or steel, of whatever shape or form, valued above four cents per pound, shall pay a duty of forty per centum ad valorem: *Provided*, That articles manufactured from iron or steel wire shall pay the maximum rate of duty which would be imposed upon any wire used in the manufacture of such articles and in addition thereto one cent per pound.

GENERAL PROVISIONS.

125. No allowance or reduction of duties for partial loss or damage in consequence of rust or of discoloration shall be made upon any description of iron or steel, or upon any article wholly or partly manufactured of iron or steel.

MANUFACTURES OF IRON AND STEEL.

126. Anchors, or parts thereof, of iron or steel, mill irons and mill cranks of wrought iron, and wrought iron for ships, and forgings of iron or steel, or of combined iron and steel, for vessels, steam engines and locomotives, or parts thereof, one and two-tenths cents per pound.

127. Axles, or parts thereof, axle bars, axle blanks, or forgings for axles, whether of iron or steel, without reference to the stage or state of manufacture, one and one-half cents per pound: *Provided*, That when iron or steel axles are imported fitted in wheels, or parts of wheels, of iron or steel, they shall be dutiable at the same rate as the wheels in which they are fitted.

128. Anvils of iron or steel, or of iron and steel combined, by what ever process made, or in whatever stage of manufacture, one and three-fourths cents per pound.

129. Blacksmiths' hammers and sledges, track tools, wedges, and crowbars, whether of iron or steel, one and one-half cents per pound.

130. Boiler or other tubes, pipes, flues, or stays of wrought iron or steel, twenty-five per centum ad valorem.

131. Bolts, with or without threads or nuts, or bolt blanks, and finished hinges or hinge blanks, whether of iron or steel, one and one-half cents per pound.

132. Card clothing manufactured from tempered steel wire, forty cents per square foot; all other, twenty cents per square foot.

133. Cast-iron pipe of every description, six-tenths of one cent per pound.

134. Cast-iron vessels, plates, stove plates, andirons, sadirons, tailors' irons, hatters' irons, and castings of iron, not specially provided for in this Act, eight-tenths of one cent per pound.

135. Castings of malleable iron not specially provided for in this Act, nine-tenths of one cent per pound.

136. Cast hollow ware, coated, glazed, or tinned, two cents per pound.

137. Chains of all kinds, made of iron or steel, thirty per centum ad valorem.

CUTLERY:

138. Penknives, pocketknives, or erasers, of all kinds, valued at not more than thirty cents per dozen, twenty-five per centum ad valorem; valued at more than thirty cents per dozen and not exceeding fifty cents per dozen, twelve cents per dozen; valued at more than fifty cents per dozen and not exceeding one dollar per dozen, twenty-five cents per dozen; valued at more than one dollar per dozen and not exceeding one dollar and fifty cents per dozen, forty cents per dozen; valued at more than one dollar and fifty cents per dozen and not exceeding three dollars per dozen, seventy-five cents per dozen; valued at more than three dollars per dozen, fifty per centum ad valorem; and in addition thereto, on all the foregoing valued at more than thirty cents per dozen and not more than three dollars per dozen, twenty-five per centum ad valorem: *Provided,* That blades, handles, or any other parts of any or either of the articles named in this paragraph, imported in any other manner than assembled in penknives, pocketknives, or erasers, shall be subject to no less rate of duty than herein provided for penknives, pocketknives, or erasers valued at more than thirty cents per dozen.

139. Swords, sword blades, and side arms, thirty-five per centum ad valorem.

140. Table and carving knives and forks, valued at more than four dollars per dozen pieces, razors and razor blades, wholly or partly finished, scissors and shears, forty-five per centum ad valorem; all other table knives, forks, steels, and all hunting, kitchen, bread, butter, vegetable, fruit, cheese, plumbers', painters', palette, and artists' knives; also all cooks', and butchers' knives, forks, and steels, thirty-five per centum ad valorem.

141. Files, file blanks, rasps, and floats, of all cuts and kinds, four inches in length and under, thirty-five cents per dozen; over four

inches in length and under nine inches, sixty cents per dozen; nine inches in length or over, one dollar per dozen.

FIREARMS :

142. Muskets, muzzle-loading shotguns, and sporting rifles, and parts thereof, twenty-five per centum ad valorem.

143. Sporting, breech-loading shotguns, combination shotguns and rifles, and pistols, and parts of all of the foregoing, thirty per centum ad valorem.

144. Sheets, plates, wares, or articles of iron, steel, or other metal, enameled or glazed with vitreous glasses, thirty-five per centum ad valorem.

NAILS, SPIKES, TACKS, AND NEEDLES :

145. Cut nails and cut spikes of iron or steel, twenty-two and one-half per centum ad valorem.

146. Horseshoe nails, hobnails, and all other wrought-iron or steel nails not specially provided for in this Act, thirty per centum ad valorem.

147. Wire nails made of wrought iron or steel, twenty-five per centum ad valorem.

148. Spikes, nuts, and washers, and horse, mule, or ox shoes, of wrought iron or steel, twenty-five per centum ad valorem.

149. Cut tacks, brads, or sprigs of all kinds, twenty-five per centum ad valorem.

150. Needles for knitting or sewing machines, crochet needles and tape needles, knitting and all other needles, not specially provided for in this Act, and bodkins of metal, twenty-five per centum ad valorem.

PLATES:

151. Steel plates engraved, stereotype plates, electrotype plates, and plates of other materials, engraved or lithographed, for printing, twenty-five per centum ad valorem.

152. Railway fish plates or splice bars, made of iron or steel, twenty-five per centum ad valorem.

153. Rivets of iron or steel, twenty-five per centum ad valorem.

SAWS:

154. Crosscut saws, six cents per linear foot; mill saws, ten cents per linear foot; pit, and drag saws, eight cents per linear foot; circular saws, twenty-five per centum ad valorem; hand, back, and all other saws, not specially provided for in this Act, twenty-five per centum ad valorem.

155. Screws, commonly called wood screws, more than two inches in length, three cents per pound; over one inch and not more than two inches in length, five cents per pound; over one-half inch and not more than one inch in length, seven cents per pound; one-half inch and less in length, ten cents per pound.

155½. Umbrella and parasol ribs, and stretcher frames, tips, runners, handles, or other parts thereof, made in whole or chief part of iron, steel, or any other metal, fifty per centum ad valorem.

156. Wheels, for railway purposes, or parts thereof, made of iron or steel, and steel-tired wheels for railway purposes, whether wholly or partly finished, and iron or steel locomotive, car, or other railway tires or parts thereof, wholly or partly manufactured, and ingots, cogged

ingots, blooms, or blanks for the same, without regard to the degree of manufacture, one and one-fourth cents per pound: *Provided*, That when wheels or parts thereof, of iron or steel, are imported with iron or steel axles fitted in them, the wheels and axles together shall be dutiable at the same rate as is provided for the wheels when imported separately.

MISCELLANEOUS METALS AND MANUFACTURES OF.

157. Aluminum, in crude form, alloys of any kind in which aluminum is the component material of chief value, ten cents per pound.

158. Argentine, albata, or German silver, unmanufactured, fifteen per centum ad valorem.

159. Brass, in bars or pigs, old brass, clippings from brass or Dutch metal, and old sheathing, or yellow metal, fit only for remanufacture, ten per centum ad valorem.

160. Bronze powder, metallics or flitters, bronze or Dutch metal, or aluminum, in leaf, forty per centum ad valorem.

COPPER:

161. Copper in rolled plates, called braziers' copper, sheets, rods, pipes, and copper bottoms, also sheathing or yellow metal of which copper is the component material of chief value, and not composed wholly or in part of iron ungalvanized, twenty per centum ad valorem.

GOLD AND SILVER:

162. Bullions and metal thread of gold, silver, or other metals, not specially provided for in this Act, twenty-five per centum ad valorem.

163. Gold leaf, thirty per centum ad valorem.

164. Silver leaf, and silver powder, thirty per centum ad valorem.

LEAD:

165. Lead ore and lead dross, three-fourths of one cent per pound: *Provided*, That silver ore and all other ores containing lead shall pay a duty of three-fourths of one cent per pound on the lead contained therein, according to sample and assay at the port of entry. The method of sampling and assaying to be that usually adopted for commercial purposes by public sampling works in the United States.

166. Lead in pigs and bars, molten and old refuse lead run into blocks and bars, and old scrap lead fit only to be remanufactured, one cent per pound: *Provided*, That in case any foreign country shall impose an export duty upon lead ore or lead dross or silver ores containing lead, exported to the United States from such country, then the duty upon such ores and lead in pigs and bars, molten and old refuse lead run into blocks and bars, and old scrap lead fit only to be remanufactured, herein provided for, when imported from such country, shall remain the same as fixed by the law in force prior to the passage of this Act.

167. Lead in sheets, pipes, shot, glaziers' lead, and lead wire, one and one-quarter cents per pound.

167½. Nickel, nickel oxide, alloy of any kind in which nickel is the component material of chief value, six cents per pound.

167¾. **Mica, twenty per centum ad valorem.**
168. Pens, metallic, except gold pens, eight cents per gross.
169. Penholder tips, penholders or parts thereof, and gold pens, twenty-five per centum ad valorem.
170. Pins, metallic, including pins with solid or glass heads, hair pins, safety pins, and hat, bonnet, shawl, and belt pins, not commercially known as jewelry, twenty-five per centum ad valorem.
170½. Quicksilver, seven cents per pound.
171. Type metal, three-fourths of one cent per pound for the lead contained therein ; and new types, fifteen per centum ad valorem.

WATCHES :
172. Chronometers, box or ship's, and parts thereof, ten per centum ad valorem.
173. Watches and clocks, or parts thereof, whether separately packed or otherwise, twenty-five per centum ad valorem.

ZINC OR SPELTER:
174. Zinc in blocks or pigs, one cent per pound.
175. Zinc in sheets, not polished nor further advanced than rolled, one and one-fourth cents per pound.
176. Zinc, old and worn-out, fit only to be remanufactured, three-fourths of one cent per pound.
177. Manufactured articles or wares, not specially provided for in this Act, composed wholly or in part of any metal, and whether partly or wholly manufactured, thirty-five per centum ad valorem.

SCHEDULE D.—WOOD AND MANUFACTURES OF.

179. Osier or willow, prepared for basket-makers' use, twenty per centum ad valorem; manufactures of osier or willow, twenty-five per centum ad valorem; chair cane, or reeds, wrought or manufactured from rattans or reeds, ten per centum ad valorem.
180. Casks and barrels, empty, sugar-box shooks, and packing boxes and packing-box shooks, of wood, not specially provided for in this Act, twenty per centum ad valorem.
180½. Tooth-picks of vegetable substance, thirty-five per centum ad valorem.
181. House or cabinet furniture, of wood, wholly or partly finished, manufactures of wood, or of which wood is the component material of chief value, not specially provided for in this Act, twenty-five per centum ad valorem.

SCHEDULE E.—SUGAR.

182. That so much of the Act entitled "An Act to reduce revenue, equalize duties, and for other purposes," approved October first, eighteen hundred and ninety, as provides for and authorizes the issue of licenses to produce sugar, and for the payment of a bounty to the producers of sugar from beets, sorghum, or sugar cane, grown in the United States, or from maple sap produced within the United States, be, and the same is hereby repealed, and hereafter it shall be unlawful to issue any license to produce sugar or to pay any bounty for the production of sugar of any kind under the said Act.
182½. There shall be levied, collected, and paid on all sugars and on all tank bottoms, sirups of cane juice or of beet juice, melada, concen-

trated melada, concrete and concentrated molasses, a duty of forty per centum ad valorem, and upon all sugars above number sixteen Dutch standard in color and upon all sugars which have been discolored there shall be levied, collected, and paid a duty of one-eighth of one cent per pound in addition to the said duty of forty per centum ad valorem; and all sugars, tank bottoms, sirups of cane juice or of beet juice, melada, concentrated melada, concrete or concentrated molasses, which are imported from or are the product of any country which at the time the same are exported therefrom pays, directly or indirectly, a bounty on the export thereof, shall pay a duty of one-tenth of one cent per pound in addition to the foregoing rates: *Provided*, That the importer of sugar produced in a foreign country, the Government of which grants such direct or indirect bounties, may be relieved from this additional duty under such regulations as the Secretary of the Treasury may prescribe, in case said importer produces a certificate of said Government that no indirect bounty has been received upon said sugar in excess of the tax collected upon the beet or cane from which it was produced, and that no direct bounty has been or shall be paid: *Provided further*, That nothing herein contained shall be so construed as to abrogate or in any manner impair or affect the provisions of the treaty of commercial reciprocity concluded between the United States and the King of the Hawaiian Islands on the thirtieth day of January, eighteen hundred and seventy-five, or the provisions of any Act of Congress heretofore passed for the execution of the same. That there shall be levied, collected, and paid on molasses testing above forty degrees and not above fifty-six degrees polariscope, a duty of two cents per gallon; if testing above fifty-six degrees polariscope, a duty of four cents per gallon.

183. Sugar candy and all confectionery, made wholly or in part of sugar, and on sugars after being refined, when tinctured, colored, or in any way adulterated, thirty-five per centum ad valorem; glucose, or grape sugar, fifteen per centum ad valorem; saccharine, twenty-five per centum ad valorem.

Schedule F.—Tobacco and Manufactures of.

184. Wrapper tobacco, unstemmed, imported in any bale, box, package, or in bulk, one dollar and fifty cents per pound; if stemmed, two dollars and twenty-five cents per pound.

185. Filler tobacco, unstemmed, imported in any bale, box, package, or in bulk, thirty-five cents per pound; if stemmed, fifty cents per pound: *Provided*, That the term wrapper tobacco, whenever used in this Act shall be taken to mean that quality of leaf tobacco known commercially as wrapper tobacco: *Provided further*, That the term filler tobacco, whenever used in this Act, shall be taken to mean all leaf tobacco unmanufactured, not commercially known as wrapper tobacco: *Provided further*, That if any leaf tobacco imported in any bale, box, package, or in bulk shall be the growth of different countries, or shall differ in quality and value, save as provided in the succeeding provision, then the entire contents of such bale, box, package, or in bulk shall be subject to the same duty as wrapper tobacco: *Provided further*, That if any bale, box, package, or bulk of leaf tobacco of uniform quality contains exceeding fifteen per centum thereof of leaves suitable in color, fineness of texture, and size for wrappers for cigars, then the entire contents of such bale, box, package, or bulk shall be subject to the same duty as wrapper tobacco: *Provided further*, That

collectors shall not permit entry to be made, except under regulations to be prescribed by the Secretary of the Treasury, of any leaf tobacco imported in any bale, box, package, or in bulk, unless the invoices covering the same shall specify in detail the character of the leaf tobacco in such bale, box, package, or in bulk, whether wrapper or filler tobacco, Quebrado or self working bales, as the case may be: *And provided further*, That in the examination for classification of any invoice of imported leaf tobacco at least one bale if less than ten bales, and one bale in every ten bales and more, if deemed necessary by the appraising officer, shall be examined by the appraiser or person authorized by law to make such examination, and for the purpose of fixing the classification and amount of duty chargeable on such invoice of leaf tobacco the examination of ten hands out of each examined bale thereof shall be taken to be a legal examination.

186. Tobacco, manufactured or unmanufactured, of all descriptions, not specially enumerated or provided for in this Act, forty cents per pound.

187. Snuff and snuff flour, manufactured of tobacco, ground dry or damp, and pickled, scented, or otherwise, of all descriptions, fifty cents per pound.

188. Cigars, cigarettes, and cheroots of all kinds, four dollars per pound and twenty-five per centum ad valorem; and paper cigars and cigarettes, including wrappers, shall be subject to the same duties as are herein imposed upon cigars.

SCHEDULE G.—AGRICULTURAL PRODUCTS AND PROVISIONS.

ANIMALS, LIVE:
189. All live animals, not specially provided for in this Act, twenty per centum ad valorem.

BREADSTUFFS AND FARINACEOUS SUBSTANCES:
190. Buckwheat, corn or maize, cornmeal, oats, rye, rye flour, wheat, and wheat flour, twenty per centum ad valorem, and oatmeal, fifteen per centum ad valorem.
191. Barley, and barley, pearled, patent, or hulled, thirty per centum ad valorem; barley malt, forty per centum ad valorem.
192. Macaroni, vermicelli, and all similar preparations, twenty per centum ad valorem.
193. Rice, cleaned, one and one-half cents per pound; uncleaned rice, or rice free of the outer hull and still having the inner cuticle on, eight-tenths of one cent per pound; rice flour and rice meal, and rice, broken, which will pass through a sieve known commercially as number twelve wire sieve, one-fourth of one cent per pound; paddy, or rice having the outer hull on, three-fourths of one cent per pound.

DAIRY PRODUCTS:
194. Butter, and substitutes therefor, four cents per pound.
195. Cheese, four cents per pound.
196. Milk, preserved or condensed, two cents per pound, including weight of packages; sugar of milk, five cents per pound.

FARM AND FIELD PRODUCTS:
197. Beans, twenty per centum ad valorem.

198. Beans, pease, mushrooms, and other vegetables, prepared or pre served, in tins, jars, bottles, or otherwise, and pickles and sauces of all kinds, thirty per centum ad valorem.

198½. Eggs, three cents per dozen.

199. Hay, two dollars per ton.

200. Honey, ten cents per gallon.

201. Hops, eight cents per pound.

202. Onions, twenty cents per bushel.

203. Pease, dried, twenty cents per bushel; split pease, fifty cents per bushel of sixty pounds; pease in cartons, papers, or other small packages, one cent per pound.

204. Potatoes, fifteen cents per bushel of sixty pounds.

SEEDS:

205. Castor beans or seeds, twenty-five cents per bushel of fifty pounds.

206. Flaxseed or linseed, poppy seed, and other oil seeds, not specially provided for in this Act, twenty cents per bushel of fifty-six pounds.

206½. Garden seeds, agricultural seeds, and other seeds not specially provided for in this Act, ten per centum ad valorem.

207. Vegetables in their natural state, not specially provided for in this Act, ten per centum ad valorem.

207½. Straw, fifteen per centum ad valorem.

207¾. Teazles, fifteen per centum ad valorem.

FISH:

208. Anchovies and sardines, packed, in oil or otherwise, in tin boxes measuring not more than five inches long, four inches wide, and three and one-half inches deep, ten cents per whole box; in half boxes, measuring not more than five inches long, four inches wide, and one and five-eighths inches deep, five cents each; in quarter boxes, measuring not more than four and three-fourths inches long, three and one-half inches wide, and one and one-fourth inches deep, two and one-half cents each; when imported in any other form, forty per centum ad valorem.

209. Fish, smoked, dried, salted, pickled, or otherwise prepared for preservation, three-fourths of one cent per pound.

210. Herrings, pickled, frozen, or salted, and salt water fish frozen or packed in ice, one-half of one cent per pound.

211. Fish in cans or packages made of tin or other material, except anchovies and sardines and fish packed in any other manner, not specially enumerated or provided for in this Act, twenty per centum ad valorem.

FRUITS AND NUTS:

Fruits—

213. Apples, green or ripe, dried, desiccated, evaporated, or prepared in any manner, twenty per centum ad valorem.

213½. Dates and pineapples, twenty per centum ad valorem.

214. Grapes, twenty per centum ad valorem.

215. Olives, green or prepared, twenty per centum ad valorem.

216. Oranges, lemons, and limes, in packages, at the rate of eight cents per cubic foot of capacity; in bulk, one dollar and fifty cents per one thousand; and in addition thereto a duty of thirty

per centum ad valorem upon the boxes or barrels containing such oranges, lemons, or limes: *Provided*, That the thin-wood, so called, comprising the sides, tops and bottoms of orange and lemon boxes of the growth and manufacture of the United States, exported as orange and lemon box shooks, may be reimported in completed form, filled with oranges and lemons, by the payment of duty at one half the rate imposed on similar boxes of entirely foreign growth and manufacture.

217. Plums, prunes, figs, raisins, and other dried grapes, including Zante currants, one and one-half cents per pound.

218. Comfits, sweetmeats, and fruits preserved in sugar, sirup, or molasses, not specially provided for in this Act, prepared or desiccated cocoanut or copra, and jellies of all kinds, thirty per centum ad valorem.

219. Fruits preserved in their own juices, twenty per centum ad valorem.

220. Orange peel and lemon peel, preserved or candied, thirty per centum ad valorem.

Nuts—

221. Almonds, not shelled, three cents per pound; clear almonds, shelled, five cents per pound.

222. Filberts and walnuts of all kinds, not shelled, two cents per pound; shelled, four cents per pound.

223. Peanuts or ground beans, twenty per centum ad valorem.

224. Cocoanuts in the shell, and other nuts shelled or unshelled, not specially provided for in this Act, twenty per centum ad valorem.

MEAT PRODUCTS:

224½. Fresh beef, mutton, and pork, twenty per centum ad valorem.

225. Extract of meat, fifteen per centum ad valorem.

225½. Lard, one cent per pound.

225¾. Meats of all kinds, prepared or preserved, not specially provided for in this Act, twenty per centum ad valorem.

226. Poultry, two cents per pound; dressed, three cents per pound.

MISCELLANEOUS PRODUCTS:

227. Chicory root, burnt or roasted, ground or granulated, or in rolls, or otherwise prepared, and not specially provided for in this Act, two cents per pound.

229. Cocoa, prepared or manufactured, not specially provided for in this Act, two cents per pound; chocolate, sweetened, flavored, or other, valued at thirty-five cents per pound or less, two cents per pound; valued at exceeding thirty-five cents per pound and chocolate confectionery, thirty-five per centum ad valorem.

230. Cocoa butter or cocoa butterine, three and one-half cents per pound.

231. Dandelion root and acorns prepared, and other articles used as coffee, or as substitutes for coffee, not specially provided for in this Act, one and one-half cents per pound.

232. Starch, including all preparations, from whatever substance produced, commonly used as starch, one and one-half cents per pound.

233. Dextrine, burnt starch, gum substitute, or British gum, one and one-half cents per pound.

234. Mustard, ground, preserved, or prepared, in bottles or otherwise, twenty-five per centum ad valorem.

234½. Orchids, lily of the valley, azaleas, palms, and other plants used for forcing under glass for cut flowers or decorative purposes, ten per centum ad valorem.

235. Spices, ground or powdered, not specially provided for in this Act, three cents per pound; capsicum or red pepper, two and one-half cents per pound, unground; sage, one cent per pound.

236. Vinegar, seven and one-half cents per gallon. The standard for vinegar shall be taken to be that strength which requires thirty-five grains of bicarbonate of potash to neutralize one ounce troy of vinegar.

SCHEDULE H.—SPIRITS, WINES, AND OTHER BEVERAGES.

SPIRITS:

237. Brandy and other spirits manufactured or distilled from grain or other materials, and not specially provided for in this Act, one dollar and eighty cents per proof gallon.

238. Each and every gauge or wine gallon of measurement shall be counted as at least one proof gallon; and the standard for determining the proof of brandy and other spirits or liquors of any kind imported shall be the same as that which is defined in the laws relating to internal revenue; but any brandy or other spirituous liquors, imported in casks of less capacity than fourteen gallons, shall be forfeited to the United States: *Provided*, That it shall be lawful for the Secretary of the Treasury, in his discretion, to authorize the ascertainment of the proof of wines, cordials, or other liquors by distillation or otherwise, in cases where it is impracticable to ascertain such proof by the means prescribed by existing law or regulations.

239. On all compounds or preparations (except as specified in the preceding paragraph of the chemical schedule relating to medicinal preparations, of which alcohol is a component part), of which distilled spirits are a component part of chief value, not specially provided for in this Act, there shall be levied a duty not less than that imposed upon distilled spirits.

240. Cordials, liquors, arrack, absinthe, kirschwasser, ratafia, and other spirituous beverages or bitters of all kinds containing spirits, and not specially provided for in this Act, one dollar and eighty cents per proof gallon.

241. No lower rate or amount of duty shall be levied, collected, and paid on brandy, spirits, and other spirituous beverages than that fixed by law for the description of first proof; but it shall be increased in proportion for any greater strength than the strength of first proof, and all imitations of brandy or spirits or wines imported by any names whatever shall be subject to the highest rate of duty provided for the genuine articles respectively intended to be represented, and in no case less than one dollar per gallon.

242. Bay rum or bay water, whether distilled or compounded, of first proof, and in proportion for any greater strength than first proof, one dollar per gallon.

WINES:

243. Champagne and all other sparkling wines, in bottles containing each not more than one quart and more than one pint, eight dollars per dozen; containing not more than one pint each and more than one-half pint, four dollars per dozen; containing one-half pint each or less, two dollars per dozen; in bottles or other vessels containing more than one quart each, in addition to eight dollars per dozen bottles, on the quantity in excess of one quart, at the rate of two dollars and fifty cents per gallon.

244. Still wines, including ginger wine or ginger cordial and vermuth, in casks or packages other than bottles or jugs, if containing fourteen per centum or less of absolute alcohol, thirty cents per gallon; if containing more than fourteen per centum of absolute alcohol, fifty cents per gallon. In bottles or jugs, per case of one dozen bottles or jugs, containing each not more than one quart and more than one pint, or twenty-four bottles or jugs containing each not more than one pint, one dollar and sixty cents per case; and any excess beyond these quantities found in such bottles or jugs shall be subject to a duty of five cents per pint or fractional part thereof, but no separate or additional duty shall be assessed on the bottles or jugs: *Provided,* That any wines, ginger cordial, or vermuth imported containing more than twenty-four per centum of alcohol shall be classed as spirits and pay duty accordingly: *And provided further,* That there shall be no constructive or other allowance for breakage, leakage, or damage on wines, liquors, cordials, or distilled spirits. Wines, cordials, brandy, and other spirituous liquors imported in bottles or jugs shall be packed in packages containing not less than one dozen bottles or jugs in each package, or duty shall be paid as if such package contained at least one dozen bottles or jugs. The percentage of alcohol in wines and fruit juices shall be determined in such manner as the Secretary of the Treasury shall by regulation prescribe.

245. Ale, porter, and beer, in bottles or jugs, thirty cents per gallon, but no separate or additional duty shall be assessed on the bottles or jugs; otherwise than in bottles or jugs, fifteen cents per gallon.

246. Malt extract, including all preparations bearing the name and commercially known as such, fluid in casks, fifteen cents per gallon; in bottles or jugs, thirty cents per gallon; solid or condensed, thirty per centum ad valorem.

247. Cherry juice and prune juice or prune wine, and other fruit juice not specially provided for in this Act, containing eighteen per centum or less of alcohol, fifty cents per gallon; if containing more than eighteen per centum of alcohol, one dollar and eighty cents per proof gallon.

248. Ginger ale or ginger beer, twenty per centum ad valorem, but no separate or additional duty shall be assessed on the bottles.

249. All imitations of natural mineral waters, and all artificial mineral waters, twenty per centum ad valorem.

SCHEDULE I.—COTTON MANUFACTURES.

250. Cotton thread and carded yarn, warps or warp yarn, in singles, whether on beams or in bundles, skeins or cops, or in any other form, except spool thread of cotton hereinafter provided for, not colored,

bleached, dyed, or advanced beyond the condition of singles by grouping or twisting two or more single yarns together, three cents per pound on all numbers up to and including number fifteen, one-fifth of a cent per number per pound on all numbers exceeding number fifteen and up to and including number thirty, and one-quarter of a cent per number per pound on all numbers exceeding number thirty; colored, bleached, dyed, combed or advanced beyond the condition of singles by grouping or twisting two or more single yarns together, whether on beams, or in bundles, skeins or cops, or in any other form, except spool thread of cotton hereinafter provided for, six cents per pound on all numbers up to and including number twenty, and on all numbers exceeding number twenty, three-tenths of a cent per number per pound: *Provided however*, That in no case shall the duty levied exceed eight cents per pound on yarns valued at not exceeding twenty-five cents per pound, nor exceed fifteen cents per pound on yarns valued at over twenty-five cents per pound and not exceeding forty cents per pound: *And provided further*, That on all yarns valued at more than forty cents per pound there shall be levied, collected and paid a duty of forty-five per centum ad valorem.

251. Spool thread of cotton, containing on each spool not exceeding one hundred yards of thread, five and one-half cents per dozen; exceeding one hundred yards on each spool, for every additional one hundred yards of thread or fractional part thereof in excess of one hundred yards, five and one-half cents per dozen spools.

252. Cotton cloth not bleached, dyed, colored, stained, painted, or printed, and not exceeding fifty threads to the square inch, counting the warp and filling, one cent per square yard; if bleached, one and one-fourth cents per square yard; if dyed, colored, stained, painted, or printed, two cents per square yard.

253. Cotton cloth, not bleached, dyed, colored, stained, painted, or printed, exceeding fifty and not exceeding one hundred threads to the square inch, counting the warp and filling, and not exceeding six square yards to the pound, one and one-fourth cents per square yard; exceeding six and not exceeding nine square yards to the pound, one and one-half cents per square yard; exceeding nine square yards to the pound, one and three-fourths cents per square yard; if bleached and not exceeding six square yards to the pound, one and one-half cents per square yard; exceeding six and not exceeding nine square yards to the pound, one and three-fourths cents per square yard; exceeding nine square yards to the pound, two and one-fourth cents per square yard; if dyed, colored, stained, painted, or printed, and not exceeding six square yards to the pound, two and three-fourths cents per square yard; exceeding six and not exceeding nine square yards to the pound, three and one-fourth cents per square yard; exceeding nine square yards to the pound, three and one-half cents per square yard: *Provided*, That on all cotton cloth not exceeding one hundred threads to the square inch, counting the warp and filling, not bleached, dyed, colored, stained, painted, or printed, valued at over seven cents per square yard, twenty-five per centum ad valorem; bleached, valued at over nine cents per square yard, twenty-five per centum ad valorem; and dyed, colored, stained, painted, or printed, valued at over twelve cents per square yard, there shall be levied, collected, and paid a duty of thirty per centum ad valorem.

254. Cotton cloth, not bleached, dyed, colored, stained, painted, or printed, exceeding one hundred and not exceeding one hundred and fifty threads to the square inch, counting the warp and filling, and not

exceeding four square yards to the pound, one and one-half cents per square yard; exceeding four and not exceeding six square yards to the pound, two cents per square yard; exceeding six and not exceeding eight square yards to the pound, two and one-half cents per square yard; exceeding eight square yards to the pound, two and three-fourths cents per square yard; if bleached, and not exceeding four square yards to the pound, two and one-half cents per square yard; exceeding four and not exceeding six square yards to the pound, three cents per square yard; exceeding six and not exceeding eight square yards to the pound, three and one-half cents per square yard; exceeding eight square yards to the pound, three and three-fourths cents per square yard; if dyed, colored, stained, painted, or printed, and not exceeding four square yards to the pound, three and one-half cents per square yard; exceeding four and not exceeding six square yards to the pound, three and three-fourths cents per square yard; exceeding six and not exceeding eight square yards to the pound, four and one-fourth cents per square yard; exceeding eight square yards to the pound, four and one-half cents per square yard: *Provided*, That on all cotton cloth exceeding one hundred and not exceeding one hundred and fifty threads to the square inch, counting the warp and filling, not bleached, dyed, colored, stained, painted, or printed, valued at over nine cents per square yard, thirty per centum ad valorem; bleached, valued at over eleven cents per square yard, thirty-five per centum ad valorem; dyed, colored, stained, painted, or printed, valued at over twelve and one-half cents per square yard, there shall be levied, collected, and paid a duty of thirty-five per centum ad valorem.

255. Cotton cloth not bleached, dyed, colored, stained, painted, or printed, exceeding one hundred and fifty and not exceeding two hundred threads to the square inch, counting the warp and filling, and not exceeding three and one-half square yards to the pound, two cents per square yard; exceeding three and one-half and not exceeding four and one-half square yards to the pound, two and three-fourths cents per square yard; exceeding four and one-half and not exceeding six square yards to the pound, three cents per square yard; exceeding six square yards to the pound, three and one-half cents per square yard; if bleached, and not exceeding three and one-half square yards to the pound, two and three-fourths cents per square yard; exceeding three and one-half and not exceeding four and one-half square yards to the pound, three and one-half cents per square yard; exceeding four and one-half and not exceeding six square yards to the pound, four cents per square yard; exceeding six square yards to the pound, four and one-fourth cents per square yard; if dyed, colored, stained, painted, or printed, and not exceeding three and one-half square yards to the pound, four and one fourth cents per square yard; exceeding three and one-half and not exceeding four and one-half square yards to the pound, four and one-half cents per square yard; exceeding four and one-half and not exceeding six square yards to the pound, four and three fourths cents per square yard; exceeding six square yards to the pound, five cents per square yard: *Provided*, That on all cotton cloth exceeding one hundred and fifty and not exceeding two hundred threads to the square inch, counting the warp and filling, not bleached, dyed, colored, stained, painted, or printed, valued at over ten cents per square yard, thirty-five per centum ad valorem; bleached, valued at over twelve cents per square yard, thirty-five per centum ad valorem; dyed, colored, stained, painted, or printed, valued at over twelve and

one-half cents per square yard, there shall be levied, collected, and paid a duty of forty per centum ad valorem.

256. Cotton cloth not bleached, dyed, colored, stained, painted, or printed, exceeding two hundred threads to the square inch, counting the warp and filling, and not exceeding two and one-half square yards to the pound, three cents per square yard; exceeding two and one half and not exceeding three and one-half square yards to the pound, three and one-half cents per square yard; exceeding three and one-half and not exceeding five square yards to the pound, four cents per square yard; exceeding five square yards to the pound, four and one-half cents per square yard; if bleached, and not exceeding two and one-half square yards to the pound, four cents per square yard; exceeding two and one half and not exceeding three and one-half square yards to the pound, four and one-half cents per square yard; exceeding three and one-half and not exceeding five square yards to the pound, five cents per square yard; exceeding five square yards to the pound, five and one-half cents per square yard; if dyed, colored, painted, or printed, and not exceeding three and one-half square yards to the pound, five and three-fourths cents per square yard; exceeding three and one-half square yards to the pound, six and one-half cents per square yard: *Provided,* That on all such cotton cloths not bleached, dyed, colored, stained, painted, or printed, valued at over twelve cents per square yard; bleached, valued at over fourteen cents per square yard; and dyed, colored, stained, painted, or printed, valued at over sixteen cents per square yard, there shall be levied, collected, and paid a duty of thirty-five per centum ad valorem.

257. The term cotton cloth, or cloth, wherever used in the foregoing paragraphs of this schedule, shall be held to include all woven fabrics of cotton in the piece, whether figured, fancy, or plain, not specially provided for in this Act, the warp and filling threads of which can be counted by unraveling or other practicable means.

258. Clothing ready made, and articles of wearing apparel of every description, handkerchiefs, and neckties or neck wear, composed of cotton or other vegetable fiber, or of which cotton or other vegetable fiber is the component material of chief value, made up or manufactured wholly or in part by the tailor, seamstress, or manufacturer, all of the foregoing not specially provided for in this Act, forty per centum ad valorem.

259. Plushes, velvets, velveteens, corduroys, and all pile fabrics composed of cotton or other vegetable fiber, not bleached, dyed, colored, stained, painted, or printed, forty per centum ad valorem; on all such goods if bleached, dyed, colored, stained, painted, or printed, forty-seven and one-half per centum ad valorem.

260. Chenille curtains, table covers, and all goods manufactured of cotton chenille, or of which cotton chenille forms the component material of chief value, forty per centum ad valorem; sleeve linings or other cloths, composed of cotton and silk, whether known as silk stripe sleeve lining, silk stripes, or otherwise, forty-five per centum ad valorem.

261. Stockings, hose and half-hose, made on knitting machines or frames, composed of cotton or other vegetable fiber and not otherwise specially provided for in this Act, thirty per centum ad valorem.

262. Stockings, hose and half-hose, selvedged, fashioned, narrowed, or shaped wholly or in part by knitting machines or frames, or knit by hand, including such as are commercially known as seamless or clocked stockings, hose or half-hose, and knitted shirts or drawers, all of the

above composed of cotton or other vegetable fiber, finished or unfinished, fifty per centum ad valorem.

263. Cords, braids, boot, shoe and corset lacings, tapes, gimps, galloons, webbing, goring, suspenders and braces, woven, braided, or twisted lamp or candle wicking, lining for bicycle tires, spindle binding, any of the above made of cotton or other vegetable fiber and whether composed in part of India rubber or otherwise, forty-five per centum ad valorem.

264. All manufactures of cotton, including cotton duck and cotton damask, in the piece or otherwise, not specially provided for in this Act, and including cloth having India rubber as a component material, thirty-five per centum ad valorem.

SCHEDULE J.—FLAX, HEMP, AND JUTE, AND MANUFACTURES OF.

265. Flax, hackled, known as "dressed line," one and one-half cents per pound.

266. Hemp, hackled, known as "dressed line," one cent per pound.

267. Yarn, made of jute, thirty per centum ad valorem.

268. Cables, cordage, and twine (except binding twine), composed in whole or in part of New Zealand hemp, istle or Tampico fiber, manila, sisal grass, or sunn, ten per centum ad valorem.

269. Hemp and jute carpets and carpetings, twenty per centum ad valorem.

272. Flax gill netting, nets, webs, and seines, forty per centum ad valorem.

273. Oilcloth for floors, stamped, painted, or printed, including linoleum, corticene, cork carpets, figured or plain, and all other oilcloth (except silk oilcloth), and waterproof cloth, not specially provided for in this Act, valued at twenty-five cents or less per square yard, twenty-five per centum ad valorem; valued above twenty-five cents per square yard, forty per centum ad valorem.

273½. Linen hydraulic hose, made in whole or in part of flax, hemp, or jute, forty per centum ad valorem.

274. Yarns or threads composed of flax or hemp, or of a mixture of either of these substances, thirty-five per centum ad valorem.

275. Collars and cuffs, composed wholly or in part of linen, thirty cents per dozen pieces, and in addition thereto thirty per centum ad valorem; shirts and all other articles of wearing apparel of every description, not specially provided for in this Act, composed wholly or in part of linen, fifty per centum ad valorem.

275½. Tapes composed of flax, woven with or without metal threads, on reels or spools, designed expressly for use in the manufacture of measuring tapes, twenty-five per centum ad valorem.

276. Laces, edgings, nettings and veilings, embroideries, insertings, neck rufflings, ruchings, trimmings, tuckings, lace window curtains, tamboured articles, and articles embroidered by hand or machinery, embroidered handkerchiefs, and articles made wholly or in part of lace, rufflings, tuckings, or ruchings, all of the above-named articles, composed of flax, jute, cotton, or other vegetable fiber, or of which these substances or either of them, or a mixture of any of them is the component material of chief value, not specially provided for in this Act, fifty per centum ad valorem.

277. All manufactures of flax, hemp, jute, or other vegetable fiber, except cotton, or of which these substances or either of them is the component material of chief value, not specially provided for in this Act, thirty-five per centum ad valorem.

SCHEDULE K.—WOOL AND MANUFACTURES OF WOOL.

279. On flocks, mungo, shoddy, garnetted waste, and carded waste, and carbonized noils, or carbonized wool, fifteen per centum ad valorem, and on wool of the sheep, hair of the camel, goat, alpaca, or other like animals, in the form of roving, roping, or tops, twenty per centum ad valorem.

280. On woolen and worsted yarns made wholly or in part of wool, worsted, the hair of the camel, goat, alpaca, or other animals, valued at not more than forty cents per pound, thirty per centum ad valorem; valued at more than forty cents per pound, forty per centum ad valorem.

281. On knit fabrics, and all fabrics made on knitting machines or frames, not including wearing apparel, and on shawls made wholly or in part of wool, worsted, the hair of the camel, goat, alpaca, or other animals, valued at not exceeding forty cents per pound, thirty-five per centum ad valorem; valued at more than forty cents per pound, forty per centum ad valorem.

282. On blankets, hats of wool, and flannels for underwear and felts for printing machines, composed wholly or in part of wool, the hair of the camel, goat, alpaca, or other animals, valued at not more than thirty cents per pound, twenty-five per centum ad valorem; valued at more than thirty and not more than forty cents per pound, thirty per centum ad valorem; valued at more than forty cents per pound, thirty-five per centum ad valorem: *Provided*, That on blankets over three yards in length the same duties shall be paid as on woolen and worsted cloths, and on flannels weighing over four ounces per square yard, the same duties as on dress goods.

283. On women's and children's dress goods, coat linings, Italian cloth, bunting, or goods of similar description or character, and on all manufactures, composed wholly or in part of wool, worsted, the hair of the camel, goat, alpaca, or other animals, including such as have India rubber as a component material, and not specially provided for in this Act, valued at not over fifty cents per pound, forty per centum ad valorem; valued at more than fifty cents per pound, fifty per centum ad valorem.

284. On clothing, ready made, and articles of wearing apparel of every description, made up or manufactured wholly or in part, not specially provided for in this Act, felts not specially provided for in this Act, all the foregoing composed wholly or in part of wool, worsted, the hair of the camel, goat, alpaca, or other animals, including those having India rubber as a component material, valued at above one dollar and fifty cents per pound, fifty per centum ad valorem; valued at less than one dollar and fifty cents per pound, forty-five per centum ad valorem.

285. On cloaks, dolmans, jackets, talmas, ulsters, or other outside garments for ladies' and children's apparel, and goods of similar description or used for like purposes, and on knit wearing apparel, composed wholly or in part of wool, worsted, the hair of the camel, goat, alpaca, or other animals, made up or manufactured wholly or in part, fifty per centum ad valorem.

286. On webbings, gorings, suspenders, braces, beltings, bindings, braids, galloons, fringes, gimps, cords, cords and tassels, dress trimmings, laces, embroideries, head nets, nettings and veilings, buttons, or barrel buttons, or buttons of other forms, for tassels or ornaments, any of the foregoing which are elastic or nonelastic, made of wool, worsted, the hair of the camel, goat, alpaca, or other animals, or of

which wool, worsted, the hair of the camel, goat, alpaca, or other animals is a component material, fifty per centum ad valorem.

287. Aubusson, Axminster, Moquette, and Chenille carpets, figured or plain, carpets woven whole for rooms, and all carpets or carpeting of like character or description, and oriental, Berlin, and other similar rugs, forty per centum ad valorem.

288. Saxony, Wilton, and Tournay velvet carpets, figured or plain, and all carpets or carpeting of like character or description, forty per centum ad valorem.

289. Brussels carpets, figured or plain, and all carpets or carpeting of like character or description, forty per centum ad valorem.

290. Velvet and tapestry velvet carpets, figured or plain, printed on the warp or otherwise, and all carpets or carpeting of like character or description, forty per centum ad valorem.

291. Tapestry Brussels carpets, figured or plain, and all carpets or carpeting of like character or description, printed on the warp or otherwise, forty-two and one half per centum ad valorem.

292. Treble ingrain, three-ply, and all chain Venetian carpets, thirty-two and one-half per centum ad valorem.

293. Wool Dutch and two-ply ingrain carpets, thirty per centum ad valorem.

294. Druggets and bockings, printed, colored, or otherwise, felt carpeting, figured or plain, thirty per centum ad valorem.

295. Carpets and carpeting of wool, flax, or cotton, or composed in part of either, not specially provided for in this Act, thirty per centum ad valorem.

296. Mats, rugs for floors, screens, covers, hassocks, bed sides, art squares, and other portions of carpets or carpeting made wholly or in part of wool, and not specially provided for in this Act, shall be subjected to the rate of duty herein imposed on carpets or carpetings of like character or description.

297. The reduction of the rates of duty herein provided for manufactures of wool shall take effect January first, eighteen hundred and ninety-five.

SCHEDULE L.—SILKS AND SILK GOODS.

298. Silk partially manufactured from cocoons or from waste silk, and not further advanced or manufactured than carded or combed silk, twenty per centum ad valorem. Thrown silk, not more advanced than singles, tram, organzine, sewing silk, twist, floss, and silk threads or yarns of every description, and spun silk in skeins, cops, warps, or on beams, thirty per centum ad valorem.

299. Velvets, chenilles, or other pile fabrics, composed of silk, or of which silk is the component material of chief value, one dollar and fifty cents per pound; plushes, composed of silk, or of which silk is the component material of chief value, one dollar per pound; but in no case shall the foregoing articles pay a less rate of duty than fifty per centum ad valorem.

300. Webbings, gorings, suspenders, braces, beltings, bindings, braids, galloons, fringes, cords, and tassels, any of the foregoing which are elastic or nonelastic, buttons, and ornaments, made of silk, or of which silk is the component material of chief value, forty-five per centum ad valorem.

301. Laces and articles made wholly or in part of lace, and embroideries, including articles or fabrics embroidered by hand or machinery,

handkerchiefs, neck rufflings and ruchings, nettings and veilings, clothing ready made, and articles of wearing apparel of every description, including knit goods made up or manufactured wholly or in part by the tailor, seamstress, or manufacturer, composed of silk, or of which silk is the component material of chief value, and beaded silk goods, not specially provided for in this Act, fifty per centum ad valorem.

302. All manufactures of silk, or of which silk is the component material of chief value, including those having India rubber as a component material, not specially provided for in this Act, forty-five per centum ad valorem.

SCHEDULE M.—PULP, PAPERS, AND BOOKS.

PULP AND PAPER:

303. Mechanically-ground wood pulp and chemical wood pulp unbleached or bleached, ten per centum ad valorem.

304. Sheathing paper and roofing-felt, ten per centum ad valorem.

306. Printing paper, unsized, sized or glued, suitable only for books and newspapers, fifteen per centum ad valorem.

307. Papers known commercially as copying paper, filtering paper, silver paper, and tissue paper, white, printed, or colored, made up in copying books, reams, or in any other form, thirty-five per centum ad valorem; albumenized or sensitized paper, and writing paper and envelopes embossed, engraved, printed or ornamented, thirty per centum ad valorem.

308. Parchment papers, and surface-coated papers, and manufactures thereof, cardboards, and photograph, autograph, and scrap albums, wholly or partially manufactured, thirty per centum ad valorem. Lithographic prints from either stone or zinc, bound or unbound (except cigar labels and bands, lettered or blank, music, and illustrations when forming a part of a periodical or newspaper and accompanying the same, or if bound in, or forming part of printed books), on paper or other material not exceeding eight-thousandths of an inch in thickness, twenty cents per pound; on paper or other material exceeding eight-thousandths of an inch and not exceeding twenty-thousandths of an inch in thickness, and exceeding thirty-five square inches cutting size in dimensions, eight cents per pound; prints exceeding eight-thousandths of an inch and not exceeding twenty-thousandths of an inch in thickness, and not exceeding thirty-five square inches cutting size in dimensions, five cents per pound; lithographic prints from either stone or zinc on cardboard or other material, exceeding twenty-thousandths of an inch in thickness, six cents per pound; lithographic cigar labels and bands, lettered or blank, printed from either stone or zinc, if printed in less than ten colors, but not including bronze or metal leaf printing, twenty cents per pound; if printed in ten or more colors, or in bronze printing, but not including metal leaf printing, thirty cents per pound; if printed in whole or in part in metal leaf, forty cents per pound.

MANUFACTURES OF PAPER:

309. Paper envelopes, twenty per centum ad valorem.

310. Paper hangings and paper for screens or fireboards, writing paper, drawing paper, and all other paper not specially provided for in this Act, twenty per centum ad valorem.

3413——3

311. Blank books of all kinds, twenty per centum ad valorem; books, including pamphlets and engravings, bound or unbound, photographs, etchings, maps, music, charts, and all printed matter not specially provided for in this Act, twenty-five per centum ad valorem.

312. Playing cards, in packs not exceeding fifty-four cards and at a like rate for any number in excess, ten cents per pack and fifty per centum ad valorem.

313. Manufactures of paper, or of which paper is the component material of chief value, not specially provided for in this Act, twenty per centum ad valorem.

SCHEDULE N.—SUNDRIES.

314. Hair pencils, brushes and feather dusters, thirty-five per centum ad valorem; brooms, twenty per centum ad valorem; bristles, sorted, bunched, or prepared in any manner, seven and one-half cents per pound.

BUTTONS AND BUTTON FORMS:

315. Button forms: Lastings, mohair, cloth, silk, or other manu factures of cloth, woven or made in patterns of such size, shape, or form, or cut in such manner as to be fit for buttons exclusively, ten per centum ad valorem.

316. Buttons commercially known as agate buttons, twenty-five per centum ad valorem; pearl and shell buttons, wholly or partially manufactured, one cent per line button measure of one-fortieth of one inch per gross and fifteen per centum ad valorem.

317. Buttons of ivory, vegetable ivory, glass, bone or horn, wholly or partially manufactured, thirty-five per centum ad valorem.

318. Shoe buttons, made of paper, board, papier maché, pulp, or other similar material not specially provided for in this Act, twenty-five per centum ad valorem.

318½. Coal, bituminous and shale, forty cents per ton; coal slack or culm such as will pass through a half-inch screen, fifteen cents per ton.

318¾. Coke, fifteen per centum ad valorem.

319. Corks, wholly or partially manufactured, ten cents per pound.

320. Dice, draughts, chess-men, chess-balls, and billiard, pool, and bagatelle balls, of ivory, bone, or other materials, fifty per centum ad valorem.

321. Dolls, doll heads, toy marbles of whatever material composed, and all other toys not composed of rubber, china, porcelain, parian, bisque, earthen or stone ware, and not specially provided for in this Act, twenty-five per centum ad valorem. This paragraph shall not take effect until January first, eighteen hundred and ninety-five.

322. Emery grains, and emery manufactured, ground, pulverized, or refined, eight-tenths of one cent per pound.

EXPLOSIVE SUBSTANCES:

323. Fire-crackers of all kinds, fifty per centum ad valorem, but no allowance shall be made for tare or damage thereon.

324. Fulminates, fulminating powders, and like articles, not specially provided for in this Act, thirty per centum ad valorem.

325. Gunpowder, and all explosive substances used for mining, blasting, artillery, or sporting purposes, when valued at twenty cents or less per pound, five cents per pound; valued above twenty cents per pound, eight cents per pound.

326. Matches, friction or lucifer, of all descriptions, twenty per centum ad valorem.

326½. Musical instruments or parts thereof (except pianoforte actions and parts thereof), strings for musical instruments not otherwise enumerated, cases for musical instruments, pitch pipes, tuning forks, tuning hammers, and metronomes, twenty-five per centum ad valorem.

327. Percussion caps, thirty per centum ad valorem; blasting caps, two dollars and seven cents per thousand caps.

328. Feathers and downs of all kinds, when dressed, colored, or manufactured, including quilts of down and other manufactures of down, and also including dressed and finished birds suitable for millinery ornaments, and artificial and ornamental feathers, fruits, grains, leaves, flowers, and stems, or parts thereof, of whatever material composed, suitable for millinery use, not specially provided for in this Act, thirty-five per centum ad valorem.

329. Furs, dressed on the skin but not made up into articles, twenty per centum ad valorem; furs not on the skin, prepared for hatters' use, twenty per centum ad valorem.

330. Fans of all kinds, except common palm-leaf fans, forty per centum ad valorem.

331. Gun wads of all descriptions, ten per centum ad valorem.

332. Hair, human, if clean or drawn but not manufactured, twenty per centum ad valorem.

332½. Hair, curled, suitable for beds or mattresses, ten per centum ad valorem.

333. Haircloth known as "crinoline cloth," six cents per square yard.

334. Haircloth known as "hair seating," twenty cents per square yard.

335. Hats for men's, women's, and children's wear, composed of the fur of the rabbit, beaver, or other animals, or of which such fur is the component material of chief value, wholly or partially manufactured, including fur hat bodies, forty per centum ad valorem.

JEWELRY AND PRECIOUS STONES:

336. Jewelry: All articles, not specially provided for in this Act, commercially known as "jewelry," and cameos in frames, thirty-five per centum ad valorem.

337. Pearls, including pearls strung but not set, ten per centum ad valorem.

338. Precious stones of all kinds, cut but not set, twenty-five per centum ad valorem; if set, and not specially provided for in this Act, including pearls set thirty per centum ad valorem; imitations of precious stones, not exceeding an inch in dimensions, not set, ten per centum ad valorem. And on uncut precious stones of all kinds, ten per centum ad valorem.

LEATHER, AND MANUFACTURES OF:

339. Sole leather, ten per centum ad valorem.

340. Bend or belting leather, and leather not specially provided for in this Act, ten per centum ad valorem.

341. Calfskins, tanned, or tanned and dressed, dressed upper leather, including patent, enameled, and japanned leather, dressed or undressed, and finished; chamois or other skins not specially

ennmerated or provided for in this Act, twenty per centum ad valorem; bookbinders' calfskins, kangaroo, sheep and goat skins, including lamb and kid skins, dressed and finished, twenty per centum ad valorem; skins for morocco, tanned but unfinished, ten per centum ad valorem; pianoforte leather and pianoforte action leather, twenty per centum ad valorem; boots and shoes, made of leather, twenty per centum ad valorem.

342. Leather cut into shoe uppers or vamps, or other forms, suitable for conversion into manufactured articles, twenty per centum ad valorem.

343. Gloves made wholly or in part of leather, whether wholly or partly manufactured, shall pay duty at the following rates, the lengths stated in each case being the extreme length when stretched to their full extent, namely :

344. Ladies' or children's "glace" finish, Schmaschen (of sheep origin), not over fourteen inches in length, one dollar per dozen pairs; over fourteen inches and not over seventeen inches in length, one dollar and fifty cents per dozen pairs; over seventeen inches in length, two dollars per dozen pairs; men's "glace" finish, Schmaschen (sheep), three dollars per dozen pairs.

345. Ladies' or children's "glace" finish, lamb or sheep, not over fourteen inches in length, one dollar and seventy-five cents per dozen pairs; over fourteen and not over seventeen inches in length, two dollars and seventy-five cents per dozen pairs; over seventeen inches in length, three dollars and seventy-five cents per dozen pairs. Men's "glace" finish, lamb or sheep, four dollars per dozen pairs.

346. Ladies' or children's "glace" finish, goat, kid, or other leather than of sheep origin, not over fourteen inches in length, two dollars and twenty-five cents per dozen pairs; over fourteen and not over seventeen inches in length, three dollars per dozen pairs; over seventeen inches in length, four dollars per dozen pairs; men's "glace" finish, kid, goat, or other leather than of sheep origin, four dollars per dozen pairs.

347. Ladies' or children's, of sheep origin, with exterior grain surface removed, by whatever name known, not over seventeen inches in length, one dollar and seventy-five cents per dozen pairs; over seventeen inches in length, two dollars and seventy-five cents per dozen pairs; men's, of sheep origin, with exterior surface removed, by whatever name known, four dollars per dozen pairs.

348. Ladies or children's kid, goat, or other leather than of sheep origin, with exterior grain surface removed, by whatever name known, not over fourteen inches in length, two dollars and twenty-five cents per dozen pairs; over fourteen inches and not over seventeen inches in length, three dollars per dozen pairs; over seventeen inches in length, four dollars per dozen pairs; men's goat, kid, or other leather than of sheep origin, with exterior grain surface removed, by whatever name known, four dollars per dozen pairs.

349. In addition to the foregoing rates, there shall be paid on all leather gloves, when lined, one dollar per dozen pairs.

350. Glove tranks, with or without the usual accompanying pieces, shall pay seventy-five per centum of the duty provided for the gloves in the fabrication of which they are suitable.

MISCELLANEOUS MANUFACTURES:

351. Manufactures of amber, asbestus, bladders, coral, cork, catgut or whipgut or wormgut, jet, paste, spar, wax, or of which these substances or either of them is the component material of chief value, not specially provided for in this Act, twenty-five per centum ad valorem.

352. Manufactures of bone, chip, grass, horn, India rubber, palm leaf, straw, weeds, or whalebone, or of which these substances or either of them is the component material of chief value, not specially provided for in this Act, twenty-five per centum ad valorem. But the terms grass and straw shall be understood to mean these substances in their natural form and structure and not the separated fiber thereof.

353. Manufactures of leather, fur, gutta-percha, vulcanized India rubber, known as hard rubber, human hair, papier-mache, plaster of Paris, indurated fiber wares, and other manufactures composed of wood or other pulp, or of which these substances or either of them is the component material of chief value, all of the above not specially provided for in this Act, thirty per centum ad valorem.

354. Manufactures of ivory, vegetable ivory, mother-of-pearl, gelatine, and shell, or of which these substances or either of them is the component material of chief value, not specially provided for in this Act, and manufactures known commercially as bead, beaded or jet trimmings or ornaments, thirty-five per centum ad valorem.

355. Masks, composed of paper or pulp, twenty-five per centum ad valorem.

356. Matting and mats made of cocoa fiber or rattan, twenty per centum ad valorem.

357. Pencils of wood filled with lead or other material, and slate pencils covered with wood, fifty per centum ad valorem; all other slate pencils, thirty per centum ad valorem.

358. Pencil leads not in wood, ten per centum ad valorem.

358½. Photographic dry plates or films, twenty-five per centum ad valorem.

359. Pipes, pipe bowls, of all materials, and all smokers' articles whatsoever, not specially provided for in this Act, including cigarette books, cigarette-book covers, pouches for smoking or chewing tobacco, and cigarette paper in all forms, fifty per centum ad valorem; all common tobacco pipes and pipe bowls made wholly of clay, valued at not more than fifty cents per gross, ten per centum ad valorem.

360. Umbrellas, parasols, and sunshades, covered with material composed wholly or in part of silk, wool, worsted, the hair of the camel, goat, alpaca, or other animals, or other material than paper, forty-five per centum ad valorem.

STICKS FOR:

361. Umbrellas, parasols, and sunshades, if plain or carved, finished or unfinished, thirty per centum ad valorem.

362. Waste, not specially provided for in this Act, ten per centum ad valorem.

FREE LIST.

SEC. 2. On and after the first day of August, eighteen hundred and ninety-four, unless otherwise provided for in this Act, the following articles, when imported, shall be exempt from duty:

363. Acids used for medicinal, chemical, or manufacturing purposes, not especially provided for in this Act.

364. Aconite.

365. Acorns, raw, dried or undried, but unground.

366. Agates, unmanufactured.

367. Albumen.

368. Alizarin, and alizarin colors or dyes, natural or artificial.

369. Amber, and amberoid unmanufactured, or crude gum.

370. Ambergris.

372. Aniline salts.

373. Any animal imported specially for breeding purposes shall be admitted free: *Provided*, That no such animal shall be admitted free unless pure bred of a recognized breed, and duly registered in the book of record established for that breed, and the Secretary of the Treasury may prescribe such additional regulations as may be required for the strict enforcement of this provision.

Cattle, horses, sheep, or other domestic animals which have strayed across the boundary line into any foreign country, or have been or may be driven across such boundary line by the owner for pasturage purposes, together with their increase, may be brought back to the United States free of duty under regulations to be prescribed by the Secretary of the Treasury.

374. Animals brought into the United States temporarily for a period not exceeding six months, for the purpose of exhibition or competition for prizes offered by any agricultural or racing association; but a bond shall be given in accordance with regulations prescribed by the Secretary of the Treasury; also, teams of animals, including their harness and tackle and the wagons or other vehicles actually owned by persons emigrating from foreign countries to the United States with their families, and in actual use for the purpose of such emigration under such regulations as the Secretary of the Treasury may prescribe; and wild animals intended for exhibition in zoological collections for scientific and educational purposes, and not for sale or profit.

375. Annatto, roucou, rocoa, o. orleans, and all extracts of.

376. Antimony ore, crude sulphite of, and antimony, as regulus or metal.

377. Apatite.

380. Argal, or argol, or crude tartar.

381. Arrow root, raw or unmanufactured.

382. Arsenic and sulphide of, or orpiment.

383. Arseniate of aniline.

384. Art educational stops, composed of glass and metal, and valued at not more than six cents per gross.

385. Articles imported by the United States.

386. Articles in a crude state used in dyeing or tanning not specially provided for in this Act.

387. Articles the growth, produce, and manufacture of the United States, when returned after having been exported, without having been advanced in value or improved in condition by any process of manufacture or other means; casks, barrels, carboys, bags, and other vessels of American manufacture exported filled with American products, or

exported empty and returned filled with foreign products, including shooks when returned as barrels or boxes; also quicksilver flasks or bottles, of either domestic or foreign manufacture, which shall have been actually exported from the United States; but proof of the identity of such articles shall be made, under general regulations to be prescribed by the Secretary of the Treasury, but the exemption of bags from duty shall apply only to such domestic bags as may be imported by the exporter thereof, and if any such articles are subject to internal tax at the time of exportation such tax shall be proved to have been paid before exportation and not refunded: *Provided*, That this paragraph shall not apply to any article upon which an allowance of drawback has been made, the reimportation of which is hereby prohibited except upon payment of duties equal to the drawbacks allowed; or to any article manufactured in bonded warehouse and exported under any provision of law: *And provided further*, That when manufactured tobacco which has been exported without payment of internal-revenue tax shall be reimported it shall be retained in the custody of the collector of customs until internal-revenue stamps in payment of the legal duties shall be placed thereon.

388. Asbestos, unmanufactured.

389. Ashes, wood and lye of, and beet-root ashes.

390. Asphaltum and bitumen, crude or dried, but not otherwise manipulated or treated.

391. Asafetida.

392½. Bagging for cotton, gunny cloth, and all similar material suitable for covering cotton, composed in whole or in part of hemp, flax, jute, or jute butts.

393. Balm of Gilead.

394. Barks, cinchona or other, from which quinine may be extracted.

395. Baryta, carbonate of, or witherite, and baryta, sulphate of, or barytes, unmanufactured, including barytes earth.

396. Bauxite, or beauxite.

397. Beeswax.

398. Bells, broken, and bell metal broken and fit only to be remanufactured.

399. All binding twine manufactured in whole or in part from New Zealand hemp, istle or Tampico fiber, sisal grass, or sunn, of single ply and measuring not exceeding six hundred feet to the pound, and manila twine not exceeding six hundred and fifty feet to the pound.

400. Bird skins, prepared for preservation, but not further advanced in manufacture.

401. Birds and land and water fowls.

402. Bismuth.

403. Bladders, and all integuments of animals, and fish sounds or bladders, crude, salted for preservation, and unmanufactured, not specially provided for in this Act.

404. Blood, dried.

405. Blue vitriol, or sulphate of copper.

406. Bologna sausages.

407. Bolting-cloths, especially for milling purposes, but not suitable for the manufacture of wearing apparel.

408. Bones, crude, or not burned, calcined, ground, steamed, or otherwise manufactured, and bone dust or animal carbon, and bone ash, fit only for fertilizing purposes.

410. Books, engravings, photographs, bound, or unbound, etchings, music, maps, and charts, which shall have been printed more than

twenty years at the date of importation, and all hydrographic charts, and scientific books and periodicals devoted to original scientific research, and publications issued for their subscribers by scientific and literary associations or academies, or publications of individuals for gratuitous private circulation, and public documents issued by foreign Governments.

411. Books and pamphlets printed exclusively in languages other than English; also books and music, in raised print, used exclusively by the blind.

412. Books, engravings, photographs, etchings, bound or unbound, maps and charts imported by authority or for the use of the United States or for the use of the Library of Congress.

413. Books, maps, music, lithographic prints, and charts, specially imported, not more than two copies in any one invoice, in good faith, for the use of any society incorporated or established for educational, philosophical, literary, or religious purposes, or for the encouragement of the fine arts, or for the use or by order of any college, academy, school, or seminary of learning in the United States, or any State or public library, subject to such regulations as the Secretary of the Treasury shall prescribe.

414. Books, libraries, usual furniture, and similar household effects of persons or families from foreign countries, if actually used abroad by them not less than one year, and not intended for any other person or persons, nor for sale.

416. Brazil paste.

417. Braids, plaits, laces, and similar manufactures composed of straw, chip, grass, palm leaf, willow, osier, or rattan, suitable for making or ornamenting hats, bonnets, and hoods.

418. Brazilian pebble, unwrought or unmanufactured.

419. Breccia, in block or slabs.

420. Bristles, crude, not sorted, bunched, or prepared.

421. Bromine.

422. Broom corn.

423. Bullion, gold or silver.

424. Burgundy pitch.

424½. Burlaps, and bags for grain made of burlaps.

425. Cabbages.

426. Old coins and medals, and other antiquities. but the term "antiquities" as used in this Act shall include only such articles as are suitable for souvenirs or cabinet collections, and which shall have been produced at any period prior to the year seventeen hundred.

427. Cadmium.

428. Calamine.

429. Camphor, crude.

430. Castor or castoreum.

431. Catgut, whipgut, or wormgut, unmanufactured, or not further manufactured than in strings or cords.

432. Cerium.

433. Chalk, unmanufactured.

434. Charcoal.

435. Chicory root, raw, dried, or undried, but unground.

436. Cider.

437. Civet, crude.

438. Chromate of iron or chromic ore.

439. Clay—Common blue clay in casks suitable for the manufacture of crucibles.

441. Coal, anthracite, and coal stores of American vessels, but none shall be unloaded.

443. Coal tar, crude, and all preparations except medicinal coal-tar preparations and products of coal tar, not colors or dyes, not specially provided for in this Act.

444. Cobalt and cobalt ore.

445. Cocculus indicus.

446. Cochineal.

447. Cocoa, or cacao, crude, leaves, and shells of.

448. Coffee.

449. Coins, gold, silver, and copper.

450. Coir, and coir yarn.

451. Copper imported in the form of ores.

452. Old copper, fit only for manufacture, clipping from new copper, and all composition metal of which copper is a component material of chief value not specially provided for in this Act.

453. Copper, regulus of, and black or coarse copper, and copper cement.

454. Copper in plates, bars, ingots, or pigs, and other forms, not manufactured, not specially provided for in this Act.

455. Copperas, or sulphate of iron.

456. Coral, marine, uncut, and unmanufactured.

457. Cork wood or cork bark, unmanufactured.

458. Cotton, and cotton waste or flocks.

459. Cotton ties of iron or steel cut to lengths, punched or not punched, with or without buckles, for baling cotton.

460. Cryolite, or kryolith.

461. Cudbear.

462. Curling stones, or quoits, and curling-stone handles.

463. Curry, and curry powder.

464. Cutch.

465. Cuttlefish bone.

466. Dandelion roots, raw, dried, or undried, but unground.

467. Diamonds; miners', glaziers', and engravers' diamonds not set, and diamond dust or bort, and jewels to be used in the manufacture of watches or clocks.

468. Divi-divi.

469. Dragon's blood.

470. Drugs, such as barks, beans, berries, balsams, buds, bulbs, bulbous roots, excrescences, fruits, flowers, dried fibers, dried insects, grains, gums and gum resin, herbs, leaves, lichens, mosses, nuts, roots and stems, spices, vegetables, seeds aromatic, seeds of morbid growth, weeds, and woods used expressly for dyeing; any of the foregoing drugs which are not edible, and which have not been advanced in value or condition by refining or grinding, or by other process of manufacture, and not specially provided for in this Act.

471. Eggs of birds, fish, and insects : *Provided, however,* That this shall not be held to include the eggs of game birds the importation of which is prohibited except specimens for scientific collections.

472. Emery ore.

473. Ergot.

474. Common palm leaf fans, and palm leaf unmanufactured.

475. Farina.

476. Fashion plates, engraved on steel or copper or on wood, colored or plain.

477. Feathers and downs for beds, and feathers and downs of all kinds, crude or not dressed, colored, or manufactured, not specially provided for in this Act.

478. Feldspar.
479. Felt, adhesive, for sheathing vessels.
480. Fibrin, in all forms.
481. Fish, frozen or packed in ice fresh.
482. Fish for bait.
483. Fish skins.
484. Flint, flints, and ground flint stones.
485. Floor matting manufactured from round or split straw, includ ing what is commonly known as Chinese matting.
486. Fossils.
487. Fruit plants, tropical and semitropical, for the purpose of propa gation or cultivation.

FRUITS AND NUTS:
489. Fruits, green, ripe, or dried not specially provided for in this Act.
490. Tamarinds.
491. Brazil nuts, cream nuts, palm nuts, and palm-nut kernels not otherwise provided for.
492. Furs, undressed; dressed fur pieces suitable only for use in the manufacture of hatter's fur.
493. Fur skins of all kinds not dressed in any manner.
494. Gambier.
495. Glass, broken, and old glass, which can not be cut for use, and fit only to be remanufactured.
496 Glass plates or disks, rough-cut or unwrought, for use in the manufacture of optical instruments, spectacles, and eyeglasses, and suitable only for such use: *Provided, however,* That such disks exceed ing eight inches in diameter may.be polished sufficiently to enable the character of the glass to be determined.

GRASSES AND FIBERS:
497. Istle or Tampico fiber, jute, jute butts, manila, sisal grass, sunn, flax straw, flax not hackled, tow of flax or hemp, hemp not hackled, hemp, flax, jute, and tow wastes, and all other textile grasses or fibrous vegetable substances, unmanufactured or undressed, not specially provided for in this Act.
498. Gold-beaters' molds and gold-beaters' skins.
499. Grease and oils, including cod oil, such as are commonly used in soap-making or in wire-drawing, or for stuffing or dressing leather, and which are fit only for such uses, not specially provided for in this Act.
500. Guano, manures, and all substances expressly used for manure.
501. Gunny bags and gunny cloths, old or refuse, fit only for remanufacture.
503. Gutta-percha, crude.
504. Hair of horse, cattle, and other animals, cleaned or uncleaned, drawn or undrawn, not specially provided for in this Act; and human hair, raw, uncleaned, and not drawn.
505. Hides and skins, raw or uncured, whether dry, salted, or pickled.
506. Hide cuttings, raw, with or without hair, and all other glue stock.
507. Hide rope.
508. Hones and whetstones.
509. Hoofs, unmanufactured.

510. Hop roots for cultivation.

511. Horns, and parts of, unmanufactured, including horn strips and tips.

512. Ice.

513. India rubber, crude, and milk of, and old scrap or refuse India rubber, which has been worn out by use and is fit only for remanufacture.

514. Indigo, and extracts or pastes of, and carmines.

515. Iodine, crude, and resublimed.

516. Ipecac.

517. Iridium.

519. Ivory, sawed or cut into logs, but not otherwise manufactured, and vegetable ivory.

520. Jalap.

521. Jet, unmanufactured.

522. Joss stick, or Joss light.

523. Junk, old.

524. Kelp.

525. Kieserite.

526. Kyanite, or cyanite, and kainite.

527. Lac-dye, crude, seed, button, stick, and shell.

528. Lac spirits.

529. Lactarine.

531. Lava, unmanufactured.

532. Leeches.

533. Lemon juice, lime juice, and sour-orange juice.

534. Licorice root, unground.

535. Lifeboats and life-saving apparatus specially imported by societies incorporated or established to encourage the saving of human life.

536. Lime, citrate of.

537. Lime, chloride of, or bleaching powder.

538. Lithographic stones not engraved.

539. Litmus, prepared or not prepared.

540. Loadstones.

541. Madder and munjeet, or Indian madder, ground or prepared, and all extracts of.

542. Magnesia, sulphate of, or Epsom salts.

543. Magnesite, or native mineral carbonate of magnesia.

544. Magnesium.

545. Magnets.

546. Manganese, oxide and ore of.

547. Manna.

548. Manuscripts.

549. Marrow, crude.

550. Marsh mallows.

551. Medals of gold, silver, or copper, and other metallic articles manufactured as trophies or prizes, and actually received or bestowed and accepted as honorary distinctions.

553. Meerschaum, crude or unmanufactured.

554. Milk, fresh.

555. Mineral waters, all not artificial, and mineral salts of the same, obtained by evaporation, when accompanied by duly authenticated certificate, showing that they are in no way artificially prepared, and are the product of a designated mineral spring; lemonade, soda-water, and all similar waters.

556. Minerals, crude, or not advanced in value or condition by

refining or grinding, or by other process of manufacture, not specially provided for in this Act.

557. Models of inventions and of other improvements in the arts, including patterns for machinery, but no article shall be deemed a model or pattern which can be fitted for use otherwise.

557½. Molasses testing not above forty degrees polariscope test, and containing twenty per centum or less of moisture.

558. Moss, seaweeds, and vegetable substances, crude or unmanufactured, not otherwise specially provided for in this Act.

559. Musk, crude, in natural pods.

560. Myrobolan.

561. Needles, hand-sewing and darning.

562. Newspapers and periodicals; but the term "periodicals" as herein used shall be understood to embrace only unbound or paper-covered publications, containing current literature of the day and issued regularly at stated periods, as weekly, monthly, or quarterly.

564. Nux vomica.

565. Oakum.

566. Ocher and ochery earths, sienna and sienna earths, umber and umber earths, not specially provided for in this Act, dry.

567. Oil cake.

568. OILS: Almond, amber, crude and rectified ambergris, anise or anise seed, aniline, aspic or spike lavender, bergamot, cajeput, caraway, cassia, cinnamon, cedrat, chamomile, citronella or lemon grass, civet, cotton seed, croton, fennel, Jasmine or Jasimine, Juglandium, Juniper, lavender, lemon, limes, mace, neroli or orange flower, enfleurage grease, nut oil or oil of nuts not otherwise specially provided for in this Act, orange oil, olive oil for manufacturing or mechanical purposes unfit for eating and not otherwise provided for in this Act, ottar of roses, palm and cocoanut, rosemary or anthoss, sesame or sesamum seed or bean, thyme, origanum red or white, valerian; and also spermaceti, whale, and other fish oils of American fisheries, and all fish and other products, of such fisheries; petroleum, crude or refined: *Provided*, That if there be imported into the United States crude petroleum, or the products of crude petroleum produced in any country which imposes a duty on petroleum or its products exported from the United States, there shall be levied, paid and collected upon said crude petroleum or its products so imported, forty per centum ad valorem.

569. Opium, crude or unmanufactured, and not adulterated, containing nine per centum and over of morphia.

570. Orange and lemon peel, not preserved, candied, or otherwise prepared.

571. Orchil, or orchil liquid.

573. Ores, of gold, silver, and nickel, and nickel matte.

574. Osmium.

575. Paintings, in oil or water colors, original drawings and sketches, and artists' proofs of etchings and engravings, and statuary, not otherwise provided for in this Act, but the term "statuary" as herein used shall be understood to include only professional productions, whether round or in relief, in marble, stone, alabaster, wood, or metal, of a statuary or sculptor, and the word "painting," as used in this Act, shall not be understood to include such as are made wholly or in part by stenciling or other mechanical process.

576. Palladium.

577. Paper stock, crude, of every description, including all grasses, fibers, rags, waste, shavings, clippings, old paper, rope ends, waste

rope, waste bagging, old or refused gunny bags or gunny cloth, and poplar or other woods, fit only to be converted into paper.

578. Paraffine.

579. Parchment and vellum.

580. Pearl, mother of, not sawed or cut, or otherwise manufactured.

581. Pease, green, in bulk or in barrels, sacks, or similar packages.

582. Peltries and other usual goods and effects of Indians passing or repassing the boundary line of the United States, under such regulations as the Secretary of the Treasury may prescribe: *Provided*, That this exemption shall not apply to goods in bales or other packages unusual among Indians.

583. Personal and household effects not merchandise of citizens of the United States dying in foreign countries.

584. Pewter and britannia metal, old, and fit only to be re-manufactured.

585. Philosophical and scientific apparatus, utensils, instruments and preparations, including bottles and boxes containing the same; statuary, casts of marble, bronze, alabaster, or plaster of Paris; paintings, drawings, and etchings, specially imported in good faith for the use of any society or institution incorporated or established for religious, philosophical, educational, scientific, or literary purposes, or for encouragement of the fine arts, and not intended for sale.

586. Phosphates, crude or native.

587. Plants, trees, shrubs, and vines of all kinds commonly known as nursery stock, not specially provided for in this Act.

588. Plaster of Paris and sulphate of lime, unground.

589. Platina, in ingots, bars, sheets, and wire.

590. Platinum, unmanufactured, and vases, retorts, and other apparatus, vessels, and parts thereof composed of platinum, adapted for chemical uses.

591. Plows, tooth and disk harrows, harvesters, reapers, agricultural drills, and planters, mowers, horserakes, cultivators, threshing machines and cotton gins: *Provided*, That all articles mentioned in this paragraph if imported from a country which lays an import duty on like articles imported from the United States, shall be subject to the duties existing prior to the passage of this Act.

592. Plumbago.

593. Plush, black, known commercially as hatters' plush, composed of silk, or of silk and cotton, and used exclusively for making men's hats.

594. Polishing-stones, and burnishing-stones.

595. Potash, crude, carbonate of, or "black salts." Caustic potash, or hydrate of, including refined in sticks or rolls. Nitrate of potash, or saltpeter, crude. Sulphate of potash, crude or refined. Chlorate of potash. Muriate of potash.

596. Professional books, implements, instruments, and tools of trade, occupation, or employment, in the actual possession at the time of persons arriving in the United States; but this exemption shall not be construed to include machinery or other articles imported for use in any manufacturing establishment, or for any other person or persons, or for sale, nor shall it be construed to include theatrical scenery, properties, and apparel, but such articles brought by proprietors or managers of theatrical exhibitions arriving from abroad for temporary use by them in such exhibitions and not for any other person and not for sale and which have been used by them abroad shall be admitted free of duty under such regulations as the Secretary of the Treasury

may prescribe; but bonds shall be given for the payment to the United States of such duties as may be imposed by law upon any and all such articles as shall not be exported within six months after such importation: *Provided*, That the Secretary of the Treasury may in his discretion extend such period for a further term of six months in case application shall be made therefor.

597. Puln.

598. Pumice.

600. Quills, prepared or unprepared, but not made up into complete articles.

601. Quinia, sulphate of, and all alkaloids or salts of cinchona bark.

602. Rags, not otherwise specially provided for in this Act.

603. Regalia and gems, statues, statuary, and specimens or casts of sculpture where specially imported in good faith for the use of any society incorporated or established solely for educational, philosophical, literary, or religious purposes, or for the encouragement of fine arts, or for the use or by order of any college, academy, school, seminary of learning, or public library in the United States; but the term "regalia" as herein used shall be held to embrace only such insignia of rank or office or emblems, as may be worn upon the person or borne in the hand during public exercises of the society or institution, and shall not include articles of furniture or fixtures, or of regular wearing apparel, nor personal property of individuals.

604. Rennets, raw or prepared.

605. Saffron and safflower, and extract of, and saffron cake.

606. Sago, crude, and sago flour.

607. Salacine.

608. Salt in bulk, and salt in bags, sacks, barrels, or other packages, but the coverings shall pay the same rate of duty as if imported separately: *Provided*, That if salt is imported from any country whether independent or a dependency which imposes a duty upon salt exported from the United States, then there shall be levied, paid, and collected upon such salt the rate of duty existing prior to the passage of this Act.

609. Sauerkraut.

610. Sausage skins.

611. Seeds; anise, canary, caraway, cardamom, coriander, cotton, croton, cummin, fennel, fenugreek, hemp, hoarhound, mustard, rape, Saint John's bread or bene, sugar beet, mangel-wurzel, sorghum or sugar cane for seed, and all flower and grass seed; bulbs and roots, not edible; all the foregoing not specially provided for in this Act.

612. Selep, or saloup.

613. Shells of all kinds, not cut, ground, or otherwise manufactured.

614. Shotgun barrels, forged, rough bored.

615. Shrimps, and other shellfish, canned or otherwise.

616. Silk, raw, or as reeled from the cocoon, but not doubled, twisted, nor advanced in manufacture in any way.

617. Silk cocoons and silk waste.

618. Silk worm's eggs.

619. Skeletons and other preparations of anatomy.

620. Snails.

621. Soda, nitrate of, or cubic nitrate, and chlorate of.

622. Sulphate of Soda, or salt cake, or niter cake.

623. Sodium.

624. Sparterre, suitable for making or ornamenting hats.

625. Specimens of natural history, botany, and mineralogy, when imported for cabinets or as objects of science, and not for sale.

SPICES:

626. Cassia, cassia vera, and cassia buds, unground.
627. Cinnamon, and chips of, unground.
628. Cloves and clove stems, unground.
629. Ginger-root, unground and not preserved or candied.
630. Mace.
631. Nutmegs.
632. Pepper, black or white, unground.
633. Pimento, unground.
635. Spunk.
636. Spurs and stilts used in the manufacture of earthen, porcelain, and stone ware.
636½. Stamps: Foreign postage or revenue stamps, canceled or uncanceled.
638. Stone and sand: Burr stone in blocks, rough or manufactured, or bound up into millstones; cliff stone, unmanufactured; pumice stone, rotten stone, and sand, crude or manufactured.
639. Storax or styrax.
640. Strontia, oxide of, and protoxide of strontian, and strontianite, or mineral carbonate of strontia.
642. Sulphur, lac or precipitated, and sulphur or brimstone, crude, in bulk, sulphur ore, as pyrites, or sulphuret of iron in its natural state, containing in excess of twenty-five per centum of sulphur, and sulphur not otherwise provided for.
643. Sulphuric acid: *Provided,* That upon sulphuric acid imported from any country, whether independent or a dependency, which imposes a duty upon sulphuric acid exported from the United States, there shall be levied, and collected the rate of duty existing prior to the passage of this Act.
644. Sweepings of silver and gold.
645. Tallow and wool grease, including that known commercially as degras or brown wool grease.
646. Tapioca, cassava or cassady.
647. Tar and pitch of wood, and pitch of coal tar.
648. Tea and tea plants.
650. Teeth, natural, or unmanufactured.
651. Terra alba.
652. Terra japonica.
653. Tin ore, cassiterite or black oxide of tin, and tin in bars, blocks, pigs, or grain or granulated.
654. Tinsel wire, lame, or lahn.
655. Tobacco stems.
656. Tonquin, tonqua, or tonka beans.
657. Tripoli.
658. Turmeric.
659. Turpentine, Venice.
660. Turpentine, spirits of.
661. Turtles.
662. Types, old, and fit only to be remanufactured.
663. Uranium, oxide and salts of.
664. Vaccine virus.
665. Valonia.
666. Verdigris, or subacetate of copper.
667. Wafers, unmedicated, and not edible.
668. Wax, vegetable or mineral.
669. Wearing apparel and other personal effects (not merchandise)

of persons arriving in the United States; but this exemption shall not be held to include articles not actually in use and necessary and appropriate for the use of such persons for the purposes of their journey and present comfort and convenience, or which are intended for any other person or persons, or for sale.

671. Whalebone, unmanufactured.

WOOD:

672. Logs, and round unmanufactured timber not specially enumerated or provided for in this Act.

673. Firewood, handle bolts, heading bolts, stave bolts, and shingle bolts, hop poles, fence posts, railroad ties, ship timber, and ship planking, not specially provided for in this Act.

674. Timber, hewn and sawed, and timber used for spars and in building wharves.

675. Timber, squared or sided.

676. Sawed boards, plank, deals, and other lumber, rough or dressed, except boards, plank, deals and other lumber of cedar, lignum vitæ, lancewood, ebony, box, granadilla, mahogany, rosewood, satinwood, and all other cabinet woods.

677. Pine clapboards.

678. Spruce clapboards.

679. Hubs for wheels, posts, last blocks, wagon blocks, oar blocks, gun blocks, heading, and all like blocks or sticks, rough hewn or sawed only.

680. Laths.

681. Pickets and palings.

682. Shingles.

683. Staves of wood of all kinds, wood unmanufactured: *Provided*, That all of the articles mentioned in paragraphs six hundred and seventy-two to six hundred and eighty-three, inclusive, when imported from any country which lays an export duty or imposes discriminating stumpage dues on any of them, shall be subject to the duties existing prior to the passage of this Act.

684. Woods, namely, cedar, lignum-vitæ, lancewood, ebony, box, granadilla, mahogany, rosewood, satinwood, and all forms of cabinet woods, in the log, rough or hewn; bamboo and rattan unmanufactured; briar root or briar wood, and similar wood unmanufactured, or not further manufactured than cut into blocks suitable for the articles into which they are intended to be converted; bamboo, reeds, and sticks of partridge, hair wood, pimento, orange, myrtle, and other woods, not otherwise specially provided for in this Act, in the rough, or not further manufactured than cut into lengths suitable for sticks for umbrellas, parasols, sunshades, whips, or walking canes; and India malacca joints, not further manufactured than cut into suitable lengths for the manufactures into which they are intended to be converted.

685. All wool of the sheep, hair of the camel, goat, alpaca, and other like animals, and all wool and hair on the skin, noils, yarn waste, card waste, bur waste, slubbing waste, roving waste, ring waste, and all waste, or rags composed wholly or in part of wool, all the foregoing not otherwise herein provided for

686. Works of art, the production of American artists residing temporarily abroad, or other works of art, including pictorial paintings on

glass, imported expressly for presentation to a national institution, or to any State or municipal corporation, or incorporated religious society, college, or other public institution, including stained or painted window glass or stained or painted glass windows; but such exemption shall be subject to such regulations as the Secretary of the Treasury may prescribe.

687. Works of art, drawings, engravings, photographic pictures, and philosophical and scientific apparatus brought by professional artists, lecturers, or scientists arriving from abroad for use by them temporarily for exhibition and in illustration, promotion, and encouragement of art, science, or industry in the United States, and not for sale, and photographic pictures, imported for exhibition by any association established in good faith and duly authorized under the laws of the United States, or of any State, expressly and solely for the promotion and encouragement of science, art, or industry, and not intended for sale, shall be admitted free of duty, under such regulations as the Secretary of the Treasury shall prescribe; but bonds shall be given for the payment to the United States of such duties as may be imposed by law upon any and all such articles as shall not be exported within six months after such importation: *Provided,* That the Secretary of the Treasury may, in his discretion, extend such period for a further term of six months in cases where applications therefor shall be made.

688. Works of art, collections in illustration of the progress of the arts, science, or manufactures, photographs, works in terra cotta, parian, pottery, or porcelain, and artistic copies of antiquities in metal or other material, hereafter imported in good faith for permanent exhibition at a fixed place by any society or institution established for the encouragement of the arts or of science, and all like articles imported in good faith by any society or association for the purpose of erecting a public monument, and not intended for sale, nor for any other purpose than herein expressed; but bonds shall be given under such rules and regulations as the Secretary of the Treasury may prescribe, for the payment of lawful duties which may accrue should any of the articles aforesaid be sold, transferred, or used contrary to this provision, and such articles shall be subject, at any time, to examination and inspection by the proper officers of the customs: *Provided,* That the privileges of this and the preceding section shall not be allowed to associations or corporations engaged in or connected with business of a private or commercial character.

689. Yams.
690. Zaffer.

SEC. 3. That there shall be levied, collected, and paid on the importation of all raw or unmanufactured articles, not enumerated or provided for in this Act, a duty of ten per centum ad valorem; and on all articles manufactured, in whole or in part, not provided for in this Act, a duty of twenty per centum ad valorem.

SEC. 4. That each and every imported article, not enumerated in this Act, which is similar, either in material, quality, texture, or the use to which it may be applied, to any article enumerated in this Act as chargeable with duty shall pay the same rate of duty which is levied on the enumerated article which it most resembles in any of the particulars before mentioned; and if any nonenumerated article equally resembles two or more enumerated articles on which different rates of duty are chargeable there shall be levied on such nonenumerated article the same rate of duty as is chargeable on the article which it resembles paying the highest rate of duty; and on articles not enumer-

. ated, manufactured of two or more materials, the duty shall be assessed at the highest rate at which the same would be chargeable if composed wholly of the component material thereof of chief value; and the words "component material of chief value," wherever used in this Act, shall be held to mean that component material which shall exceed in value any other single component material of the article; and the value of each component material shall be determined by the ascertained value of such material in its condition as found in the article. If two or more rates of duty shall be applicable to any imported article it shall pay duty at the highest of such rates.

Sec. 5. That all articles of foreign manufacture, such as are usually or ordinarily marked, stamped, branded, or labeled, and all packages containing such or other imported articles, shall, respectively, be plainly marked, stamped, branded, or labeled in legible English words, so as to indicate the country of their origin and the quantity of their contents; and until so marked, stamped, branded, or labeled they shall not be delivered to the importer should any article of imported merchandise be marked, stamped, branded, or labeled so as to indicate a quantity, number, or measurement in excess of the quantity, number, or measurement actually contained in such article, no delivery of the same shall be made to the importer until the mark, stamp, brand, or label, as the case may be, shall be changed so as to conform to the facts of the case.

Sec. 6. That no article of imported merchandise which shall copy or simulate the name or trade-mark of any domestic manufacture or manufacturer shall be admitted to entry at any custom-house of the United States. And in order to aid the officers of the customs in enforcing this prohibition any domestic manufacturer who has adopted trade-marks may require his name and residence and a description of his trade-marks to be recorded in books which shall be kept for that purpose in the Department of the Treasury under such regulations as the Secretary of the Treasury shall prescribe, and may furnish to the Department facsimiles of such trade-marks; and thereupon the Secretary of the Treasury shall cause one or more copies of the same to be transmitted to each collector or other proper officer of the customs.

Sec. 7. That all materials of foreign production which may be necessary for the construction of vessels built in the United States for foreign account and ownership or for the purpose of being employed in the foreign trade including the trade between the Atlantic and Pacific ports of the United States, and all such materials necessary for the building of their machinery, and all articles necessary for their outfit and equipment, after the passage of this Act, may be imported in bond under such regulations as the Secretary of the Treasury may prescribe; and upon proof that such materials have been used for such purposes no duties shall be paid thereon. But vessels receiving the benefit of this section shall not be allowed to engage in the coastwise trade of the United States more than two months in any one year except upon the payment to the United States of the duties of which a rebate is herein allowed: *Provided*, That vessels built in the United States for foreign account and ownership shall not be allowed to engage in the coastwise trade of the United States.

Sec. 8. That all articles of foreign production needed for the repair of American vessels engaged in foreign trade, including the trade between the Atlantic and Pacific ports of the United States, may be withdrawn from bonded warehouses free of duty, under such regulations as the Secretary of the Treasury may prescribe.

SEC. 9. That all articles manufactured in whole or in part of imported materials, or of materials subject to internal-revenue tax, and intended for exportation without being charged with duty and without having an internal-revenue stamp affixed thereto shall, under such regulations as the Secretary of the Treasury may prescribe, in order to be so manufactured and exported be made and manufactured in bonded warehouses similar to those known and designated in Treasury Regulations as bonded warehouses, class six: *Provided*, That the manufacturer of such articles shall first give satisfactory bonds for the faithful observance of all the provisions of law and of such regulations as shall be prescribed by the Secretary of the Treasury: *Provided further*, That the manufacture of distilled spirits from grain, starch, molasses or sugar, including all dilutions or mixtures of them or either of them, shall not be permitted in such manufacturing warehouses.

Whenever goods manufactured in any bonded warehouse established under the provisions of the preceding paragraph shall be exported directly therefrom or shall be duly laden for transportation and immediate exportation under the supervision of the proper officer who shall be duly designated for that purpose, such goods shall be exempt from duty and from the requirements relating to revenue stamps.

Any materials used in the manufacture of such goods, and any packages, coverings, vessels, brands, and labels used in putting up the same may, under the regulations of the Secretary of the Treasury, be conveyed without the payment of revenue tax or duty into any bonded manufacturing warehouse, and imported goods may, under the aforesaid regulations, be transferred without the exaction of duty from any bonded warehouse into any bonded manufacturing warehouse; but this privilege shall not be held to apply to implements, machinery, or apparatus to be used in the construction or repair of any bonded manufacturing warehouse or for the prosecution of the business carried on therein.

No articles or materials received into such bonded manufacturing warehouse shall be withdrawn or removed therefrom except for direct shipment and exportation or for transportation and immediate exportation in bond under the supervision of the officer duly designated therefor by the collector of the port, who shall certify to such shipment and exportation, or ladening for transportation, as the case may be, describing the articles by their mark or otherwise, the quantity, the date of exportation, and the name of the vessel. All labor performed and services rendered under these provisions shall be under the supervision of a duly designated officer of the customs and at the expense of the manufacturer.

A careful account shall be kept by the collector of all merchandise delivered by him to any bonded manufacturing warehouse, and a sworn monthly return, verified by the customs officers in charge, shall be made by the manufacturers containing a detailed statement of all imported merchandise used by him in the manufacture of exported articles.

Before commencing business the proprietor of any manufacturing warehouse shall file with the Secretary of the Treasury a list of all the articles intended to be manufactured in such warehouse and state the formula of manufacture and the names and quantities of the ingredients to be used therein.

Articles manufactured under these provisions may be withdrawn under such regulations as the Secretary of the Treasury may prescribe for transportation and delivery into any bonded warehouse at an exterior port for the sole purpose of immediate export therefrom.

The provisions of Revised Statutes thirty-four hundred and thirty-three shall, so far as may be practicable, apply to any bonded manufacturing warehouse established under this Act and to the merchandise conveyed therein.

SEC. 10. That all persons are prohibited from importing into the United States from any foreign country any obscene book, pamphlet, paper, writing, advertisement, circular, print, picture, drawing, or other representation, figure, or image on or of paper or other material, or any cast, instrument, or other article of an immoral nature, or any drug or medicine, or any article whatever for the prevention of conception or for causing unlawful abortion, or any lottery ticket or any advertisement of any lottery. No such articles, whether imported separately or contained in packages with other goods entitled to entry, shall be admitted to entry; and all such articles shall be proceeded against, seized, and forfeited by due course of law. All such prohibited articles and the package in which they are contained in the course of importation shall be detained by the officer of customs, and proceedings taken against the same as hereinafter prescribed, unless it appears to the satisfaction of the collector of customs that the obscene articles contained in the package were inclosed therein without the knowledge or consent of the importer, owner, agent, or consignee: *Provided*, That the drugs hereinbefore mentioned, when imported in bulk and not put up for any of the purposes hereinbefore specified, are excepted from the operation of this section.

SEC. 11. That whoever, being an officer, agent, or employee of the Government of the United States, shall knowingly aid or abet any person engaged in any violation of any of the provisions of law prohibiting importing, advertising, dealing in, exhibiting, or sending or receiving by mail obscene or indecent publications or representations, or means for preventing conception or procuring abortion, or other articles of indecent or immoral use or tendency, shall be deemed guilty of a misdemeanor, and shall for every offense be punishable by a fine of not more than five thousand dollars, or by imprisonment at hard labor for not more than ten years, or both.

SEC. 12. That any judge of any district or circuit court of the United States, within the proper district, before whom complaint in writing of any violation of the two preceding sections is made, to the satisfaction of such judge, and founded on knowledge or belief, and if upon belief, setting forth the grounds of such belief, and supported by oath or affirmation of the complainant, may issue, conformably to the Constitution, a warrant directed to the marshal or any deputy marshal in the proper district, directing him to search for, seize, and take possession of any such article or thing mentioned in the two preceding sections, and to make due and immediate return thereof to the end that the same may be condemned and destroyed by proceedings, which shall be conducted in the same manner as other proceedings in the case of municipal seizure, and with the same right of appeal or writ of error.

SEC. 13. That machinery for repair may be imported into the United States without payment of duty, under bond, to be given in double the appraised value thereof, to be withdrawn and exported after said machinery shall have been repaired; and the Secretary of the Treasury is authorized and directed to prescribe such rules and regulations as may be necessary to protect the revenue against fraud and secure the identity and character of all such importations when again withdrawn and exported, restricting and limiting the export and withdrawal to the same port of entry where imported, and also limiting all bonds to a period of time of not more than six months from the date of the importation.

SEC. 14. That a discriminating duty of ten per centum ad valorem, in addition to the duties imposed by law, shall be levied, collected, and paid on all goods, wares, or merchandise which shall be imported in vessels not of the United States; but this discriminating duty shall not apply to goods, wares, and merchandise which shall be imported in vessels not of the United States, entitled, by treaty or any Act of Congress, to be entered in the ports of the United States on payment of the same duties as shall then be paid on goods, wares, and merchandise imported in vessels of the United States.

SEC. 15. That no goods, wares, or merchandise, unless in cases provided for by treaty, shall be imported into the United States from any foreign port or place, except in vessels of the United States, or in such foreign vessels as truly and wholly belong to the citizens or subjects of that country of which the goods are the growth, production, or manufacture, or from which such goods, wares, or merchandise can only be, or most usually are, first shipped for transportation. All goods, wares, or merchandise imported contrary to this section, and the vessel wherein the same shall be imported, together with her cargo, tackle, apparel, and furniture, shall be forfeited to the United States; and such goods, wares, or merchandise, ship, or vessel, and cargo shall be liable to be seized, prosecuted, and condemned in like manner, and under the same regulations, restrictions, and provisions as have been heretofore established for the recovery, collection, distribution, and remission of forfeitures to the United States by the several revenue laws.

SEC. 16. That the preceding section shall not apply to vessels or goods, wares, or merchandise imported in vessels of a foreign nation which does not maintain a similar regulation against vessels of the United States.

SEC. 17. That the importation of neat cattle and the hides of neat cattle from any foreign country into the United States is prohibited: *Provided*, That the operation of this section shall be suspended as to any foreign country or countries, or any parts of such country or countries, whenever the Secretary of the Treasury shall officially determine, and give public notice thereof that such importation will not tend to the introduction or spread of contagious or infectious diseases among the cattle of the United States; and the Secretary of the Treasury is hereby authorized and empowered, and it shall be his duty, to make all necessary orders and regulations to carry this section into effect, or to suspend the same as herein provided, and to send copies thereof to the proper officers in the United States, and to such officers or agents of the United States in foreign countries as he shall judge necessary.

SEC. 18. That any person convicted of a willful violation of any of the provisions of the preceding section shall be fined not exceeding five hundred dollars, or imprisoned not exceeding one year, or both, in the discretion of the court.

SEC. 19. That upon the reimportation of articles once exported of the growth, product, or manufacture of the United States, upon which no internal tax has been assessed or paid, or upon which such tax has been paid and refunded by allowance or drawback, there shall be levied, collected, and paid a duty equal to the tax imposed by the internal-revenue laws upon such articles, except articles manufactured in bonded warehouses and exported pursuant to law, which shall be subject to the same rate of duty as if originally imported.

SEC. 20. That whenever any vessel laden with merchandise in whole or in part subject to duty has been sunk in any river, harbor, bay, or waters subject to the jurisdiction of the United States, and within its limits, for the period of two years, and is abandoned by the owner thereof, any person who may raise such vessel shall be permitted to bring any merchandise recovered therefrom into the port nearest to the place where such vessel was so raised free from the payment of any duty thereupon, but under such regulations as the Secretary of the Treasury may prescribe.

SEC. 21. That the works of manufacturers engaged in smelting or refining metals, or both smelting and refining, in the United States may be designated as bonded warehouses under such regulations as the Secretary of the Treasury may prescribe: *Provided*, That such manufacturers shall first give satisfactory bonds to the Secretary of the Treasury. Ores or metals in any crude form requiring smelting or refining to make them readily available in the arts, imported into the United States to be smelted or refined and intended to be exported in a refined but unmanufactured state, shall, under such rules as the Secretary of the Treasury may prescribe, and under the direction of the proper officer, be removed in original packages or in bulk from the vessel or other vehicle on which they have been imported, or from the bonded warehouse in which the same may be, into the bonded warehouse in which such smelting or refining, or both, may be carried on, for the purpose of being smelted or refined, or both, without payment of duties thereon, and may there be smelted or refined, together with other metals of home or foreign production: *Provided*, That each day a quantity of refined metal equal to the amount of imported metal smelted or refined that day shall be set aside, and such metal so set aside shall not be taken from said works except for transportation to another bonded warehouse or for exportation, under the direction of the proper officer having charge thereof as aforesaid, whose certificate, describing the articles by their marks or otherwise, the quantity, the date of importation, and the name of vessel or other vehicle by which it was imported, with such additional particulars as may from time to time be required, shall be received by the collector of customs as sufficient evidence of the exportation of the metal, or it may be removed under such regulations as the Secretary of the Treasury may prescribe, upon entry and payment of duties, for domestic consumption. All labor performed and services rendered under these regulations shall be under the supervision of an officer of the customs, to be appointed by the Secretary of the Treasury, and at the expense of the manufacturer.

SEC. 22. That where imported materials on which duties have been paid are used in the manufacture of articles manufactured or produced in the United States, there shall be allowed on the exportation of such articles a drawback equal in amount to the duties paid on the materials used, less one per centum of such duties: *Provided*, That when the articles exported are made in part from domestic materials the imported materials, or the parts of the articles made from such materials, shall so appear in the completed articles that the quantity or measure thereof may be ascertained: *And provided further*, That the drawback on any article allowed under existing law shall be continued at the rate herein provided. That the imported materials used in the manufacture or production of articles entitled to drawback of customs duties when exported shall, in all cases where drawback of duties paid on such materials is claimed, be identified, the quantity of such materials used and the amount of duties paid thereon shall be ascertained, the facts of the manufacture or production of such articles in the United States and their exportation therefrom shall be determined, and the drawback due thereon shall be paid to the manufacturer, producer, or exporter, to the agent of either or to the person to whom such manufacturer, producer, exporter, or agent shall in writing order such drawback paid, under such regulations as the Secretary of the Treasury shall prescribe.

SEC. 23. That the collector or chief officer of the customs at any port of entry or delivery shall issue a license to any reputable and competent person desiring to transact business as a custom-house broker. Such license shall be granted for a period of one year, and may be revoked for cause at any time by the Secretary of the Treasury. From and after the first day of August, eighteen hundred and ninety-four, no person shall transact business as a custom-house broker without a license granted in accordance with this provision; but this Act shall not be so construed as to prohibit any importer from transacting business at a custom-house pertaining to his own importations.

SEC. 24. That all goods, wares, articles, and merchandise manufactured wholly or in part in any foreign country by convict labor shall not be entitled to entry at any of the ports of the United States, and the importation thereof is hereby prohibited, and the Secretary of the Treasury is authorized to prescribe such regulations as may be necessary for the enforcement of this provision.

SEC. 25. That the value of foreign coin as expressed in the money of account of the United States shall be that of the pure metal of such coin of standard value; and the values of the standard coins in circulation of the various nations of the world shall be estimated quarterly by the Director of the Mint, and be proclaimed by the Secretary of the Treasury immediately after the passage of this Act and thereafter quarterly on the first day of January, April, July, and October in each year. And the values so proclaimed shall be followed in estimating the value of all foreign merchandise exported to the United States during the quarter for which the value is proclaimed, and the date of the consular certification of any invoice shall, for the purposes of this section, be considered the date of exportation: *Provided*, That the Secretary of the Treasury may order the reliquidation of any entry at a different value, whenever satisfactory evidence shall be produced to him showing that the value in United States currency of the foreign money specified in the invoice was, at the date of certification, at least ten per centum more or less than the value proclaimed during the quarter in which the consular certification occurred.

SEC. 26. That section twenty-eight hundred and four of the Revised Statutes be amended so as to read:

"SEC. 2804. No cigars shall be imported unless the same are packed in boxes of not more than five hundred cigars in each box; and no entry of any imported cigars shall be allowed of less quantity than three thousand in a single package; and all cigars on importation shall be placed in public store or bonded warehouse, and shall not be removed therefrom until the same shall have been inspected and a stamp affixed to each box indicating such inspection, and also a serial number to be recorded in the custom-house. And the Secretary of the Treasury is hereby authorized to provide the requisite stamps, and to make all necessary regulations for carrying the above provisions of law into effect."

SEC. 27. That from and after the first day of January, eighteen hun-

dred and ninety-five, and until the first day of January, nineteen hun
dred, there shall be assessed, levied, collected, and paid annually upon
the gains, profits, and income received in the preceding calendar year
by every citizen of the United States, whether residing at home or
abroad, and every person residing therein, whether said gains, profits,
or income be derived from any kind of property, rents, interest, dividends, or salaries, or from any profession, trade, employment, or voca-
tion carried on in the United States or elsewhere, or from any other
source whatever, a tax of two per centum on the amount so derived
over and above four thousand dollars, and a like tax shall be levied,
collected, and paid annually upon the gains, profits, and income from
all property owned and of every business, trade, or profession carried
on in the United States by persons residing without the United States.
And the tax herein provided for shall be assessed, by the Commissioner
of Internal Revenue and collected, and paid upon the gains, profits,
and income for the year ending the thirty-first day of December next
preceding the time for levying, collecting, and paying said tax.

SEC. 28. That in estimating the gains, profits, and income of any
person there shall be included all income derived from interest upon
notes, bonds, and other securities, except such bonds of the United
States the principal and interest of which are by the law of their issu-
ance exempt from all Federal taxation; profits realized within the year
from sales of real estate purchased within two years previous to the
close of the year for which income is estimated; interest received or
accrued upon all notes, bonds, mortgages, or other forms of indebtedness bearing interest, whether paid or not, if good and collectible, less
the interest which has become due from said person or which has been
paid by him during the year; the amount of all premium on bonds,
notes, or coupons; the amount of sales of live stock, sugar, cotton,
wool, butter, cheese, pork, beef, mutton, or other meats, hay, and
grain, or other vegetable or other productions, being the growth or
produce of the estate of such person, less the amount expended in the
purchase or production of said stock or produce, and not including any
part thereof consumed directly by the family; money and the value of
all personal property acquired by gift or inheritance; all other gains,
profits, and income derived from any source whatever except that portion of the salary, compensation, or pay received for services in the
civil, military, naval, or other service of the United States, including
Senators, Representatives, and Delegates in Congress, from which the
tax has been deducted, and except that portion of any salary upon which
the employer is required by law to withhold, and does withhold the tax
and pays the same to the officer authorized to receive it. In computing
incomes the necessary expenses actually incurred in carrying on any business, occupation, or profession shall be deducted and also all interest due
or paid within the year by such person on existing indebtedness. And
all national, State, county, school, and municipal taxes, not including
those assessed against local benefits, paid within the year shall be
deducted from the gains, profits, or income of the person who has
actually paid the same, whether such person be owner, tenant, or
mortgagor; also losses actually sustained during the year, incurred in
trade or arising from fires, storms, or shipwreck, and not compensated
for by insurance or otherwise, and debts ascertained to be worthless,
but excluding all estimated depreciation of values and losses within
the year on sales of real estate purchased within two years previous to
the year for which income is estimated: *Provided*, That no deduction
shall be made for any amount paid out for new buildings, permanent

improvements, or betterments, made to increase the value of any property or estate: *Provided further*, That only one deduction of four thousand dollars shall be made from the aggregate income of all the members of any family, composed of one or both parents, and one or more minor children, or husband and wife; that guardians shall be allowed to make a deduction in favor of each and every ward, except that in case where two or more wards are comprised in one family, and have joint property interests, the aggregate deduction in their favor shall not exceed four thousand dollars: *And provided further*, That in cases where the salary or other compensation paid to any person in the employment or service of the United States shall not exceed the rate of four thousand dollars per annum, or shall be by fees, or uncertain or irregular in the amount or in the time during which the same shall have accrued or been earned, such salary or other compensation shall be included in estimating the annual gains, profits, or income of the person to whom the same shall have been paid, and shall include that portion of any income or salary upon which a tax has not been paid by the employer, where the employer is required by law to pay on the excess over four thousand dollars: *Provided also*, That in computing the income of any person, corporation, company, or association there shall not be included the amount received from any corporation, company, or association as dividends upon the stock of such corporation, company, or association if the tax of two per centum has been paid upon its net profits by said corporation, company, or association as required by this Act.

Sec. 29. That it shall be the duty of all persons of lawful age having an income of more than three thousand five hundred dollars for the taxable year, computed on the basis herein prescribed, to make and render a list or return, on or before the day provided by law, in such form and manner as may be directed by the Commissioner of Internal Revenue, with the approval of the Secretary of the Treasury, to the collector or a deputy collector of the district in which they reside, of the amount of their income, gains, and profits, as aforesaid; and all guardians and trustees, executors, administrators, agents, receivers, and all persons or corporations acting in any fiduciary capacity, shall make and render a list or return, as aforesaid, to the collector or a deputy collector of the district in which such person or corporation acting in a fiduciary capacity resides or does business, of the amount of income, gains, and profits of any minor or person for whom they act, but persons having less than three thousand five hundred dollars income are not required to make such report; and the collector or deputy collector, shall require every list or return to be verified by the oath or affirmation of the party rendering it, and may increase the amount of any list or return if he has reason to believe that the same is understated; and in case any such person having a taxable income shall neglect or refuse to make and render such list and return, or shall render a willfully false or fraudulent list or return, it shall be the duty of the collector or deputy collector, to make such list, according to the best information he can obtain, by the examination of such person, or any other evidence, and to add fifty per centum as a penalty to the amount of the tax due on such list in all cases of willful neglect or refusal to make and render a list or return; and in all cases of a willfully false or fraudulent list or return having been rendered to add one hundred per centum as a penalty to the amount of tax ascertained to be due, the tax and the additions thereto as a penalty to be assessed and collected in the manner provided for in other cases of willful neglect or refusal to render a list or return, or of rendering a false or fraudulent return: *Provided,* That any person, or corporation in his, her, or its own behalf, or as such fiduciary, shall be permitted to declare, under oath or affirmation, the form and manner of which shall be prescribed by the Commissioner of Internal Revenue, with the approval of the Secretary of the Treasury, that he, she, or his or her, or its ward or beneficiary, was not possessed of an income of four thousand dollars, liable to be assessed according to the provisions of this Act; or may declare that he, she, or it, or his, her, or its ward or beneficiary has been assessed and has paid an income tax elsewhere in the same year, under authority of the United States, upon all his, her, or its income, gains, or profits, and upon all the income, gains, or profits for which he, she, or it is liable as such fiduciary, as prescribed by law; and if the collector or deputy collector shall be satisfied of the truth of the declaration, such person or corporation shall thereupon be exempt from income tax in the said district for that year; or if the list or return of any person or corporation, company, or association shall have been increased by the collector or deputy collector, such person or corporation, company, or association may be permitted to prove the amount of income liable to be assessed; but such proof shall not be considered as conclusive of the facts, and no deductions claimed in such cases shall be made or allowed until approved by the collector or deputy collector. Any person or company, corporation, or association feeling aggrieved by the decision of the deputy collector, in such cases may appeal to the collector of the district, and his decision thereon, unless reversed by the Commissioner of Internal Revenue, shall be final. If dissatisfied with the decision of the collector such person or corporation, company, or association may submit the case, with all the papers, to the Commissioner of Internal Revenue for his decision, and may furnish the testimony of witnesses to prove any relevant facts having served notice to that effect upon the Commissioner of Internal Revenue, as herein prescribed.

Such notice shall state the time and place at which, and the officer before whom, the testimony will be taken; the name, age, residence, and business of the proposed witness, with the questions to be propounded to the witness, or a brief statement of the substance of the testimony he is expected to give: *Provided,* That the Government may at the same time and place take testimony upon like notice to rebut the testimony of the witnesses examined by the person taxed.

The notice shall be delivered or mailed to the Commissioner of Internal Revenue a sufficient number of days previous to the day fixed for taking the testimony, to allow him, after its receipt, at least five days, exclusive of the period required for mail communication with the place at which the testimony is to be taken, in which to give, should he so desire, instructions as to the cross-examination of the proposed witness. Whenever practicable, the affidavit or deposition shall be taken before a collector or deputy collector of internal revenue, in which case reasonable notice shall be given to the collector or deputy collector of the time fixed for taking the deposition or affidavit:

Provided further, That no penalty shall be assessed upon any person or corporation, company, or association for such neglect or refusal or for making or rendering a willfully false or fraudulent return, except after reasonable notice of the time and place of hearing, to be prescribed by the Commissioner of Internal Revenue so as to give the person charged an opportunity to be heard.

SEC. 30. The taxes on incomes herein imposed shall be due and payable on or before the first day of July in each year; and to any sum

or sums annually due and unpaid after the first day of July as aforesaid, and for ten days after notice and demand thereof by the collector,
there shall be levied, in addition thereto, the sum of five per centum
on the amount of taxes unpaid, and interest at the rate of one per
centum per month upon said tax from the time the same becomes due,
as a penalty, except from the estates of deceased, insane, or insolvent
persons.

SEC. 31. Any nonresident may receive the benefit of the exemptions
hereinbefore provided for by filing with the deputy collector of any
district a true list of all his property and sources of income in the
United States and complying with the provisions of section twenty-
nine of this Act as if a resident. In computing income he shall include
all income from every source, but unless he be a citizen of the United
States he shall only pay on that part of the income which is derived
from any source in the United States. In case such nonresident fails
to file such statement, the collector of each district shall collect the tax
on the income derived from property situated in his district, subject to
income tax, making no allowance for exemptions, and all property
belonging to such nonresident shall be liable to distraint for tax:
Provided, That nonresident corporations shall be subject to the same
laws as to tax as resident corporations, and the collection of the tax
shall be made in the same manner as provided for collections of taxes
against nonresident persons.

SEC. 32. That there shall be assessed, levied, and collected, except
as herein otherwise provided, a tax of two per centum annually on the
net profits or income above actual operating and business expenses,
including expenses for materials purchased for manufacture or bought
for resale, losses, and interest on bonded and other indebtedness of all
banks, banking institutions, trust companies, saving institutions, fire,
marine, life, and other insurance companies, railroad, canal, turnpike,
canal navigation, slack water, telephone, telegraph, express, electric
light, gas, water, street railway companies, and all other corporations,
companies, or associations doing business for profit in the United
States, no matter how created and organized, but not including part-
nerships.

That said tax shall be paid on or before the first day of July in each
year; and if the president or other chief officer of any corporation,
company, or association, or in the case of any foreign corporation, company, or association, the resident manager or agent shall neglect or
refuse to file with the collector of the internal-revenue district in which
said corporation, company, or association shall be located or be engaged
in business, a statement verified by his oath or affirmation, in such
form as shall be prescribed by the Commissioner of Internal Revenue,
with the approval of the Secretary of the Treasury, showing the
amount of net profits or income received by said corporation, company,
or association during the whole calendar year last preceding the date
of filing said statement as hereinafter required, the corporation, company, or association making default shall forfeit as a penalty the sum
of one thousand dollars and two per centum on the amount of taxes
due, for each month until the same is paid, the payment of said penalty
to be enforced as provided in other cases of neglect and refusal to make
return of taxes under the internal-revenue laws.

The net profits or income of all corporations, companies, or associations shall include the amounts paid to shareholders, or carried to the
account of any fund, or used for construction, enlargement of plant, or

any other expenditure or investment paid from the net annual profits made or acquired by said corporations, companies, or associations.

That nothing herein contained shall apply to States, counties, or municipalities; nor to corporations, companies, or associations organized and conducted solely for charitable, religious, or educational purposes, including fraternal beneficiary societies, orders, or associations operating upon the lodge system and providing for the payment of life, sick, accident, and other benefits to the members of such societies, orders, or associations and dependents of such members; nor to the stocks, shares, funds, or securities held by any fiduciary or trustee for charitable, religious, or educational purposes; nor to building and loan associations or companies which make loans only to their shareholders; nor to such savings banks, savings institutions or societies as shall, first, have no stockholders or members except depositors and no capital except deposits; secondly, shall not receive deposits to an aggregate amount, in any one year, of more than one thousand dollars from the same depositor; thirdly, shall not allow an accumulation or total of deposits, by any one depositor, exceeding ten thousand dollars; fourthly, shall actually divide and distribute to its depositors, ratably to deposits, all the earnings over the necessary and proper expenses of such bank, institution, or society, except such as shall be applied to surplus; fifthly, shall not possess, in any form, a surplus fund exceeding ten per centum of its aggregate deposits; nor to such savings banks, savings institutions, or societies composed of members who do not participate in the profits thereof and which pay interest or dividends only to their depositors; nor to that part of the business of any savings bank, institution, or other similar association having a capital stock, that is conducted on the mutual plan solely for the benefit of its depositors on such plan, and which shall keep its accounts of its business conducted on such mutual plan separate and apart from its other accounts.

Nor to any insurance company or association which conducts all its business solely upon the mutual plan, and only for the benefit of its policy holders or members, and having no capital stock and no stock or shareholders, and holding all its property in trust and in reserve for its policy holders or members; nor to that part of the business of any insurance company having a capital stock and stock and shareholders, which is conducted on the mutual plan, separate from its stock plan of insurance, and solely for the benefit of the policy holders and members insured on said mutual plan, and holding all the property belonging to and derived from said mutual part of its business in trust and reserve for the benefit of its policy holders and members insured on said mutual plan.

That all State, county, municipal, and town taxes paid by corporations, companies, or associations, shall be included in the operating and business expenses of such corporations, companies, or associations.

SEC. 33. That there shall be levied, collected, and paid on all salaries of officers, or payments for services to persons in the civil, military, naval, or other employment or service of the United States, including Senators and Representatives and Delegates in Congress, when exceeding the rate of four thousand dollars per annum, a tax of two per centum on the excess above the said four thousand dollars; and it shall be the duty of all paymasters and all disbursing officers under the Government of the United States, or persons in the employ thereof, when making any payment to any officers or persons as aforesaid, whose compensation is determined by a fixed salary, or upon settling or adjusting the accounts of such officers or persons, to deduct and withhold the aforesaid tax of two per centum; and the pay roll, receipts, or account of officers or persons paying such tax as aforesaid shall be made to exhibit the fact of such payment. And it shall be the duty of the accounting officers of the Treasury Department, when auditing the accounts of any paymaster or disbursing officer, or any officer withholding his salary from moneys received by him, or when settling or adjusting the accounts of any such officer to require evidence that the taxes mentioned in this section have been deducted and paid over to the Treasurer of the United States, or other officer authorized to receive the same. Every corporation which pays to any employee a salary or compensation exceeding four thousand dollars per annum shall report the same to the collector or deputy collector of his district and said employee shall pay thereon, subject to the exemptions herein provided for, the tax of two per centum on the excess of his salary over four thousand dollars: *Provided,* That salaries due to State, county, or municipal officers shall be exempt from the income tax herein levied

SEC. 34. That sections thirty-one hundred and sixty-seven, thirty-one hundred and seventy-two, thirty-one hundred and seventy-three, and thirty-one hundred and seventy-six of the Revised Statutes of the United States as amended are hereby amended so as to read as follows :

SEC. 3167. That it shall be unlawful for any collector, deputy collector, agent, clerk or other officer or employe of the United States to divulge or to make known in any manner whatever not provided by law to any person the operations, style of work or apparatus of any manufacturer or producer visited by him in the discharge of his official duties, or the amount or source of income, profits, losses, expenditures, or any particular thereof, set forth or disclosed in any income return by any person or corporation, or to permit any income return or copy thereof or any book containing any abstract or particulars thereof, to be seen or examined by any person except as provided by law ; and it shall be unlawful for any person to print or publish in any manner whatever not provided by law, any income return or any part thereof or the amount or source of income, profits, losses, or expenditures appearing in any income return ; and any offense against the foregoing provision shall be a misdemeanor and be punished by a fine not exceeding one thousand dollars or by imprisonment not exceeding one year, or both, at the discretion of the court ; and if the offender be an officer or employe of the United States he shall be dismissed from office and be incapable thereafter of holding any office under the Government.

"SEC. 3172. That every collector shall, from time to time, cause his deputies to proceed through every part of his district and inquire after and concerning all persons therein who are liable to pay any internal revenue tax, and all persons owning or having the care and management of any objects liable to pay any tax, and to make a list of such persons and enumerate said objects.

"SEC. 3173. That it shall be the duty of any person, partnership, firm, association, or corporation, made liable to any duty, special tax, or other tax imposed by law, when not otherwise provided for, in case of a special tax, on or before the thirty-first day of July in each year, in case of income tax on or before the first Monday of March in each year, and in other cases before the day on which the taxes accrue, to make a list or return, verified by oath or affirmation, to the collector or a deputy collector of the district where located, of the articles or objects, including the amount of annual income, charged with a duty or tax, the quantity of goods, wares, and merchandise made or sold, and charged with a tax, the several rates and aggregate amount, according to the forms and regulations to be prescribed by the Commissioner of Internal Revenue, with the approval of the Secretary of the Treasury, for which such person, partnership, firm, association, or corporation is liable: *Provided*, That if any person liable to pay any duty or tax, or owning, possessing, or having the care or management of property, goods, wares, and merchandise, articles or objects liable to pay any duty, tax, or license, shall fail to make and exhibit a list or return required by law, but shall consent to disclose the particulars of any and all the property, goods, wares, and merchandise, articles and objects liable to pay any duty or tax, or any business or occupation liable to pay any tax as aforesaid, then, and in that case, it shall be the duty of the collector or deputy collector to make such list or return, which, being distinctly read, consented to, and signed and verified by oath or affirmation by the person so owning, possessing, or having the care and management as aforesaid, may be received as the list of such person: *Provided further*, That in case no annual list or return has been rendered by such person to the collector or deputy collector as required by law, and the person shall be absent from his or her residence or place of business at the time the collector or a deputy collector shall call for the annual list or return, it shall be the duty of such collector or deputy collector to leave at such place of residence or business, with some one of suitable age and discretion, if such be present, otherwise to deposit in the nearest post-office a note or memorandum addressed to such person, requiring him or her to render to such collector or deputy collector the list or return required by law, within ten days from the date of such note or memorandum, verified by oath or affirmation. And if any person on being notified or required as aforesaid shall refuse or neglect to render such list or return within the time required as aforesaid or whenever any person who is required to deliver a monthly or other return of objects subject to tax fails to do so at the time required, or delivers any return which, in the opinion of the collector, is false or fraudulent, or contains any undervaluation or understatement, it shall be lawful for the collector to summon such person, or any other person having possession, custody, or care of books of account containing entries relating to the business of such person, or any other person he may deem proper, to appear before him and produce such books, at a time and place named in the summons, and to give testimony or answer interrogatories, under oath, respecting any objects liable to tax or the returns thereof. The collector may summon any person residing or found within the State in which his district lies; and when the person intended to be summoned does not reside and can not be found within such State, he may enter any collection district where such person may be found, and there make the examination herein authorized. And to this end he may there exercise all the authority which he might lawfully exercise in the district for which he was commissioned.

"SEC. 3176. When any person, corporation, company, or association refuses or neglects to render any return or list required by law, or renders a false or fraudulent return or list, the collector or any deputy collector shall make, according to the best information which he can obtain, including that derived from the evidence elicited by the examination of the collector, and on his own view and information, such list or return, according to the form prescribed, of the income, property, and objects liable to tax owned or possessed or under the care or management of such person, or corporation, company, or association and the Commissioner of Internal Revenue shall assess all taxes not paid by stamps, including the amount, if any, due for special tax, income or other tax, and in case of any return of a false or fraudulent list or valuation intentionally he shall add one hundred per centum to such tax; and in case of a refusal or neglect, except in cases of sickness or absence, to make a list or return, or to verify the same as aforesaid, he shall add fifty per centum to such tax. In case of neglect occasioned by sickness or absence as aforesaid the collector may allow such further time for making and delivering such list or return as he may deem necessary, not exceeding thirty days. The amount so added to the tax shall be collected at the same time and in the same manner as the tax unless the neglect or falsity is discovered after the tax has been paid, in which case the amount so added shall be collected in the same manner as the tax; and the list or return so made and subscribed by such collector or deputy collector shall be held prima facie good and sufficient for all legal purposes."

SEC. 35. That every corporation, company, or association doing business for profit shall make and render to the collector of its collection district, on or before the first Monday of March in every year, beginning with the year eighteen hundred and ninety-five, a full return, verified by oath or affirmation, in such form as the Commissioner of Internal Revenue may prescribe, of all the following matters for the whole calendar year last preceding the date of such return:

First. The gross profits of such corporation, company, or association, from all kinds of business of every name and nature.

Second. The expenses of such corporation, company, or association, exclusive of interest, annuities, and dividends.

Third. The net profits of such corporation, company, or association, without allowance for interest, annuities, or dividends.

Fourth. The amount paid on account of interest, annuities, and dividends, stated separately.

Fifth. The amount paid in salaries of four thousand dollars or less to each person employed.

Sixth. The amount paid in salaries of more than four thousand dollars to each person employed, and the name and address of each of such persons and the amount paid to each.

SEC. 36. That it shall be the duty of every corporation, company, or association doing business for profit to keep full, regular, and accurate books of account, upon which all its transactions shall be entered from day to day, in regular order, and whenever a collector or deputy collector of the district in which any corporation, company, or association is assessable shall believe that a true and correct return of the income of such corporation, company, or association has not been made, he shall make an affidavit of such belief and of the grounds on which it is founded, and file the same with the Commissioner of Internal Revenue, and if said Commissioner shall, on examination thereof, and after full hearing upon notice given to all parties, conclude there is good ground for such belief, he shall issue a request in writing to such corporation, company, or association to permit an inspection of the books of such corporation, company, or association to be made; and if such corporation, company, or association shall refuse to comply with such request, then the collector or deputy collector of the district shall make from such information as he can obtain an estimate of the amount of such income and then add fifty per centum thereto, which said assessment so made shall then be the lawful assessment of such income.

SEC. 37. That it shall be the duty of every collector of internal revenue, to whom any payment of any taxes other than the tax represented by an adhesive stamp or other engraved stamp is made under the provisions of this Act, to give to the person making such payment a full written or printed receipt, expressing the amount paid and the particular account for which such payment was made; and whenever such payment is made such collector shall, if required, give a separate receipt for each tax paid by any debtor, on account of payments made to or to be made by him to separate creditors in such form that such debtor can conveniently produce the same separately to his several creditors in satisfaction of their respective demands to the amounts specified in such receipts; and such receipts shall be sufficient evidence in favor of such debtor, to justify him in withholding the amount therein expressed from his next payment to his creditor; but such creditor may, upon giving to his debtor a full written receipt, acknowledging the payment to him of whatever sum may be actually paid, and accepting the amount of tax paid as aforesaid (specifying the same) as a further satisfaction of the debt to that amount, require the surrender to him of such collector's receipt.

SEC. 38. That on and after the first day of August, eighteen hundred and ninety-four, there shall be levied, collected, and paid, by adhesive stamps, a tax of two cents for and upon every pack of playing cards containing not more than fifty-four cards, manufactured and sold or removed, and also upon every pack in the stock of any dealer on and after that date; and the Commissioner of Internal Revenue, with the approval of the Secretary of the Treasury, shall make regulations as to dies and adhesive stamps.

SEC. 39. That in all cases where an adhesive stamp is used for denoting the tax imposed by this Act upon playing cards, except as hereinafter provided, the person using or affixing the same shall write thereon the initials of his name and the date on which such stamp is attached or used, so that it may not again be used. And every person who fraudulently makes use of an adhesive stamp to denote any tax imposed by this Act without so effectually canceling and obliterating such stamp shall forfeit the sum of fifty dollars. The Commissioner of Internal Revenue is authorized to prescribe such method for the cancellation of stamps as substitute for, or in addition to the method prescribed in this section as he may deem expedient and effectual. And he is authorized, in his discretion, to make the application of such method imperative upon the manufacturers of playing cards.

SEC. 40. That every manufacturer of playing cards shall register with the collector of the district his name or style, place of residence, trade, or business, and the place where such business is to be carried on, and a failure to register as herein provided and required shall subject such person to a penalty of fifty dollars.

SEC. 41. That the Commissioner of Internal Revenue shall cause to be prepared, for payment of the tax upon playing cards, suitable stamps denoting the tax thereon. Such stamps shall be furnished to collectors requiring them, and collectors shall, if there be any manufacturers of playing cards within their respective districts, keep on hand at all times a supply equal in amount to two months' sales thereof, and shall sell the same only to such manufacturers as have registered as required by law and to importers of playing cards, who are required to affix the same to imported playing cards, and to persons who are required by law to affix the same to stocks of playing cards on hand when the tax thereon imposed first takes effect. Every collector shall keep an account of the number and denominate values of the stamps sold by him to each manufacturer and to other persons above described.

SEC. 42. That if any person shall forge or counterfeit, or cause or procure to be forged or counterfeited, any stamp, die, plate, or other instrument, or any part of any stamp, die, plate, or other instrument which shall have been provided or may hereafter be provided, made, or used in pursuance of the provisions of this Act or of any previous provisions of law on the same subjects, or shall forge, counterfeit, or resemble, or cause or procure to be forged, counterfeited, or resembled the impression or any part of the impression of any such stamp, die, plate, or other instrument, as aforesaid, upon any paper, or shall stamp or mark or cause or procure to be stamped or marked any paper with any such forged or counterfeited stamp, die, plate, or other instrument or part of any stamp, die, plate, or other instrument, as aforesaid, with intent to defraud the United States of any of the taxes hereby imposed or any part thereof; or if any person shall utter, or sell, or expose to sale any paper, article, or thing having thereupon the impression of any such counterfeited stamp, die, plate, or other instrument, or any part of any stamp, die, plate, or other instrument, or any such forged, counterfeited, or resembled impression, or part of impression, as aforesaid, knowing the same to be forged, counterfeited, or resembled; or if any person shall knowingly use or permit the use of any stamp, die, plate, or other instrument which shall have been so provided, made, or used, as aforesaid, with intent to defraud the United States; or if any person shall fraudulently cut, tear, or remove, or cause or procure to be cut, torn, or removed, the impression of any stamp, die, plate, or other instrument, which shall have been provided, made, or used in pursuance of this Act, or of any previous provisions of law on the same subjects, from any paper, or any instrument or writing charged or chargeable with any of the taxes imposed by law; or if any person shall fraudulently use, join, fix, or place, or cause to be used, joined, fixed, or placed, to, with, or upon any paper, or any instrument or writing charged or chargeable with any of the taxes hereby imposed, any adhesive stamp, or the impression of any stamp, die, plate, or other instrument, which shall have been provided, made, or used in pursuance of law, and which shall have been cut, torn, or removed from any other paper or any instrument or writing charged or chargeable with any of the taxes imposed by law; or if any person shall willfully remove or cause to be removed, alter or cause to be altered, the canceling or defacing marks on any adhesive stamp, with intent to use the same, or to cause the use of the same, after it shall have been once used, or shall knowingly or willfully sell or buy such washed or restored stamps or offer the same for sale, or give or expose the same to any person for use, or knowingly use the same, or prepare the same with intent for the further use thereof; or if any person shall knowingly and without lawful excuse (the proof whereof shall lie on the person accused) have in his possession any washed, restored, or altered stamps, which have been removed from any article, paper, instrument, or writing, then, and in every such case, every person so offending, and every person knowingly and willfully aiding, abetting, or assisting in committing any such offense as aforesaid, shall, on conviction thereof, forfeit the said counterfeit, washed, restored, or altered stamps and the articles upon which they are placed and be punished by fine not exceeding one thousand dollars, or by imprisonment and confinement to hard labor not exceeding five years, or both, at the discretion of the court. And the fact that any adhesive stamp so bought, sold, offered for sale, used, or had in possession as aforesaid, has been washed or restored by

3413——5·

removing or altering the canceling or defacing marks thereon, shall be prima-facie proof that such stamp has been once used and removed by the possessor thereof from some paper, instrument, or writing charged with taxes imposed by law, in violation of the provisions of this section.

SEC. 43. That whenever any person makes, prepares, and sells or removes for consumption or sale, playing cards, whether of domestic manufacture or imported, upon which a tax is imposed by law, without affixing thereto an adhesive stamp denoting the tax before mentioned, he shall incur a penalty of fifty dollars for every omission to affix such stamp: *Provided*, That playing cards may be removed from the place of manufacture for export to a foreign country, without payment of tax, or affixing stamps thereto, under such regulations and the filing of such bonds as the Commissioner of Internal Revenue, with the approval of the Secretary of the Treasury, may prescribe.

SEC. 44. That every manufacturer or maker of playing cards who, after the same are so made, and the particulars hereinbefore required as to stamps have been complied with, takes off, removes, or detaches, or causes, or permits, or suffers to be taken off, or removed, or detached, any stamp, or who uses any stamp, or any wrapper or cover to which any stamp is affixed, to cover any other article or commodity than that originally contained in such wrapper or cover, with such stamp when first used, with the intent to evade the stamp duties, shall, for every such article, respectively, in respect of which any such offense is committed, be subject to a penalty of fifty dollars, to be recovered together with the costs thereupon accruing; and every such article or commodity as aforesaid shall also be forfeited.

SEC. 45. That every maker or manufacturer of playing cards who, to evade the tax or duty chargeable thereon, or any part thereof, sells, exposes for sale, sends out, removes, or delivers any playing cards before the duty thereon has been fully paid, by affixing thereon the proper stamp, as provided by law, or who, to evade as aforesaid, hides or conceals, or causes to be hidden or concealed, or removes or conveys away, or deposits, or causes to be removed or conveyed away from or deposited in any place, any such article or commodity, shall be subject to a penalty of fifty dollars, together with the forfeiture of any such article or commodity.

SEC. 46. That the tax on playing cards shall be paid by the manufacturer thereof. Every person who offers or exposes for sale playing cards, whether the articles so offered or exposed are of foreign manufacture and imported or are of domestic manufacture, shall be deemed the manufacturer thereof, and subject to all the duties, liabilities, and penalties imposed by law in regard to the sale of domestic articles without the use of the proper stamps denoting the tax paid thereon, and all such articles of foreign manufacture shall, in addition to the import duties imposed on the same, be subject to the stamp tax prescribed in this Act.

SEC. 47. That whenever any article upon which a tax is required to be paid by means of a stamp is sold or removed for sale by the manufacturer thereof, without the use of the proper stamp, in addition to the penalties imposed by law for such sale or removal, it shall be the duty of the Commissioner of Internal Revenue, within a period of not more than two years after such removal or sale, upon such information as he can obtain, to estimate the amount of the tax which has been omitted to be paid, and to make an assessment therefor upon the manufacturer or producer of such article. He shall certify such assessment to the collector, who shall immediately demand payment of such tax, and upon the neglect or refusal of payment by such manufacturer or producer, shall proceed to collect the same in the manner provided for the collection of other assessed taxes.

SEC. 48. That on and after the passage of this Act there shall be levied and collected on all distilled spirits in bond at that time, or that have been or that may be then or thereafter produced in the United States, on which the tax is not paid before that day, a tax of one dollar and ten cents on each proof gallon, or wine gallon when below proof, and a proportionate tax at a like rate on all fractional parts of such proof or wine gallon: *Provided*, That in computing the tax on any package of spirits all fractional parts of a gallon, less than one tenth, shall be excluded.

The Commissioner of Internal Revenue, with the approval of the Secretary of the Treasury, shall prescribe and furnish suitable stamps denoting the payment of the internal-revenue tax imposed by this section; and until such stamps are prepared and furnished, the stamps now used to denote the payment of the internal-revenue tax on distilled spirits shall be affixed to all packages containing distilled spirits on which the tax imposed by this section is paid; and the Commissioner of Internal Revenue shall, by assessment or otherwise, cause to be collected the tax on any fractional gallon contained in each of such packages as ascertained by the original gauge, or regauge when made, before or at the time of removal of such packages from warehouse or other place of storage; and all provisions of existing laws relating to stamps denoting the payment of internal-revenue tax on distilled spirits, so far as applicable, are hereby extended to the stamps provided for in this section.

That the tax herein imposed shall be paid by the distiller of the spirits, on or before their removal from the distillery or place of storage, except in case the removal therefrom without payment of tax is authorized by law; and (upon spirits lawfully deposited in any distillery warehouse, or other bonded warehouse, established under internal-revenue laws) within eight years from the date of the original entry for deposit in any distillery warehouse, or from the date of original gauge of fruit brandy deposited in special-bonded warehouse, except in case of withdrawal therefrom without payment of tax as authorized by law.

SEC. 49. That warehousing bonds and transportation and warehousing bonds, conditioned for the payment of the taxes on all distilled spirits entered for deposit into distillery or special bonded warehouses on and after the passage of this Act, shall be given by the distiller of said spirits as required by existing laws, conditioned, however, for payment of taxes at the rate imposed by this Act and before removal from warehouse and within eight years; as to fruit brandy, from the date of the original gauge, and as to all other spirits from the date of the original entry for deposit, and all warehousing bonds or transportation and warehousing bonds conditioned for the payment of the taxes on distilled spirits entered for deposit into distillery or special bonded warehouses prior to that date shall continue in full force and effect for the time named in said bonds, except where new or additional bonds are required under existing law.

The Commissioner of Internal Revenue may require the distillers of the spirits to give bonds for the additional tax, and before the expiration of the original bonds shall prescribe rules and regulations for re-entry for deposit and for new bonds as provided for spirits originally entered for deposit under this Act, and conditioned for payment of tax at the rate imposed by this Act and before removal of the spirits from warehouse, and within eight years; as to fruit brandy, from the date of the original gauge, and as to all other spirits from the date of original entry for deposit. If the distiller of the spirits fails or refuses to give the bond for the additional tax, or to re-enter and re-bond the spirits, the Commissioner of Internal Revenue may proceed to collect the tax as now provided by law for failure or refusal to give warehousing bonds on original entry into distillery warehouse or special-bonded warehouse, and the provisions of section four of the Act of May twenty-eighth, eighteen hundred and eighty (twenty-first Statutes, one hundred and forty-five), so far as applicable, are hereby extended to bonds given under the provisions of this section: *Provided*, That the distiller may, at his option and under such regulations as the Commissioner of Internal Revenue, with the approval of the Secretary of the Treasury, shall prescribe, execute an annual bond for the spirits so deposited in lieu of the bonds herein provided.

Sec. 50. That the distiller of any distilled spirits deposited in any distillery warehouse, or special-bonded warehouse, or in any general-bonded warehouse established under the provisions of this Act may, prior to the expiration of four years from the date of original gauge as to fruit brandy, or original entry as to all other spirits, file with the collector a notice giving a description of the packages containing the spirits, and request a regauge of the same, and thereupon the collector shall direct a gauger to regauge the spirits, and to mark upon each such package the number of gauge or wine gallons and proof gallons therein contained. If upon such regauging it shall appear that there has been a loss of distilled spirits from any cask or package, without the fault or negligence of the distiller thereof, taxes shall be collected only on the quantity of distilled spirits contained in such cask or package at the time of the withdrawal thereof from the distillery warehouse or other bonded warehouse: *Provided, however*, That the allowance which shall be made for such loss of spirits as aforesaid shall not exceed one proof gallon for two months or part thereof; one and one-half gallons for three and four months; two gallons for five and six months; two and one-half gallons for seven and eight months; three gallons for nine and ten months; three and one-half gallons for eleven and twelve months; four gallons for thirteen, fourteen, and fifteen months; four and one-half gallons for sixteen, seventeen, and eighteen months; five gallons for nineteen, twenty, and twenty-one months; five and one-half gallons for twenty-two, twenty-three, and twenty-four months; six gallons for twenty-five, twenty-six, and twenty-seven months; six and one-half gallons for twenty-eight, twenty-nine, and thirty months; seven gallons for thirty-one, thirty-two, and thirty-three months; seven and one-half gallons for thirty-four, thirty-five, and thirty-six months; eight gallons for thirty-seven, thirty-eight, thirty-nine, and forty months; eight and one-half gallons for forty-one, forty-two, forty-three, and forty-four months; nine gallons for forty-five, forty-six, forty-seven, and forty-eight months; and no further allowance shall be made: *And provided further*, That in case such spirits shall remain in warehouse after the same have been regauged, the packages containing the spirits shall, at the time of withdrawal from warehouse and at such other times as the Commissioner of Internal Revenue may direct, be again regauged or inspected; and if found to contain a larger quantity than shown by the first regauge, the tax shall be collected and paid on the quantity contained in each such package as shown by the original gauge: *And provided further*, That taxes shall be collected on the quantity contained in each cask or package as shown by the original gauge, where the distiller does not request a regauge before the expiration of four years from the date of original entry or gauge: *Provided also,* That the foregoing allowance of loss shall apply only to casks or packages of a capacity of forty or more wine gallons, and that the allowance for loss on casks or packages of less capacity than forty gallons shall not exceed one-half the amount allowed on said forty-gallon cask or package; but no allowance shall be made on casks or packages of less capacity than twenty gallons: *And provided further,* That the proof of such distilled spirits shall not in any case be computed at the time of withdrawal at less than one hundred per centum.

SEC. 51. That the Commissioner of Internal Revenue shall be, and is hereby, authorized, in his discretion and upon the execution of such bond as he may prescribe, to establish one or more warehouses, not exceeding ten in number in any one collection district, to be known and designated as general bonded warehouses, and to be used exclusively for the storage of spirits distilled from materials other than fruit, each of which warehouses shall be in the charge of a storekeeper or storekeeper and gauger to be appointed, assigned, transferred, and paid in the same manner as such officers for distillery warehouses are now appointed, assigned, transferred, and paid. Every such warehouse shall be under the control of the collector of internal revenue of the district in which such warehouse is located, and shall be in the joint custody of the storekeeper and proprietor thereof, and kept securely locked, and shall at no time be unlocked or opened or remain open except in the presence of such storekeeper or other person who may be designated to act for him, as provided in the case of distillery warehouses; and such warehouses shall be under such further regulations as the Commissioner of Internal Revenue, with the approval of the Secretary of the Treasury, may prescribe.

SEC. 52. That any distilled spirits made from materials other than fruit, and lawfully deposited in a distillery warehouse, may, upon application of the distiller thereof, be removed from such distillery warehouse to any general bonded warehouse established under the provisions of the preceding section; and the removal of said spirits to said general bonded warehouse shall be under such regulations, and after making such entries and executing and filing with the collector of the district in which the spirits were manufactured, such bonds and bills of lading, and the giving of such other additional security, as may be prescribed by the Commissioner of Internal Revenue and approved by the Secretary of the Treasury.

SEC. 53. That all spirits intended for deposit in a general bonded warehouse, before being removed from the distillery warehouse, shall have affixed to each package an engraved stamp indicative of such intention, to be provided and furnished to the several collectors as in the case of other stamps, and to be charged to them and accounted for in the same manner.

SEC. 54. That any spirits removed in bond as aforesaid may, upon its arrival at a general bonded warehouse, be deposited therein upon making such entries, filing such bonds and other securities, and under such regulations as shall be prescribed by the Commissioner of Internal Revenue, with the approval of the Secretary of the Treasury. It shall be one of the conditions of the warehousing bond covering such spirits that the principal named in said bond shall pay the tax on the spirits as specified in the entry or cause the same to be paid within eight years from the date of the original entry of the same into the distillery warehouse, and before withdrawal, except as hereinafter provided.

SEC. 55. That any spirits may be withdrawn once and no more from one general bonded warehouse for transportation to another general bonded warehouse, and when intended to be so withdrawn, shall have affixed thereto another general bonded warehouse stamp indicative of such intention; and the withdrawal of such spirits, and their transfer to and entry into such general bonded warehouse shall be under such regulations and upon the filing of such notices, entries, bonds, and bill of lading as the Commissioner of Internal Revenue, with the approval of the Secretary of the Treasury, may, from time to time, prescribe; and the bonds covering spirits in general bonded warehouses shall be given by distillers of the spirits, and shall be renewed at such times as the Commissioner of Internal Revenue may, by regulations, require.

SEC. 56. That the provisions of existing law in regard to the withdrawal of distilled spirits from warehouses upon payment of tax, or for exportation, or for transfer to a manufacturing warehouse, and as to the gauging, marking, branding, and stamping of the spirits upon such withdrawals, and in regard to withdrawals for the use of the United States or scientific institutions or colleges of learning, including the provisions for allowance for loss by accidental fire or other unavoidable accident, are hereby extended and made applicable to spirits deposited in general bonded warehouses under this Act.

SEC. 57. Whenever distilling shall have been suspended at any distillery for a period or periods aggregating six months during any calendar year, and the quantity of spirits remaining in the distillery warehouse does not exceed five thousand proof gallons, or whenever, in the opinion of the Commissioner of Internal Revenue, any distillery warehouse or general bonded warehouse is unsafe or unfit for use, or the merchandise therein is liable to loss or great wastage, he may in either such case discontinue such warehouse and require the merchandise therein to be transferred to such other warehouse as he may designate, and within such time as he may prescribe; and all the provisions of section thirty-two hundred and seventy-two of the Revised Statutes of the United States relating to transfers of spirits from warehouses, including those imposing penalties, are hereby made applicable to transfers to or from general bonded warehouses established under this Act.

SEC. 58. The tax upon any distilled spirits removed from a distillery warehouse for deposit in a general bonded warehouse, and in respect of which any requirement of this Act is not complied with, shall, at any time when knowledge of such fact is obtained by the Commissioner of Internal Revenue, be assessed by him upon the distiller of the same, and returned to the collector, who shall immediately demand payment of such tax, and upon the neglect of payment by the distiller shall proceed to collect the same by distraint. But this provision shall not exclude any other remedy or proceeding provided by law to enforce the payment of the tax. If it shall appear at any time that there has been a loss of distilled spirits from any cask or package deposited in a general bonded warehouse or special bonded warehouse, other than the loss provided for in section thirty-two hundred and twenty-one of the Revised Statutes of the United States, which, in the opinion of the Commissioner of Internal Revenue, is excessive, he may instruct the collector of the district in which the loss has occurred to require the withdrawal from warehouse of such cask or package of distilled spirits and to collect the tax accrued upon the original quantity of distilled spirits entered into the warehouse in such cask or package, less only the allowance for loss provided by law. If the said tax is not paid on demand the collector shall report the amount due, as shown by the original gauge, upon his next monthly list, and it shall be assessed and collected as other taxes are assessed and collected.

SEC. 59. That in case any distilled spirits removed from a distillery warehouse for deposit in a general bonded warehouse shall fail to be deposited in such general bonded warehouse within ten days after such removal, or within the time specified in any bond given on such removal, or if any distilled spirits deposited in any general bonded warehouse shall be taken therefrom, for export or otherwise, without full compliance with the provisions of this Act, and with the requirements of any regulations made thereunder, and with the terms of any bond given on such removal, or if any distilled spirits which have been deposited in a general bonded warehouse shall be found elsewhere, not having been removed therefrom according to law, any person who shall be guilty of such failure, or any person who shall in any manner violate any provision of the next preceding eleven sections of this Act, shall be subject, on conviction, to a fine of not less than one hundred dollars nor more than five thousand dollars, or to imprisonment for not less than three months nor more than three years for every such failure or violation; and the spirits as to which such failure or violation, or unlawful removal shall take place shall be forfeited to the United States.

SEC. 60. That all assessments made under the provisions of section thirty-three hundred and nine of the Revised Statutes of the United States, and Acts amendatory thereof, shall be at the rate of tax imposed by this Act on each proof gallon.

SEC. 61. Any manufacturer finding it necessary to use alcohol in the arts, or in any medicinal or other like compound, may use the same under regulations to be prescribed by the Secretary of the Treasury, and on satisfying the collector of internal revenue for the district wherein he resides or carries on business that he has complied with such regulations and has used such alcohol therein, and exhibiting and delivering up the stamps which show that a tax has been paid thereon, shall be entitled to receive from the Treasury of the United States a rebate or repayment of the tax so paid.

SEC. 62. That no distiller who has given the required bond and who sells only distilled spirits of his own production at the place of manufacture, or at the place of storage in bond, in the original packages to which the tax-paid stamps are affixed, shall be required to pay the special tax of a wholesale liquor dealer on account of such sales: *Provided*, That he shall be required to keep the book prescribed by section thirty-three hundred and eighteen of the Revised Statutes of the United States, or so much as shall show the date when he sent out any spirits, the serial numbers of the packages containing same, the kind and quality of the spirits in wine gallons and taxable gallons, the serial numbers of the stamps on the packages, and the name and residence of the person to whom sent; and the provisions of section five of an Act entitled "An Act to amend the laws relating to internal revenue," approved March fifth, eighteen hundred and seventy-nine, as to transcripts, shall apply to such books. Any failure, by reason of refusal or willful neglect, to furnish the transcript by him shall subject the spirits owned or distilled by him to forfeiture.

SEC. 63. That storekeepers, and storekeepers and gaugers, when transferred from one distillery to another, either in the same district or in different districts, shall receive compensation not exceeding four dollars per day during the time necessarily occupied in traveling from one distillery to the other, together with actual and necessary traveling expenses.

SEC. 64. That the officer holding the combined office of storekeeper and gauger, under the provisions of the legislative, executive, and judicial appropriation Act, approved August fifteenth, eighteen hundred and seventy-six (Nineteenth Statutes, page one hundred and fifty-two), may be assigned by the Commissioner of Internal Revenue to perform the separate duties of a storekeper at any distillery, or at any general or special bonded warehouse, or to perform any of the duties of a gauger under the internal-revenue laws. And the said officer, before entering upon the discharge of such separate duties, shall give a bond to be approved by the Commissioner of Internal Revenue for the faithful discharge of his duties in such form and for such amount as the Commissioner may prescribe.

SEC. 65. That internal-revenue gaugers may be assigned to duty at distilleries, rectifying houses, or wherever gauging is required to be done, and transferred from one place of duty to another, by the Commissioner of Internal Revenue, in like manner as storekeepers and storekeepers and gaugers are now assigned and transferred.

SEC. 66. That section thirty-three hundred and twenty of the Revised Statutes of the United States, as amended, be further amended by striking out all after said number and substituting the following:

" Whenever any cask or package, containing five wine gallons or more, is filled for shipment, sale, or delivery on the premises of any rectifier who has paid the special tax required by law, it shall be inspected and gauged by a United States gauger whose duty it shall be to mark and brand the same and place thereon an engraved stamp, which shall state the date when affixed and the number of proof gallons, and shall be in such form as shall be prescribed by the Commissioner of Internal Revenue with the approval of the Secretary of the Treasury: *Provided,* That when such cask or package is filled on the premises of a rectifier rectifying less than five hundred barrels a year, counting forty gallons of proof spirits to the barrel, it may be gauged, marked, branded, and stamped by a United States gauger, or it may be gauged, marked, branded, and stamped by the rectifier, as the Commissioner of Internal Revenue, with the approval of the Secretary of the Treasury, may by regulations prescribe.

SEC. 67. That whenever any person intending to commence or to continue the business of a distiller shall execute a bond under the provisions of section thirty-two hundred and sixty of the Revised Statutes of United States, and file the same with the collector of internal revenue for the district in which he proposes to distill, the collector may refuse to approve said bond if the person offering the same shall have been previously convicted, in a court of competent jurisdiction, of any fraudulent noncompliance with any of the provisions of law relating to the duties and business of distillers, or if the Commissioner of Internal Revenue, with the approval of the Secretary of the Treasury, shall have compromised such an offense with the person upon the payment of penalties or otherwise, and, in case of such refusal, the person so proposing to distill may appeal to the Commissioner of Internal Revenue, whose decision in the matter shall be final.

SEC. 68. That section forty-three of the Act approved October first, eighteen hundred and ninety, entitled "An Act to reduce the revenue and equalize duties on imports, and for other purposes," be amended so as to read as follows:

"That the wine spirits mentioned in section forty-two of this Act is the product resulting from the distillation of fermented grape juice and shall be held to include the product commonly known as grape brandy; and the pure sweet wine which may be fortified free of tax, as provided in said section, is fermented grape juice only, and shall contain no other substance of any kind whatever introduced before, at the time of, or after fermentation and such sweet wine shall contain not less than four per centum of saccharine matter, which saccharine strength may be determined by testing with Balling's saccharometer or must scale, such sweet wine, after the evaporation of the spirit contained therein, and restoring the sample tested to original volume by addition of water : *Provided*, That the addition of pure boiled or condensed grape must, or pure chrystallized cane or beet sugar to the pure grape juice aforesaid, or the fermented product of such grape juice prior to the fortification provided for by this Act for the sole purpose of perfecting sweet wines according to commercial standard, shall not be excluded by the definition of pure, sweet wine aforesaid : *Provided further*, That the cane or beet sugar so used shall not be in excess of ten per cent of the weight of wines to be fortified under this Act."

SEC. 69. Every person whose business it is to manufacture tobacco or snuff for himself, or who employs others to manufacture tobacco or snuff, whether such manufacture be by cutting, pressing, grinding, crushing, or rubbing of any raw or leaf-tobacco, or otherwise preparing raw or leaf tobacco, or manufactured or partially manufactured tobacco or snuff, or the putting up for use or consumption of scraps, waste, clippings, stems, or deposits of tobacco resulting from any process of handling tobacco, or by the working or preparation of leaf-tobacco, tobacco-stems, scraps, clippings, or waste, by sifting, twisting, screening, or any other process, shall be regarded as a manufacturer of tobacco.

Every person shall also be regarded as a manufacturer of tobacco whose business it is to sell leaf tobacco in quantities less than a hogshead, case or bale; or who sells directly to consumers, or to persons other than duly registered dealers in leaf tobacco, or duly registered manufacturers of tobacco, snuff or cigars, or to persons who purchase in packages for export; and all tobacco so sold by such persons shall be regarded as manufactured tobacco, and such manufactured tobacco shall be put up and prepared by such manufacturer in such packages only as the Commissioner of Internal Revenue with the approval of the Secretary of the Treasury shall prescribe : *Provided*, That farmers and growers of tobacco who sell leaf tobacco of their own growth and raising shall not be regarded as manufacturers of tobacco; and so much of section three thousand two hundred and forty-four of the Revised Statutes of the United States, and acts amendatory thereof, as are in conflict with this Act are hereby repealed : *Provided further*, That section twenty-seven, chapter twelve hundred and forty-four, page eight hundred and sixty-three, volume one, of Supplement to the Revised Statutes of the United States, be amended by striking out all after the word "repealed," in line five of said section, as follows: "*Provided, however*, That it shall be the duty of every farmer or planter producing and selling leaf tobacco, on demand of any internal-revenue officer or other authorized agent of the Treasury Department, to furnish said officer or agent a true and complete statement, verified by oath, of all of his sales of leaf tobacco, the number of hogsheads, cases, or pounds, with the name and residence, in each instance, of the person to whom sold and the place to which it is shipped; and every farmer or planter who willfully refuses to furnish such information, or who knowingly makes false statements as to any of the facts aforesaid, shall be guilty of a misdemeanor and shall be liable to a penalty not exceeding five hundred dollars." That section thirty-three hundred and sixty-one of the Revised Statutes is hereby repealed.

SEC. 70. That the Act of June twentieth, eighteen hundred and seventy-six (Nineteenth United States Statutes, page sixty), be amended by inserting after the words "imported into the United States by such firm or partnership" the following: "Or for any other purpose connected with the general transaction of business at any custom-house."

SEC. 71. That section three of an Act approved October first, eighteen hundred and ninety, entitled "An Act to reduce the revenue and equalize duties on imports, and for other purposes," is hereby repealed; but nothing herein contained shall be held to abrogate, or in any way affect such reciprocal commercial arrangements as have been heretofore made and now exist between the United States and foreign countries, except where such arrangements are inconsistent with the provisions of this Act.

SEC. 72. All Acts and parts of Acts inconsistent with the provisions of this Act are hereby repealed, but the repeal of existing laws or modifications thereof embraced in this Act shall not affect any act done, or any right accruing or accrued, or any suit or proceeding had or commenced in any civil cause before the said repeal or modifications; but all rights and liabilities under said laws shall continue and may be enforced in the same manner as if said repeal or modifications had not been made. Any offenses committed and all penalties or forfeitures or liabilities incurred prior to the passage of this Act under any statute embraced in or changed, modified, or repealed by this Act may be prosecuted or punished in the same manner and with the same effect as if this Act had not been passed. All Acts of limitation, whether applicable to civil causes and proceedings or to the prosecution of offenses or for the recovery of penalties or forfeitures embraced in or modified, changed, or repealed by this Act shall not be affected thereby; and all suits, proceedings, or prosecutions, whether civil or criminal, for causes arising or acts done or committed prior to the passage of this Act, may be commenced and prosecuted within the same time and with the same effect as if this Act had not been passed: *And provided further*, That nothing in this Act shall be construed to repeal the provisions of section three thousand and fifty-eight of the Revised Statutes as amended by the Act approved February twenty-third, eighteen hundred and eighty-seven, in respect to the abandonment of merchandise to underwriters or the salvors of property, and the ascertainment of duties thereon.

SEC. 73. That every combination, conspiracy, trust, agreement, or contract is hereby declared to be contrary to public policy, illegal, and void, when the same is made by or between two or more persons or corporations either of whom is engaged in importing any article from any foreign country into the United States, and when such combination, conspiracy, trust, agreement, or contract is intended to operate in restraint of lawful trade, or free competition in lawful trade or commerce, or to increase the market price in any part of the United States of any article or articles imported or intended to be imported into the United States, or of any manufacture into which such imported article enters or is intended to enter. Every person who is or shall hereafter be engaged in the importation of goods or any commodity from any foreign country in violation of this section of this Act, or who shall combine or conspire with another to violate the same, is guilty of a misdemeanor, and, on conviction thereof in any court of the United States, such person shall be fined in a sum not less than one hundred dollars and not exceeding five thousand dollars, and shall be further punished by imprisonment, in the discretion of the court, for a term not less than three months nor exceeding twelve months.

SEC. 74. That the several circuit courts of the United States are hereby invested with jurisdiction to prevent and restrain violations of section seventy-three of this Act; and it shall be the duty of the several district attorneys of the United States, in their respective districts, under the direction of the Attorney-General, to institute proceedings in equity to prevent and restrain such violations. Such proceedings may be by way of petitions setting forth the case and praying that such violations shall be enjoined or otherwise prohibited. When the parties complained of shall have been duly notified of such petition the court shall proceed, as soon as may be, to the hearing and determination of the case; and pending such petition and before final decree, the court may at any time make such temporary restraining order or prohibition as shall be deemed just in the premises.

SEC. 75. That whenever it shall appear to the court before which any proceeding under the seventy-fourth section of this Act may be pending, that the ends of justice require that other parties should be brought before the court, the court may cause them to be summoned, whether they reside in the district in which the court is held or not; and subpœnas to that end may be served in any district by the marshal thereof.

SEC. 76. That any property owned under any contract or by any combination, or pursuant to any conspiracy (and being the subject thereof) mentioned in section seventy-three of this Act, and being in the course of transportation from one State to another, or to or from a Territory, or the District of Columbia, shall be forfeited to the United States, and may be seized and condemned by like proceedings as those provided by law for the forfeiture, seizure, and condemnation of property imported into the United States contrary to law.

SEC. 77. That any person who shall be injured in his business or property by any other person or corporation by reason of anything forbidden or declared to be unlawful by this Act may sue therefor in any circuit court of the United States in the district in which the defendant resides or is found, without respect to the amount in controversy, and shall recover threefold the damages by him sustained, and the costs of suit, including a reasonable attorney's fee.

Received by the President, August 15, 1894.

[NOTE BY THE DEPARTMENT OF STATE.—The foregoing act having been presented to the President of the United States for his approval, and not having been returned by him to the house of Congress in which it originated within the time prescribed by the Constitution of the United States, has become a law without his approval.]
August 28, 1894.

INDEX TO TARIFF,

AUGUST 28, 1894.

83

88

3413——7

THE TARIFF

ON

IMPORTS INTO THE UNITED STATES

AND THE

FREE LIST,

AS

CONTAINED IN ACT OF JULY 24, 1897.

SCHEDULES.

An Act To provide revenue for the Government and to encourage the industries of the United States.

Be it enacted by the Senate and House of Representatives of the United States of America in Congress assembled, That on and after the passage of this Act, unless otherwise specially provided for in this Act, there shall be levied, collected, and paid upon all articles imported from foreign countries, and mentioned in the schedules herein contained, the rates of duty which are, by the schedules and paragraphs, respectively prescribed, namely:

SCHEDULE A.—CHEMICALS, OILS, AND PAINTS.

1. ACIDS: Acetic or pyroligneous acid, not exceeding the specific gravity of one and forty-seven one-thousandths, three-fourths of one cent per pound; exceeding the specific gravity of one and forty-seven one-thousandths, two cents per pound; boracic acid, five cents per pound; chromic acid and lactic acid, three cents per pound; citric acid, seven cents per pound; salicylic acid, ten cents per pound; sulphuric acid or oil of vitriol not specially provided for in this Act, one-fourth of one cent per pound; tannic acid or tannin, fifty cents per pound; gallic acid, ten cents per pound; tartaric acid, seven cents per pound; all other acids not specially provided for in this Act, twenty-five per centum ad valorem.

2. All alcoholic perfumery, including cologne water and other toilet waters and toilet preparations of all kinds, containing alcohol or in the preparation of which alcohol is used, and alcoholic compounds not specially provided for in this Act, sixty cents per pound and forty-five per centum ad valorem.

3. Alkalies, alkaloids, distilled oils, essential oils, expressed oils, rendered oils, and all combinations of the foregoing, and all chemical compounds and salts not specially provided for in this Act, twenty-five per centum ad valorem.

4. Alumina, hydrate of, or refined bauxite, six-tenths of one cent per pound; alum, alum cake, patent alum, sulphate of alumina, and aluminous cake, and alum in crystals or ground, one-half of one cent per pound.

5. Ammonia, carbonate of, one and one-half cents per pound; muriate of, or sal ammoniac, three-fourths of one cent per pound; sulphate of, three-tenths of one cent per pound.

6. Argols or crude tartar or wine lees crude, containing not more than forty per centum of bitartrate of potash, one cent per pound; containing more than forty per centum of bitartrate of potash, one and one-half cents per pound; tartars and lees crystals, or partly refined argols, containing not more than ninety per centum of bitartrate of potash, and tartrate of soda or potassa, or Rochelle salts, four cents per pound; containing more than ninety per centum of bitartrate of potash, five cents per pound; cream of tartar and patent tartar, six cents per pound.

7. Blacking of all kinds, twenty-five per centum ad valorem.

103

8. Bleaching powder, or chloride of lime, one-fifth of one cent per pound.

9. Blue vitriol or sulphate of copper, one-half of one cent per pound.

10. Bone char, suitable for use in decolorizing sugars, twenty per centum ad valorem.

11. Borax, five cents per pound; borates of lime or soda, or other borate material not otherwise provided for, containing more than thirty-six per centum of anhydrous boracic acid, four cents per pound; borates of lime or soda, or other borate material not otherwise provided for, containing not more than thirty-six per centum of anhydrous boracic acid, three cents per pound.

12. Camphor, refined, six cents per pound.

13. Chalk (not medicinal nor prepared for toilet purposes) when ground, precipitated naturally or artificially, or otherwise prepared, whether in the form of cubes, blocks, sticks or disks, or otherwise, including tailors', billiard, red, or French chalk, one cent per pound. Manufactures of chalk not specially provided for in this Act, twenty-five per centum ad valorem.

14. Chloroform, twenty cents per pound.

15. Coal-tar dyes or colors, not specially provided for in this Act, thirty per centum ad valorem; all other products or preparations of coal tar, not colors or dyes and not medicinal, not specially provided for in this Act, twenty per centum ad valorem.

16. Cobalt, oxide of, twenty-five cents per pound.

17. Collodion and all compounds of pyroxylin, whether known as celluloid or by any other name, fifty cents per pound; rolled or in sheets, unpolished, and not made up into articles, sixty cents per pound; if in finished or partly finished articles, and articles of which collodion or any compound of pyroxylin is the component material of chief value, sixty-five cents per pound and twenty-five per centum ad valorem.

18. Coloring for brandy, wine, beer, or other liquors, fifty per centum ad valorem.

19. Copperas or sulphate of iron, one-fourth of one cent per pound.

20. Drugs, such as barks, beans, berries, balsams, buds, bulbs, bulbous roots, excrescences, fruits, flowers, dried fibers, dried insects, grains, gums and gum resin, herbs, leaves, lichens, mosses, nuts, nutgalls, roots, stems, spices, vegetables, seeds (aromatic, not garden seeds), seeds of morbid growth, weeds, and woods used expressly for dyeing; any of the foregoing which are drugs and not edible, but which are advanced in value or condition by refining, grinding, or other process, and not specially provided for in this Act, one-fourth of one cent per pound, and in addition thereto ten per centum ad valorem.

21. Ethers: Sulphuric, forty cents per pound; spirits of nitrous ether, twenty-five cents per pound; fruit ethers, oils, or essences, two dollars per pound; ethers of all kinds not specially provided for in this Act, one dollar per pound: *Provided,* That no article of this paragraph shall pay a less rate of duty than twenty-five per centum ad valorem.

22. Extracts and decoctions of logwood and other dyewoods, and extracts of barks, such as are commonly used for dyeing or tanning, not specially provided for in this Act, seven-eighths of one cent per pound; extracts of quebracho and of hemlock bark, one-half of one cent per pound; extracts of sumac, and of woods other than dyewoods, not specially provided for in this Act, five-eighths of one cent per pound.

23. Gelatin, glue, isinglass or fish glue, and prepared fish bladders or fish sounds, valued at not above ten cents per pound, two and one-

half cents per pound; valued at above ten cents per pound and not above thirty-five cents per pound, twenty-five per centum ad valorem; valued above thirty-five cents per pound, fifteen cents per pound and twenty per centum ad valorem.

24. Glycerin, crude, not purified, one cent per pound; refined, three cents per pound.

25. Indigo, extracts, or pastes of, three-fourths of one cent per pound; carmined, ten cents per pound.

26. Ink and ink powders, twenty-five per centum ad valorem.

27. Iodine, resublimed, twenty cents per pound.

28. Iodoform, one dollar per pound.

29. Licorice, extracts of, in paste, rolls, or other forms, four and one-half cents per pound.

30. Chicle, ten cents per pound.

31. Magnesia, carbonate of, medicinal, three cents per pound; calcined, medicinal, seven cents per pound; sulphate of, or Epsom salts, one-fifth of one cent per pound.

OILS:
32. Alizarin assistant, sulpho-ricinoleic acid, and ricinoleic acid, by whatever name known, whether liquid, solid, or in paste, in the manufacture of which fifty per centum or more of castor oil is used, thirty cents per gallon; in the manufacture of which less than fifty per centum of castor oil is used, fifteen cents per gallon; all other alizarin assistant, not specially provided for in this Act, thirty per centum ad valorem.

33. Castor oil, thirty-five cents per gallon.

34. Cod-liver oil, fifteen cents per gallon.

35. Cotton-seed oil, four cents per gallon of seven and one-half pounds weight.

36. Croton oil, twenty cents per pound.

37. Flaxseed, linseed, and poppy-seed oil, raw, boiled, or oxidized, twenty cents per gallon of seven and one-half pounds weight.

38. Fusel oil, or amylic alcohol, one-fourth of one cent per pound.

39. Hemp-seed oil and rape-seed oil, ten cents per gallon.

40. Olive oil, not specially provided for in this Act, forty cents per gallon; in bottles, jars, tins, or similar packages, fifty cents per gallon.

41. Peppermint oil, fifty cents per pound.

42. Seal, herring, whale, and other fish oil, not specially provided for in this Act, eight cents per gallon.

43. Opium, crude or unmanufactured, and not adulterated, containing nine per centum and over of morphia, one dollar per pound; morphia or morphine, sulphate of, and all alkaloids or salts of opium, one dollar per ounce; aqueous extract of opium, for medicinal uses, and tincture of, as laudanum, and other liquid preparations of opium, not specially provided for in this Act, forty per centum ad valorem; opium containing less than nine per centum of morphia, and opium prepared for smoking, six dollars per pound; but opium prepared for smoking and other preparations of opium deposited in bonded warehouses shall not be removed therefrom without payment of duties, and such duties shall not be refunded.

PAINTS, COLORS, AND VARNISHES:
44. Baryta, sulphate of, or barytes, including barytes earth, unmanufactured, seventy-five cents per ton; manufactured, five dollars and twenty-five cents per ton.

45. Blues, such as Berlin, Prussian, Chinese, and all others, containing ferrocyanide of iron, in pulp, dry or ground in or mixed with oil or water, eight cents per pound.
46. Blanc-fixe, or artificial sulphate of barytes, and satin white, or artificial sulphate of lime, one-half of one cent per pound.
47. Black, made from bone, ivory, or vegetable substance, by whatever name known, including bone black and lampblack, dry or ground in oil or water, twenty-five per centum ad valorem.
48. Chrome yellow, chrome green, and all other chromium colors in the manufacture of which lead and bichromate of potash or soda are used, in pulp, dry, or ground in or mixed with oil or water, four and one-half cents per pound.
49. Ocher and ochery earths, sienna and sienna earths, and umber and umber earths, not specially provided for, when crude or not powdered, washed or pulverized, one-eighth of one cent per pound; if powdered, washed or pulverized, three-eighths of one cent per pound; if ground in oil or water, one and one-half cents per pound.
50. Orange mineral, three and three-eighths cents per pound.
51. Red lead, two and seven-eighths cents per pound.
52. Ultramarine blue, whether dry, in pulp, or mixed with water, and wash blue containing ultramarine, three and three-fourths cents per pound.
53. Varnishes, including so-called gold size or japan, thirty-five per centum ad valorem; spirit varnishes, one dollar and thirty-two cents per gallon and thirty-five per centum ad valorem.
54. Vermilion red, and other colors containing quicksilver, dry or ground in oil or water, ten cents per pound; when not containing quicksilver but made of lead or containing lead, five cents per pound.
55. White lead, white paint and pigment containing lead, dry or in pulp, or ground or mixed with oil, two and seven-eighths cents per pound.
56. Whiting and Paris white, dry, one-fourth of one cent per pound; ground in oil, or putty, one cent per pound.
57. Zinc, oxide of, and white paint or pigment containing zinc, but not containing lead, dry, one cent per pound; ground in oil, one and three-fourth cents per pound; sulfid of zinc white, or white sulphide of zinc, one and one-fourth cents per pound; chloride of zinc and sulphate of zinc, one cent per pound.
58. All paints, colors, pigments, lakes, crayons, smalts and frostings, whether crude or dry or mixed, or ground with water or oil or with solutions other than oil, not otherwise specially provided for in this Act, thirty per centum ad valorem ; all paints, colors and pigments, commonly known as artists' paints or colors, whether in tubes, pans, cakes or other forms, thirty per centum ad valorem.
59. Paris green, and London purple, fifteen per centum ad valorem.
60. Lead: Acetate of, white, three and one-fourth cents per pound; brown, gray, or yellow, two and one-fourth cents per pound; nitrate of, two and one-half cents per pound; litharge, two and three-fourth cents per pound.
61. Phosphorus, eighteen cents per pound.

POTASH:
62. Bichromate and chromate of, three cents per pound.
63. Caustic or hydrate of, refined, in sticks or rolls, one cent per pound; chlorate of, two and one-half cents per pound.

64. Hydriodate, iodide, and iodate of, twenty-five cents per pound.
65. Nitrate of, or saltpeter, refined, one-half cent per pound.
66. Prussiate of, red, eight cents per pound; yellow, four cents per pound; cyanide of potassium, twelve and one-half per centum ad valorem.

PREPARATIONS:
67. Medicinal preparations containing alcohol, or in the preparation of which alcohol is used, not specially provided for in this Act, fifty-five cents per pound, but in no case shall the same pay less than twenty-five per centum ad valorem.
68. Medicinal preparations not containing alcohol or in the preparation of which alcohol is not used, not specially provided for in this Act, twenty-five per centum ad valorem; calomel and other mercurial medicinal preparations, thirty-five per centum ad valorem.
69. Plasters, healing or curative, of all kinds, and court-plaster, thirty-five per centum ad valorem.
70. Preparations used as applications to the hair, mouth, teeth, or skin, such as cosmetics, dentifrices, pastes, pomades, powders, and other toilet articles, and articles of perfumery, whether in sachets or otherwise, not containing alcohol or in the manufacture of which alcohol is not used, and not specially provided for in this Act, fifty per centum ad valorem.
71. Santonin, and all salts thereof containing eighty per centum or over of santonin, one dollar per pound.

SOAP:
72. Castile soap, one and one-fourth cents per pound; fancy, perfumed, and all descriptions of toilet soap, including so-called medicinal or medicated soaps, fifteen cents per pound; all other soaps not specially provided for in this Act, twenty per centum ad valorem.

SODA:
73. Bicarbonate of soda, or supercarbonate of soda, or saleratus, and other alkalies containing fifty per centum or more of bicarbonate of soda, three-fourths of one cent per pound.
74. Bichromate and chromate of soda, two cents per pound.
75. Crystal carbonate of soda, or concentrated soda crystals, or monohydrate, or sesquicarbonate of soda, three-tenths of one cent per pound; chlorate of soda two cents per pound.
76. Hydrate of, or caustic soda, three-fourths of one cent per pound; nitrite of soda, two and one-half cents per pound; hypo-sulphite and sulphide of soda, one-half of one cent per pound.
77. Sal soda, or soda crystals, not concentrated, two-tenths of one cent per pound.
78. Soda ash, three-eighths of one cent per pound; arseniate of soda, one and one-fourth cents per pound.
79. Silicate of soda, or other alkaline silicate, one-half of one cent per pound.
80. Sulphate of soda, or salt cake, or niter cake, one dollar and twenty-five cents per ton.
81. Sea moss, ten per centum ad valorem.
82. Sponges, twenty per centum ad valorem; manufactures of sponges, or of which sponge is the component material of chief value, not specially provided for in this Act, forty per centum ad valorem.

83. Strychnia, or strychnine, and all salts thereof, thirty cents per ounce.

84. Sulphur, refined or sublimed, or flowers of, eight dollars per ton.

85. Sumac, ground, three-tenths of one cent per pound.

86. Vanillin, eighty cents per ounce.

SCHEDULE B.—EARTHS, EARTHENWARE, AND GLASSWARE.

BRICK AND TILE:

87. Fire-brick, weighing not more than ten pounds each, not glazed; enameled, ornamented, or decorated in any manner, one dollar and twenty-five cents per ton; glazed, enameled, ornamented, or decorated, forty-five per centum ad valorem; brick, other than fire-brick, not glazed, enameled, painted, vitrified, ornamented, or decorated in any manner, twenty-five per centum ad valorem; if glazed, enameled, painted, vitrified, ornamented, or decorated in any manner, forty-five per centum ad valorem.

88. Tiles, plain unglazed, one color, exceeding two square inches in size, four cents per square foot; glazed, encaustic, ceramic mosaic, vitrified, semi-vitrified, flint, spar, embossed, enameled, ornamental, hand painted, gold decorated, and all other earthenware tiles, valued at not exceeding forty cents per square foot, eight cents per square foot; exceeding forty cents per square foot, ten cents per square foot and twenty-five per centum ad valorem.

CEMENT, LIME, AND PLASTER:

89. Roman, Portland, and other hydraulic cement, in barrels, sacks, or other packages, eight cents per one hundred pounds, including weight of barrel or package; in bulk, seven cents per one hundred pounds; other cement, twenty per centum ad valorem.

90. Lime, five cents per one hundred pounds, including weight of barrel or package.

91. Plaster rock or gypsum, crude, fifty cents per ton; if ground or calcined, two dollars and twenty-five cents per ton; pearl hardening for paper makers' use, twenty per centum ad valorem.

92. Pumice stone, wholly or partially manufactured, six dollars per ton; unmanufactured, fifteen per centum ad valorem.

CLAYS OR EARTHS:

93. Clays or earths, unwrought or unmanufactured, not specially provided for in this Act, one dollar per ton; wrought or manufactured, not specially provided for in this Act, two dollars per ton; china clay or kaolin, two dollars and fifty cents per ton; limestone rock asphalt containing not more than fifteen per centum of bitumen, fifty cents per ton; asphaltum and bitumen, not specially provided for in this Act, crude, if not dried, or otherwise advanced in any manner, one dollar and fifty cents per ton; if dried or otherwise advanced in any manner, three dollars per ton; bauxite, or beauxite, crude, not refined or otherwise advanced in condition from its natural state, one dollar per ton; fullers' earth, unwrought and unmanufactured, one dollar and fifty cents per ton; wrought or manufactured, three dollars per ton.

EARTHENWARE AND CHINA:
94. Common yellow, brown, or gray earthenware, plain, embossed, or salt-glazed common stoneware, and crucibles, all the foregoing not decorated in any manner, twenty-five per centum ad valorem; Rockingham earthenware not decorated, forty per centum ad valorem.

95. China, porcelain, parian, bisque, earthen, stone, and crockery ware, including clock cases with or without movements, plaques, ornaments, toys, toy tea sets, charms, vases and statuettes, painted, tinted, stained, enameled, printed, gilded, or otherwise decorated or ornamented in any manner, sixty per centum ad valorem; if plain white and without superadded ornamentation of any kind, fifty-five per centum ad valorem.

96. All other china, porcelain, parian, bisque, earthen, stone, and crockery ware, and manufactures thereof, or of which the same is the component material of chief value, by whatever name known, not specially provided for in this Act, if painted, tinted, stained, enameled, printed, gilded, or otherwise decorated or ornamented in any manner, sixty per centum ad valorem; if not ornamented or decorated, fifty-five per centum ad valorem.

97. Articles and wares composed wholly or in chief value of earthy or mineral substances, or carbon, not specially provided for in this Act, if not decorated in any manner, thirty-five per centum ad valorem; if decorated, forty-five per centum ad valorem.

98. Gas retorts, three dollars each; lava tips for burners, ten cents per gross and fifteen per centum ad valorem; carbous for electric lighting, ninety cents per hundred; filter tubes, forty-five per centum ad valorem; porous carbon pots for electric batteries, without metallic connections, twenty per centum ad valorem.

GLASS AND GLASSWARE:
99. Plain green or colored, molded or pressed, and flint, lime, or lead glass bottles, vials, jars, and covered or uncovered demijohns and carboys, any of the foregoing, filled or unfilled, not otherwise specially provided for, and whether their contents be dutiable or free, (except such as contain merchandise subject to an ad valorem rate of duty, or to a rate of duty based in whole or in part upon the value thereof, which shall be dutiable at the rate applicable to their contents) shall pay duty as follows: If holding more than one pint, one cent per pound; if holding not more than one pint and not less than one-fourth of a pint, one and one-half cents per pound; if holding less than one-fourth of a pint, fifty cents per gross: *Provided*, That none of the above articles shall pay a less rate of duty than forty per centum ad valorem.

100. Glass bottles, decanters, or other vessels or articles of glass, cut, engraved, painted, colored, stained, silvered, gilded, etched, frosted, printed in any manner or otherwise ornamented, decorated, or ground (except such grinding as is necessary for fitting stoppers), and any articles of which such glass is the component material of chief value, and porcelain, opal and other blown glassware; all the foregoing, filled or unfilled, and whether their contents be dutiable or free, sixty per centum ad valorem.

101. Unpolished, cylinder, crown, and common window glass, not exceeding ten by fifteen inches square, one and three-eighths cents per pound; above that, and not exceeding sixteen by twenty-four inches square, one and seven-eighths cents per pound; above that, and not exceeding twenty-four by thirty inches square, two and three-eighths cents per pound; above that, and not exceeding twenty-four by thirty-six inches square, two and seven-eighths cents per pound; above that, and not exceeding thirty by forty inches square, three and three-eighths cents per pound; above that, and not exceeding forty by sixty inches square, three and seven-eighths cents per pound; above that, four and three-eighths cents per pound: *Provided*, That unpolished cylinder, crown, and common window glass, imported in boxes, shall contain fifty square feet, as nearly as sizes will permit, and the duty shall be computed thereon according to the actual weight of glass.

102. Cylinder and crown glass, polished, not exceeding sixteen by twenty-four inches square, four cents per square foot; above that, and not exceeding twenty-four by thirty inches square, six cents per square foot; above that, and not exceeding twenty-four by sixty inches square, fifteen cents per square foot; above that, twenty cents per square foot.

103. Fluted, rolled, ribbed, or rough plate glass, or the same containing a wire netting within itself, not including crown, cylinder, or common window glass, not exceeding sixteen by twenty-four inches square, three-fourths of one cent per square foot; above that, and not exceeding twenty-four by thirty inches square, one and one-fourth cents per square foot; all above that, one and three-fourths cents per square foot; and all fluted, rolled, ribbed, or rough plate glass, weighing over one hundred pounds per one hundred square feet, shall pay an additional duty on the excess at the same rates herein imposed: *Provided*, That all of the above plate glass, when ground, smoothed, or otherwise obscured, shall be subject to the same rate of duty as cast polished plate glass unsilvered.

104. Cast polished plate glass, finished or unfinished and unsilvered, not exceeding sixteen by twenty-four inches square, eight cents per square foot; above that, and not exceeding twenty-four by thirty inches square, ten cents per square foot; above that, and not exceeding twenty-four by sixty inches square, twenty-two and one-half cents per square foot; all above that, thirty-five cents per square foot.

105. Cast polished plate glass, silvered, cylinder and crown glass, silvered, and looking-glass plates, exceeding in size one hundred and forty-four square inches and not exceeding sixteen by twenty-four inches square, eleven cents per square foot; above that, and not exceeding twenty-four by thirty inches square, thirteen cents per square foot; above that, and not exceeding twenty-four by sixty inches square, twenty-five cents per square foot; all above that, thirty-eight cents per square foot.

106. But no looking-glass plates or plate glass, silvered, when framed, shall pay a less rate of duty than that imposed upon similar glass of like description not framed, but shall pay in addition thereto upon such frames the rate of duty applicable thereto when imported separate.

107. Cast polished plate glass, silvered or unsilvered, and cylinder, crown, or common window glass, silvered or unsilvered, when bent, ground, obscured, frosted, sanded, enameled, beveled, etched, embossed, engraved, flashed, stained, colored, painted, or otherwise ornamented or decorated, shall be subject to a duty of five per centum ad valorem in addition to the rates otherwise chargeable thereon.

108. Spectacles, eyeglasses, and goggles, and frames for the same, or parts thereof, finished or unfinished, valued at not over forty cents per dozen, twenty cents per dozen and fifteen per centum ad valorem; valued at over forty cents per dozen and not over one dollar and fifty cents per dozen, forty-five cents per dozen and twenty per centum ad valorem; valued at over one dollar and fifty cents per dozen, fifty per centum ad valorem.

109. Lenses of glass or pebble, ground and polished to a spherical, cylindrical, or prismatic form, and ground and polished plano or coquill glasses, wholly or partly manufactured, with the edges unground, forty-five per centum ad valorem; if with their edges ground or beveled, ten cents per dozen pairs and forty-five per centum ad valorem.

110. Strips of glass, not more than three inches wide, ground or polished on one or both sides to a cylindrical or prismatic form, and glass slides for magic lanterns, forty-five per centum ad valorem.

111. Opera and field glasses, telescopes, microscopes, photographic and projecting lenses and optical instruments, and frames or mountings for the same; all the foregoing not specially provided for in this Act, forty-five per centum ad valorem.

112. Stained or painted glass windows, or parts thereof, and all mirrors, not exceeding in size one hundred and forty-four square inches, with or without frames or cases, and all glass or manufactures of glass or paste, or of which glass or paste is the component material of chief value, not specially provided for in this Act, forty-five per centum ad valorem.

113. Fusible enamel, twenty-five per centum ad valorem.

MARBLE AND STONE, AND MANUFACTURES OF:

114. Marble in block, rough or squared only, sixty-five cents per cubic foot; onyx in block, rough or squared, one dollar and fifty cents per cubic foot; marble or onyx, sawed or dressed, over two inches in thickness, one dollar and ten cents per cubic foot; slabs or paving tiles of marble or onyx, containing not less than four superficial inches, if not more than one inch in thickness, twelve cents per superficial foot; if more than one inch and not more than one and one-half inches in thickness, fifteen cents per superficial foot; if more than one and one-half inches and not more than two inches in thickness, eighteen cents per superficial foot; if rubbed in whole or in part, three cents per superficial foot in addition; mosaic cubes of marble, onyx, or stone, not exceeding two cubic inches in size, if loose, one cent per pound and twenty per centum ad valorem; if attached to paper or other material, twenty cents per superficial foot and thirty-five per centum ad valorem.

115. Manufactures of agate, alabaster, chalcedony, chrysolite, coral, cornelian, garnet, jasper, jet, malachite, marble, onyx, rock crystal, or spar, including clock cases with or without

movements, not specially provided for in this Act, fifty per centum ad valorem.

Stone—

116. Burr stones, manufactured or bound up into millstones, fifteen per centum ad valorem.

117. Freestone, granite, sandstone, limestone, and other building or monumental stone, except marble and onyx, unmanufactured or undressed, not specially provided for in this Act, twelve cents per cubic foot.

118. Freestone, granite, sandstone, limestone, and other building or monumental stone, except marble and onyx, not specially provided for in this Act, hewn, dressed, or polished, fifty per centum ad valorem.

119. Grindstones, finished or unfinished, one dollar and seventy-five cents per ton.

Slate—

120. Slates, slate chimney-pieces, mantels, slabs for tables, roofing slates, and all other manufactures of slate, not specially provided for in this Act, twenty per centum ad valorem.

SCHEDULE C.—METALS AND MANUFACTURES OF.

121. Iron ore, including manganiferous iron ore, and the dross or residuum from burnt pyrites, forty cents per ton: *Provided*, That in levying and collecting the duty on iron ore no deduction shall be made from the weight of the ore on account of moisture which may be chemically or physically combined therewith; basic slag, ground or unground, one dollar per ton.

122. Iron in pigs, iron kentledge, spiegeleisen, ferro-manganese, ferro-silicon, wrought and cast scrap iron, and scrap steel, four dollars per ton; but nothing shall be deemed scrap iron or scrap steel except waste or refuse iron or steel fit only to be remanufactured.

123. Bar iron, square iron, rolled or hammered, comprising flats not less than one inch wide nor less than three-eighths of one inch thick, round iron not less than seven-sixteenths of one inch in diameter, six-tenths of one cent per pound.

124. Round iron, in coils or rods, less than seven-sixteenths of one inch in diameter, and bars or shapes of rolled or hammered iron, not specially provided for in this Act, eight-tenths of one cent per pound: *Provided*, That all iron in slabs, blooms, loops, or other forms less finished than iron in bars, and more advanced than pig iron, except castings, shall be subject to a duty of five-tenths of one cent per pound: *Provided further*, That all iron bars, blooms, billets, or sizes or shapes of any kind, in the manufacture of which charcoal is used as fuel, shall be subject to a duty of twelve dollars per ton.

125. Beams, girders, joists, angles, channels, car-truck channels, T T, columns and posts or parts or sections of columns and posts, deck and bulb beams, and building forms, together with all other structural shapes of iron or steel, whether plain or punched, or fitted for use, five-tenths of one cent per pound.

126. Boiler or other plate iron or steel, except crucible plate steel and saw plates hereinafter provided for, not thinner than number ten wire gauge, sheared or unsheared, and skelp iron or steel sheared or rolled in grooves, valued at one cent per pound or less, five-tenths of one cent per pound; valued above one cent and not above two cents per pound, six-tenths of one cent per pound; valued above two cents and not above

four cents per pound, one cent per pound; valued at over four cents per pound, twenty-five per centum ad valorem: *Provided,* That all sheets or plates of iron or steel thinner than number ten wire gauge shall pay duty as iron or steel sheets.

127. Iron or steel anchors or parts thereof, one and one-half cents per pound; forgings of iron or steel, or of combined iron and steel, of whatever shape or whatever degree or stage of manufacture, not specially provided for in this Act, thirty-five per centum ad valorem; anti-friction ball forgings of iron or steel, or of combined iron and steel, forty-five per centum ad valorem.

128. Hoop, band, or scroll iron or steel, not otherwise provided for in this Act, valued at three cents per pound or less, eight inches or less in width, and less than three-eighths of one inch thick and not thinner than number ten wire gauge, five-tenths of one cent per pound; thinner than number ten wire gauge and not thinner than number twenty wire gauge, six-tenths of one cent per pound; thinner than number twenty wire gauge, eight-tenths of one cent per pound: *Provided,* That barrel hoops of iron or steel, and hoop or band iron or hoop or band steel flared, splayed or punched, with or without buckles or fastenings, shall pay one-tenth of one cent per pound more duty than that imposed on the hoop or band iron or steel from which they are made; steel bands or strips, untempered, suitable for making band saws, three cents per pound and twenty per centum ad valorem; if tempered, or tempered and polished, six cents per pound and twenty per centum ad valorem.

129. Hoop or band iron, or hoop or band steel, cut to lengths, or wholly or partly manufactured into hoops or ties, coated or not coated with paint or any other preparation, with or without buckles or fastenings, for baling cotton or any other commodity, five-tenths of one cent per pound.

130. Railway bars, made of iron or steel, and railway bars made in part of steel, T rails, and punched iron or steel flat rails, seven-twentieths of one cent per pound; railway fish-plates or splice-bars, made of iron or steel, four-tenths of one cent per pound.

131. Sheets of iron or steel, common or black, of whatever dimensions, and skelp iron or steel, valued at three cents per pound or less, thinner than number ten and not thinner than number twenty wire gauge, seven-tenths of one cent per pound; thinner than number twenty wire gauge and not thinner than number twenty-five wire gauge, eight-tenths of one cent per pound; thinner than number twenty-five wire gauge and not thinner than number thirty-two wire gauge, one and one-tenth cents per pound; thinner than number thirty-two wire gauge, one and two-tenths cents per pound; corrugated or crimped, one and one-tenth cents per pound: *Provided,* That all sheets of common or black iron or steel not thinner than number ten wire gauge shall pay duty as plate iron or plate steel.

132. All iron or steel sheets or plates, and all hoop, band, or scroll iron or steel, excepting what are known commercially as tin plates, terne plates, and taggers tin, and hereinafter provided for, when galvanized or coated with zinc, spelter, or other metals, or any alloy of those metals, shall pay two-tenths of one cent per pound more duty than if the same was not so galvanized or coated.

133. Sheets of iron or steel, polished, planished, or glanced, by whatever name designated, two cents per pound: *Provided,* That plates or sheets of iron or steel, by whatever name designated, other than the polished, planished, or glanced herein provided for, which have been pickled or cleaned by acid, or by any other material or process, or which

are cold-rolled, smoothed only, not polished, shall pay two-tenths of one cent per pound more duty than the corresponding gauges of common or black sheet iron or steel.

134. Sheets or plates of iron or steel, or taggers iron or steel, coated with tin or lead, or with a mixture of which these metals, or either of them, is a component part, by the dipping or any other process, and commercially known as tin plates, terne plates, and taggers tin, one and one-half cents per pound.

135. Steel ingots, cogged ingots, blooms, and slabs, by whatever process made; die blocks or blanks; billets and bars and tapered or beveled bars; mill shafting; pressed, sheared, or stamped shapes; saw plates, wholly or partially manufactured; hammer molds or swaged steel; gun-barrel molds not in bars; alloys used as substitutes for steel in the manufacture of tools; all descriptions and shapes of dry sand, loam, or iron-molded steel castings; sheets and plates and steel in all forms and shapes not specially provided for in this Act, all of the above valued at one cent per pound or less, three-tenths of one cent per pound; valued above one cent and not above one and four-tenths cents per pound, four-tenths of one cent per pound; valued above one and four-tenths cents and not above one and eight-tenths cents per pound, six-tenths of one cent per pound; valued above one and eight-tenths cents and not above two and two-tenths cents per pound, seven-tenths of one cent per pound; valued above two and two-tenths cents and not above three cents per pound, nine-tenths of one cent per pound; valued above three cents per pound and not above four cents per pound, one and two-tenths cents per pound; valued above four cents and not above seven cents per pound, one and three-tenths cents per pound; valued above seven cents and not above ten cents per pound, two cents per pound; valued above ten cents and not above thirteen cents per pound, two and four-tenths cents per pound: valued above thirteen cents and not above sixteen cents per pound, two and eight-tenths cents per pound; valued above sixteen cents per pound, four and seven-tenths cents per pound.

WIRE:
136. Wire rods: Rivet, screw, fence, and other iron or steel wire rods, whether round, oval, flat, or square, or in any other shape, and nail rods, in coils or otherwise, valued at four cents or less per pound, four-tenths of one cent per pound; valued over four cents per pound, three-fourths of one cent per pound: *Provided*, That all round iron or steel rods smaller than number six wire gauge shall be classed and dutiable as wire: *Provided further*, That all iron or steel wire rods which have been tempered or treated in any manner or partly manufactured shall pay an additional duty of one-half of one cent per pound.

137. Round iron or steel wire, not smaller than number thirteen wire gauge, one and one-fourth cents per pound; smaller than number thirteen and not smaller than number sixteen wire gauge, one and one-half cents per pound; smaller than number sixteen wire gauge, two cents per pound: *Provided*, That all the foregoing valued at more than four cents per pound shall pay forty per centum ad valorem. Iron or steel or other wire not specially provided for in this Act, including such as is commonly known as hat wire, or bonnet wire, crinoline wire, corset wire, needle wire, piano wire, clock wire. and watch wire, whether flat or otherwise, and corset clasps, corset steels and dress steels, and

sheet steel in strips, twenty-five one-thousandths of an inch thick or thinner, any of the foregoing, whether uncovered or covered with cotton, silk, metal, or other material, valued at more than four cents per pound, forty-five per centum ad valorem: *Provided*, That articles manufactured from iron, steel, brass, or copper wire, shall pay the rate of duty imposed upon the wire used in the manufacture of such articles, and in addition thereto one and one-fourth cents per pound, except that wire rope and wire strand shall pay the maximum rate of duty which would be imposed upon any wire used in the manufacture thereof, and in addition thereto one cent per pound; and on iron or steel wire coated with zinc, tin, or any other metal, two-tenths of one cent per pound in addition to the rate imposed on the wire from which it is made.

GENERAL PROVISIONS.

138. No allowance or reduction of duties for partial loss or damage in consequence of rust or of discoloration shall be made upon any description of iron or steel, or upon any article wholly or partly manufactured of iron or steel, or upon any manufacture of iron or steel.

139. All metal produced from iron or its ores, which is cast and malleable, of whatever description or form, without regard to the percentage of carbon contained therein, whether produced by cementation, or converted, cast, or made from iron or its ores, by the crucible, Bessemer, Clapp-Griffith, pneumatic, Thomas-Gilchrist, basic, Siemens-Martin, or open-hearth process, or by the equivalent of either, or by a combination of two or more of the processes, or their equivalents, or by any fusion or other process which produces from iron or its ores a metal either granular or fibrous in structure, which is cast and malleable, excepting what is known as malleable-iron castings, shall be classed and denominated as steel.

140. No article not specially provided for in this Act, which is wholly or partly manufactured from tin plate, terne plate, or the sheet, plate, hoop, band, or scroll iron or steel herein provided for, or of which such tin plate, terne plate, sheet, plate, hoop, band, or scroll iron or steel shall be the material of chief value, shall pay a lower rate of duty than that imposed on the tin plate, terne plate, or sheet, plate, hoop, band, or scroll iron or steel from which it is made, or of which it shall be the component thereof of chief value.

141. On all iron or steel bars or rods of whatever shape or section which are cold rolled, cold drawn, cold hammered, or polished in any way in addition to the ordinary process of hot rolling or hammering, there shall be paid one-fourth of one cent per pound in addition to the rates provided in this Act on bars or rods of whatever section or shape which are hot rolled; and on all strips, plates, or sheets of iron or steel of whatever shape, other than the polished, planished, or glanced sheet-iron or sheet-steel hereinbefore provided for, which are cold rolled, cold hammered, blued, brightened, tempered, or polished by any process to such perfected surface finish or polish better than the grade of cold rolled, smoothed only, hereinbefore provided for, there shall be paid one cent per pound in addition to the rates provided in this Act upon plates, strips, or sheets of iron or steel of common or black finish; and on steel circular saw plates there shall be paid one-half of one cent per pound in addition to the rate provided in this Act for steel saw plates.

MANUFACTURES OF IRON AND STEEL.

142. Anvils of iron or steel, or of iron and steel combined, by whatever process made, or in whatever stage of manufacture, one and seven-eighths cents per pound.

143. Axles, or parts thereof, axle bars, axle blanks, or forgings for axles, whether of iron or steel, without reference to the stage or state of manufacture, valued at not more than six cents per pound, one cent per pound: *Provided*, That when iron or steel axles are imported fitted in wheels, or parts of wheels, of iron or steel, they shall be dutiable at the same rate as the wheels in which they are fitted.

144. Blacksmiths' hammers and sledges, track tools, wedges, and crowbars, whether of iron or steel, one and one-half cents per pound.

145. Bolts, with or without threads or nuts, or bolt-blanks, and finished hinges or hinge-blanks, whether of iron or steel, one and one-half cents per pound.

146. Card-clothing manufactured from tempered steel wire, forty-five cents per square foot; all other, twenty cents per square foot.

147. Cast-iron pipe of every description, four-tenths of one cent per pound.

148. Cast-iron vessels, plates, stove-plates, andirons, sad-irons, tailors' irons, hatters' irons, and castings of iron, not specially provided for in this Act, eight-tenths of one cent per pound.

149. Castings of malleable iron not specially provided for in this Act, nine-tenths of one cent per pound.

150. Cast hollow-ware, coated, glazed, or tinned, two cents per pound.

151. Chain or chains of all kinds, made of iron or steel, not less than three-fourths of one inch in diameter, one and one-eighth cents per pound; less than three-fourths of one inch and not less than three-eighths of one inch in diameter, one and three-eighths cents per pound; less than three-eighths of one inch in diameter and not less than five-sixteenths of one inch in diameter, one and seven-eighths cents per pound; less than five-sixteenths of one inch in diameter, three cents per pound; but no chain or chains of any description shall pay a lower rate of duty than forty-five per centum ad valorem.

152. Lap welded, butt welded, seamed, or jointed iron or steel boiler tubes, pipes, flues, or stays, not thinner than number sixteen wire gauge, two cents per pound; welded cylindrical furnaces, made from plate metal, two and one-half cents per pound; all other iron or steel tubes, finished, not specially provided for in this Act, thirty-five per centum ad valorem.

CUTLERY:

153. Penknives or pocketknives, clasp knives, pruning knives, and budding knives of all kinds, or parts thereof, and erasers or manicure knives, or parts thereof, wholly or partly manufactured, valued at not more than forty cents per dozen, forty per centum ad valorem; valued at more than forty cents per dozen and not exceeding fifty cents per dozen, one cent per piece and forty per centum ad valorem; valued at more than fifty cents per dozen and not exceeding one dollar and twenty-five cents per dozen, five cents per piece and forty per centum ad valorem; valued at more than one dollar and twenty-five cents per dozen and not exceeding three dollars per dozen, ten cents per piece and forty per centum ad valorem; valued at more than three dollars per dozen, twenty cents per piece and forty per centum

ad valorem: *Provided*, That blades, handles, or other parts of either or any of the foregoing articles, imported in any other manner than assembled in finished knives or erasers, shall be subject to no less rate of duty than herein provided for penknives, pocketknives, clasp knives, pruning knives, manicure knives, and erasers valued at more than fifty and not more than one dollar and fifty cents per dozen. Razors and razor blades, finished or unfinished, valued at less than one dollar and fifty cents per dozen, fifty cents per dozen and fifteen per centum ad valorem; valued at one dollar and fifty cents per dozen and less than three dollars per dozen, one dollar per dozen and fifteen per centum ad valorem; valued at three dollars per dozen or more, one dollar and seventy-five cents per dozen and twenty per centum ad valorem. Scissors and shears, and blades for the same, finished or unfinished, valued at not more than fifty cents per dozen, fifteen cents per dozen and fifteen per centum ad valorem; valued at more than fifty cents and not more than one dollar and seventy-five cents per dozen, fifty cents per dozen and fifteen per centum ad valorem; valued at more than one dollar and seventy-five cents per dozen, seventy-five cents per dozen and twenty-five per centum ad valorem.

154. Swords, sword-blades, and side-arms, thirty-five per centum ad valorem.

155. Table, butchers', carving, cooks', hunting, kitchen, bread, butter, vegetable, fruit, cheese, plumbers', painters', palette, artists', and shoe knives, forks and steels, finished or unfinished, with handles of mother-of-pearl, shell or ivory, sixteen cents each; with handles of deer horn, twelve cents each; with handles of hard rubber, solid bone, celluloid or any pyroxyline material, five cents each; with handles of any other material than those above mentioned, one and one-half cents each, and in addition, on all the above articles, fifteen per centum ad valorem: *Provided*, That none of the above-named articles shall pay a less rate of duty than forty-five per centum ad valorem.

156. Files, file-blanks, rasps, and floats, of all cuts and kinds, two and one-half inches in length and under, thirty cents per dozen; over two and one-half inches in length and not over four and one-half inches, fifty cents per dozen; over four and one-half inches in length and under seven inches, seventy-five cents per dozen; seven inches in length and over, one dollar per dozen.

FIREARMS:

157. Muskets, muzzle-loading shotguns, rifles, and parts thereof, twenty-five per centum ad valorem.

158. Double-barreled, sporting, breech-loading shotguns, combination shotguns and rifles, valued at not more than five dollars, one dollar and fifty cents each and in addition thereto fifteen per centum ad valorem; valued at more than five dollars and not more than ten dollars, four dollars each and in addition thereto fifteen per centum ad valorem each; valued at more than ten dollars, six dollars each; double barrels for sporting breech-loading shotguns and rifles further advanced in manufacture than rough bored only, three dollars each; stocks for double-barreled sporting breech-loading shotguns and rifles wholly or partially manu-

factured, three dollars each; and in addition thereto on all such guns and rifles, valued at more than ten dollars each, and on such stocks and barrels, thirty-five per centum ad valorem; on all other parts of such guns or rifles, and fittings for such stocks or barrels, finished or unfinished, fifty per centum ad valorem: *Provided*, That all double-barrel sporting breech-loading shotguns and rifles imported without a lock or locks or other fittings shall be subject to a duty of six dollars each and thirty-five per centum ad valorem; single-barreled breech-loading shotguns, or parts thereof, except as otherwise specially provided for in this Act, one dollar each and thirty-five per centum ad valorem. Revolving pistols or parts thereof, seventy-five cents each and twenty-five per centum ad valorem.

159. Sheets, plates, wares, or articles of iron, steel, or other metal, enameled or glazed with vitreous glasses, forty per centum ad valorem.

NAILS, SPIKES, TACKS, AND NEEDLES:

160. Cut nails and cut spikes of iron or steel, six-tenths of one cent per pound.

161. Horseshoe nails, hob nails, and all other wrought iron or steel nails not specially provided for in this Act, two and one-fourth cents per pound.

162. Wire nails made of wrought iron or steel, not less than one inch in length and not lighter than number sixteen wire gauge, one-half of one cent per pound; less than one inch in length and lighter than number sixteen wire gauge, one cent per pound.

163. Spikes, nuts, and washers, and horse, mule, or ox shoes, of wrought iron or steel, one cent per pound.

164. Cut tacks, brads, or sprigs, not exceeding sixteen ounces to the thousand, one and one-fourth cents per thousand; exceeding sixteen ounces to the thousand, one and one-half cents per pound.

165. Needles for knitting or sewing machines, including latch needles, one dollar per thousand and twenty-five per centum ad valorem; crochet needles and tape needles, knitting and all other needles, not specially provided for in this Act, and bodkins of metal, twenty-five per centum ad valorem.

PLATES:

166. Steel plates engraved, stereotype plates, electrotype plates, and plates of other materials, engraved or lithographed, for printing, twenty-five per centum ad valorem.

167. Rivets of iron or steel, two cents per pound.

SAWS:

168. Crosscut saws, six cents per linear foot; mill saws, ten cents per linear foot; pit, and drag saws, eight cents per linear foot; circular saws, twenty-five per centum ad valorem; steel band saws, finished or further advanced than tempered and polished, ten cents per pound and twenty per centum ad valorem; hand, back, and all other saws, not specially provided for in this Act, thirty per centum ad valorem.

169. Screws, commonly called wood screws, made of iron or steel, more than two inches in length, four cents per pound; over one inch and not more than two inches in length, six cents per pound; over one-half inch and not more than one inch in length, eight and one-half cents per pound; one-half inch and less in length, twelve cents per pound.

170. Umbrella and parasol ribs and stretchers, composed in chief value of iron, steel, or other metal, in frames or otherwise, fifty per centum ad valorem.

171. Wheels for railway purposes, or parts thereof, made of iron or steel, and steel tired wheels for railway purposes, whether wholly or partly finished, and iron or steel locomotive, car, or other railway tires or parts thereof, wholly or partly manufactured, one and one-half cents per pound; and ingots, cogged ingots, blooms, or blanks for the same, without regard to the degree of manufacture, one and one-fourth cents per pound: *Provided*, That when wheels for railway purposes, or parts thereof, of iron or steel, are imported with iron or steel axles fitted in them, the wheels and axles together shall be dutiable at the same rate as is provided for the wheels when imported separately.

MISCELLANEOUS METALS AND MANUFACTURES OF.

172. Aluminum, and alloys of any kind in which aluminum is the component material of chief value, in crude form, eight cents per pound; in plates, sheets, bars, and rods, thirteen cents per pound.

173. Antimony, as regulus or metal, three-fourths of one cent per pound.

174. Argentine, albata, or German silver, unmanufactured, twenty-five per centum ad valorem.

175. Bronze powder, twelve cents per pound; bronze or Dutch-metal or aluminum, in leaf, six cents per package of one hundred leaves.

176. Copper in rolled plates, called braziers' copper, sheets, rods, pipes, and copper bottoms, two and one-half cents per pound: sheathing or yellow metal of which copper is the component material of chief value, and not composed wholly or in part of iron ungalvanized, two cents per pound.

GOLD AND SILVER:

177. Gold leaf, one dollar and seventy-five cents per package of five hundred leaves.

178. Silver leaf, seventy-five cents per package of five hundred leaves.

179. Tinsel wire, lame or lahn, made wholly or in chief value of gold, silver, or other metal, five cents per pound; bullions and metal threads, made wholly or in chief value of tinsel wire, lame or lahn, five cents per pound and thirty-five per centum ad valorem: laces, embroideries, braids, galloons, trimmings, or other articles, made wholly or in chief value of tinsel wire, lame or lahn, bullions, or metal threads, sixty per centum ad valorem.

180. Hooks and eyes, metallic, whether loose, carded or otherwise, including weight of cards, cartons, and immediate wrappings and labels, five and one-half cents per pound and fifteen per centum ad valorem.

LEAD:

181. Lead-bearing ore of all kinds, one and one-half cents per pound on the lead contained therein: *Provided*, That on all importations of lead-bearing ores the duties shall be estimated at the port of entry, and a bond given in double the amount of such estimated duties for the transportation of the ores by common carriers bonded for the transportation of appraised or unappraised merchandise to properly equipped sampling or smelting establishments, whether designated as bonded warehouses or otherwise. On the arrival of the ores at such establishments

they shall be sampled according to commercial methods under the supervision of Government officers, who shall be stationed at such establishments, and who shall submit the samples thus obtained to a Government assayer, designated by the Secretary of the Treasury, who shall make a proper assay of the sample, and report the result to the proper customs officers, and the import entries shall be liquidated thereon, except in case of ores that shall be removed to a bonded warehouse to be refined for exportation as provided by law. And the Secretary of the Treasury is authorized to make all necessary regulations to enforce the provisions of this paragraph.

182. Lead dross, lead bullion or base bullion, lead in pigs and bars, lead in any form not specially provided for in this Act, old refuse lead run into blocks and bars, and old scrap lead fit only to be remanufactured; all the foregoing, two and one-eighth cents per pound; lead in sheets, pipe, shot, glaziers' lead and lead wire, two and one-half cents per pound.

183. Metallic mineral substances in a crude state, and metals unwrought, not specially provided for in this Act, twenty per centum ad valorem; monazite sand and thorite, six cents per pound.

184. Mica, unmanufactured, or rough trimmed only, six cents per pound and twenty per centum ad valorem; mica, cut or trimmed, twelve cents per pound and twenty per centum ad valorem.

185. Nickel, nickel oxide, alloy of any kind in which nickel is a component material of chief value, in pigs, ingots, bars, or sheets, six cents per pound.

186. Pens, metallic, except gold pens, twelve cents per gross.

187. Penholder tips, penholders or parts thereof, and gold pens, twenty-five per centum ad valorem.

188. Pins with solid heads, without ornamentation, including hair, safety, hat, bonnet, and shawl pins; any of the foregoing composed wholly of brass, copper, iron, steel, or other base metal, not plated, and not commonly known as jewelry, thirty-five per centum ad valorem.

189. Quicksilver, seven cents per pound. The flasks, bottles, or other vessels in which quicksilver is imported shall be subject to the same rate of duty as they would be subjected to if imported empty.

190. Type metal, one and one-half cents per pound for the lead contained therein; new types, twenty-five per centum ad valorem.

191. Watch movements, whether imported in cases or not, if having not more than seven jewels, thirty-five cents each; if having more than seven jewels and not more than eleven jewels, fifty cents each: if having more than eleven jewels and not more than fifteen jewels, seventy-five cents each: if having more than fifteen jewels and not more than seventeen jewels, one dollar and twenty-five cents each; it having more than seventeen jewels, three dollars each, and in addition thereto, on all the foregoing, twenty-five per centum ad valorem; watch cases and parts of watches, including watch dials, chronometers, box or ship, and parts thereof, clocks and parts thereof, not otherwise provided for in this Act, whether separately packed or otherwise, not composed wholly or in part of china, porcelain, parian, bisque or earthenware, forty per centum ad valorem; all jewels for use in the manufacture of watches or clocks, ten per centum ad valorem.

192. Zinc in blocks or pigs, one and one-half cents per pound; in sheets, two cents per pound; old and worn-out, fit only to be remanufactured, one cent per pound.

193. Articles or wares not specially provided for in this Act, composed

wholly or in part of iron, steel, lead, copper, nickel, pewter, zinc, gold, silver, platinum, aluminum or other metal, and whether partly or wholly manufactured, forty-five per centum ad valorem.

SCHEDULE D.—WOOD AND MANUFACTURES OF.

194. Timber hewn, sided, or squared (not less than eight inches square), and round timber used for spars or in building wharves, one cent per cubic foot.

195. Sawed boards, planks, deals, and other lumber of whitewood, sycamore, and basswood, one dollar per thousand feet board measure; sawed lumber, not specially provided for in this Act, two dollars per thousand feet board measure; but when lumber of any sort is planed or finished, in addition to the rates herein provided, there shall be levied and paid for each side so planed or finished fifty cents per thousand feet board measure; and if planed on one side and tongued and grooved, one dollar per thousand feet board measure; and if planed on two sides and tongued and grooved, one dollar and fifty cents per thousand feet board measure; and in estimating board measure under this schedule no deduction shall be made on board measure on account of planing, tongueing and grooving: *Provided,* That if any country or dependency shall impose an export duty upon saw logs, round unmanufactured timber, stave bolts, shingle bolts, or heading bolts, exported to the United States, or a discriminating charge upon boom sticks, or chains used by American citizens in towing logs, the amount of such export duty, tax, or other charge, as the case may be, shall be added as an additional duty to the duties imposed upon the articles mentioned in this paragraph when imported from such country or dependency.

196. Paving posts, railroad ties, and telephone, trolley, electric-light and telegraph poles of cedar or other woods, twenty per centum ad valorem.

197. Kindling wood in bundles not exceeding one-quarter of a cubic foot each, three-tenths of one cent per bundle; if in larger bundles, three-tenths of one cent for each additional quarter of a cubic foot or fractional part thereof.

198. Sawed boards, planks, deals, and all forms of sawed cedar, lignum-vitæ, lancewood, ebony, box, granadilla, mahogany, rosewood, satinwood, and all other cabinet woods not further manufactured than sawed, fifteen per centum ad valorem; veneers of wood, and wood, unmanufactured, not specially provided for in this Act, twenty per centum ad valorem.

199. Clapboards, one dollar and fifty cents per thousand.

200. Hubs for wheels, posts, heading bolts, stave bolts, last-blocks, wagon-blocks, oar-blocks, heading-blocks, and all like blocks or sticks, rough-hewn, sawed or bored, twenty per centum ad valorem; fence posts, ten per centum ad valorem.

201. Laths, twenty-five cents per one thousand pieces.

202. Pickets, palings and staves of wood, of all kinds, ten per centum ad valorem.

203. Shingles, thirty cents per thousand.

204. Casks, barrels, and hogsheads, (empty), sugar-box shooks, and packing-boxes (empty), and packing-box shooks, of wood, not specially provided for in this Act, thirty per centum ad valorem.

205. Boxes, barrels, or other articles containing oranges, lemons, limes, grape fruit, shaddocks or pomelos, thirty per centum ad valorem: *Provided,* That the thin wood, so called, comprising the sides, tops and

bottoms of orange and lemon boxes of the growth and manufacture of the United States, exported as orange and lemon box shooks, may be reimported in completed form, filled with oranges and lemons, by the payment of duty at one-half the rate imposed on similar boxes of entirely foreign growth and manufacture.

206. Chair cane or reeds, wrought or manufactured from rattans or reeds, ten per centum ad valorem; osier or willow prepared for basket makers' use, twenty per centum ad valorem; manufactures of osier or willow, forty per centum ad valorem.

207. Toothpicks of wood or other vegetable substance, two cents per one thousand and fifteen per centum ad valorem; butchers' and packers' skewers of wood, forty cents per thousand.

208. House or cabinet furniture, of wood, wholly or partly finished, and manufactures of wood, or of which wood is the component material of chief value, not specially provided for in this Act, thirty-five per centum ad valorem.

SCHEDULE E.—SUGAR, MOLASSES, AND MANUFACTURES OF.

209. Sugars not above number sixteen Dutch standard in color, tank bottoms, sirups of cane juice, melada, concentrated melada, concrete and concentrated molasses, testing by the polariscope not above seventy-five degrees, ninety-five one-hundredths of one cent per pound, and for every additional degree shown by the polariscopic test, thirty-five one-thousandths of one cent per pound additional, and fractions of a degree in proportion; and on sugar above number sixteen Dutch standard in color, and on all sugar which has gone through a process of refining, one cent and ninety-five one-hundredths of one-cent per pound; molasses testing above forty degrees and not above fifty-six degrees, three cents per gallon; testing fifty-six degrees and above, six cents per gallon; sugar drainings and sugar sweepings shall be subject to duty as molasses or sugar, as the case may be, according to polariscopic test: *Provided*, That nothing herein contained shall be so construed as to abrogate or in any manner impair or affect the provisions of the treaty of commercial reciprocity concluded between the United States and the King of the Hawaiian Islands on the thirtieth day of January, eighteen hundred and seventy-five, or the provisions of any Act of Congress heretofore passed for the execution of the same.

210. Maple sugar and maple sirup, four cents per pound; glucose or grape sugar, one and one-half cents per pound; sugar cane in its natural state, or unmanufactured, twenty per centum ad valorem.

211. Saccharine, one dollar and fifty cents per pound and ten per centum ad valorem.

212. Sugar candy and all confectionery not specially provided for in this Act, valued at fifteen cents per pound or less, and on sugars after being refined, when tinctured, colored or in any way adulterated, four cents per pound and fifteen per centum ad valorem; valued at more than fifteen cents per pound, fifty per centum ad valorem. The weight and the value of the immediate coverings, other than the outer packing case or other covering, shall be included in the dutiable weight and the value of the merchandise.

SCHEDULE F.—TOBACCO AND MANUFACTURES OF.

213. Wrapper tobacco, and filler tobacco when mixed or packed with more than fifteen per centum of wrapper tobacco, and all leaf tobacco

the product of two or more countries or dependencies when mixed or packed together, if unstemmed, one dollar and eighty-five cents per pound; if stemmed, two dollars and fifty cents per pound; filler tobacco not specially provided for in this Act, if unstemmed, thirty-five cents per pound; if stemmed, fifty cents per pound.

214. The term wrapper tobacco as used in this Act means that quality of leaf tobacco which is suitable for cigar wrappers, and the term filler tobacco means all other leaf tobacco. Collectors of customs shall not permit entry to be made, except under regulations to be prescribed by the Secretary of the Treasury, of any leaf tobacco, unless the invoices of the same shall specify in detail the character of such tobacco, whether wrapper or filler, its origin and quality. In the examination for classification of any imported leaf tobacco, at least one bale, box, or package in every ten, and at least one in every invoice, shall be examined by the appraiser or person authorized by law to make such examination, and at least ten hands shall be examined in each examined bale, box, or package.

215. All other tobacco, manufactured or unmanufactured, not specially provided for in this Act, fifty-five cents per pound.

216. Snuff and snuff flour, manufactured of tobacco, ground dry, or damp, and pickled, scented, or otherwise, of all descriptions. fifty-five cents per pound.

217. Cigars, cigarettes, cheroots of all kinds, four dollars and fifty cents per pound and twenty-five per centum ad valorem; and paper cigars and cigarettes, including wrappers, shall be subject to the same duties as are herein imposed upon cigars.

SCHEDULE G.—AGRICULTURAL PRODUCTS AND PROVISIONS.

ANIMALS, LIVE:

218. Cattle, if less than one year old, two dollars per head; all other cattle if valued at not more than fourteen dollars per head, three dollars and seventy-five cents per head; if valued at more than fourteen dollars per head, twenty-seven and one-half per centum ad valorem.

219. Swine. one dollar and fifty cents per head.

220. Horses and mules, valued at one hundred and fifty dollars or less per head, thirty dollars per head; if valued at over one hundred and fifty dollars, twenty-five per centum ad valorem.

221. Sheep, one year old or over, one dollar and fifty cents per head; less than one year old, seventy-five cents per head.

222. All other live animals, not specially provided for in this Act, twenty per centum ad valorem.

BREADSTUFFS AND FARINACEOUS SUBSTANCES:

223. Barley, thirty cents per bushel of forty-eight pounds.

224. Barley-malt, forty-five cents per bushel of thirty-four pounds.

225. Barley, pearled, patent, or hulled, two cents per pound.

226. Buckwheat, fifteen cents per bushel of forty-eight pounds.

227. Corn or maize, fifteen cents per bushel of fifty-six pounds.

228. Corn meal, twenty cents per bushel of forty-eight pounds.

229. Macaroni, vermicelli, and all similar preparations, one and one-half cents per pound.

230. Oats, fifteen cents per bushel.

231. Oatmeal and rolled oats, one cent per pound; oat hulls, ten cents per hundred pounds.

232. Rice, cleaned, two cents per pound; uncleaned rice, or rice free of the outer hull and still having the inner cuticle on, one and one-fourth cents per pound; rice flour, and rice meal, and rice broken which will pass through a sieve known commercially as number twelve wire sieve, one-fourth of one cent per pound; paddy, or rice having the outer hull on, three-fourths of one cent per pound.

233. Rye, ten cents per bushel; rye flour, one-half of one cent per pound.

234. Wheat, twenty-five cents per bushel.

235. Wheat flour, twenty-five per centum ad valorem.

DAIRY PRODUCTS:

236. Butter, and substitutes therefor, six cents per pound.

237. Cheese, and substitutes therefor, six cents per pound.

238. Milk, fresh, two cents per gallon.

239. Milk, preserved or condensed, or sterilized by heating or other processes, including weight of immediate coverings, two cents per pound; sugar of milk, five cents per pound.

FARM AND FIELD PRODUCTS:

240. Beans, forty-five cents per bushel of sixty pounds.

241. Beans, pease, and mushrooms, prepared or preserved, in tins, jars, bottles, or similar packages, two and one-half cents per pound, including the weight of all tins, jars, and other immediate coverings; all vegetables, prepared or preserved, including pickles and sauces of all kinds, not specially provided for in this Act, and fish paste or sauce, forty per centum ad valorem.

242. Cabbages, three cents each.

243. Cider, five cents per gallon.

244. Eggs, not specially provided for in this Act, five cents per dozen.

245. Eggs, yolk of, twenty-five per centum ad valorem; albumen, egg or blood, three cents per pound; dried blood, when soluble, one and one-half cents per pound.

246. Hay, four dollars per ton.

247. Honey, twenty cents per gallon.

248. Hops, twelve cents per pound; hop extract and lupulin, fifty per centum ad valorem.

249. Onions, forty cents per bushel; garlic, one cent per pound.

250. Pease, green, in bulk or in barrels, sacks, or similar packages, and seed pease, forty cents per bushel of sixty pounds; pease, dried, not specially provided for, thirty cents per bushel; split pease, forty cents per bushel of sixty pounds; pease in cartons, papers, or other small packages, one cent per pound.

251. Orchids, palms, dracænas, crotons and azaleas, tulips, hyacinths, narcissi, jonquils, lilies, lilies of the valley, and all other bulbs, bulbous roots, or corms, which are cultivated for their flowers, and natural flowers of all kinds, preserved or fresh, suitable for decorative purposes, twenty-five per centum ad valorem.

252. Stocks, cuttings or seedlings of Myrobolan plum, Mahaleb or Mazzard cherry, three years old or less, fifty cents per thousand plants and fifteen per centum ad valorem; stocks, cuttings or seedlings of pear, apple, quince and the St. Julien plum, three years old or less, and evergreen seedlings, one dollar per thousand plants and fifteen per centum ad valorem;

rose plants, budded, grafted, or grown on their own roots, two and one-half cents each; stocks, cuttings and seedlings of all fruit and ornamental trees, deciduous and evergreen, shrubs and vines, manetti, multiflora, and brier rose, and all trees, shrubs, plants and vines, commonly known as nursery or greenhouse stock, not specially provided for in this Act, twenty-five per centum ad valorem.

253. Potatoes, twenty-five cents per bushel of sixty pounds.

254. Seeds: Castor beans or seeds, twenty-five cents per bushel of fifty pounds; flaxseed or linseed and other oil seeds not specially provided for in this Act, twenty-five cents per bushel of fifty-six pounds; poppy seed, fifteen cents per bushel; but no drawback shall be allowed upon oil cake made from imported seed, nor shall any allowance be made for dirt or other impurities in any seed; seeds of all kinds not specially provided for in this Act, thirty per centum ad valorem.

255. Straw, one dollar and fifty cents per ton.

256. Teazles, thirty per centum ad valorem.

257. Vegetables in their natural state, not specially provided for in this Act, twenty-five per centum ad valorem.

FISH:

258. Fish known or labeled as anchovies, sardines, sprats, brislings, sardels, or sardellen, packed in oil or otherwise, in bottles, jars, tin boxes or cans, shall be dutiable as follows: When in packages containing seven and one-half cubic inches or less, one and one-half cents per bottle, jar, box or can; containing more than seven and one-half and not more than twenty-one cubic inches, two and one-half cents per bottle, jar, box or can; containing more than twenty-one and not more than thirty-three cubic inches, five cents per bottle, jar, box or can; containing more than thirty-three and not more than seventy cubic inches, ten cents per bottle, jar, box or can; if in other packages, forty per centum ad valorem. All other fish, (except shellfish), in tin packages, thirty per centum ad valorem; fish in packages containing less than one-half barrel, and not specially provided for in this Act, thirty per centum ad valorem.

259. Fresh-water fish not specially provided for in this Act, one-fourth of one cent per pound.

260. Herrings, pickled or salted, one-half of one cent per pound; herrings, fresh, one-fourth of one cent per pound.

261. Fish, fresh, smoked, dried, salted, pickled, frozen, packed in ice or otherwise prepared for preservation, not specially provided for in this Act, three-fourths of one cent per pound; fish, skinned or boned, one and one-fourth cents per pound; mackerel, halibut or salmon, fresh, pickled or salted, one cent per pound.

FRUITS AND NUTS:

262. Apples, peaches, quinces, cherries; plums, and pears, green or ripe, twenty-five cents per bushel; apples, peaches, pears, and other edible fruits, including berries, when dried, desiccated, evaporated or prepared in any manner, not specially provided for in this Act, two cents per pound; berries, edible, in their natural condition, one cent per quart; cranberries, twenty-five per centum ad valorem.

263. Comfits, sweetmeats, and fruits preserved in sugar, molasses, spirits, or in their own juices, not specially provided for in this

Act, one cent per pound and thirty-five per centum ad valorem; if containing over ten per centum of alcohol and not specially provided for in this Act, thirty-five per centum ad valorem and in addition two dollars and fifty cents per proof gallon on the alcohol contained therein in excess of ten per centum; jellies of all kinds, thirty-five per centum ad valorem; pineapples preserved in their own juice, twenty-five per centum ad valorem.

264. Figs, plums, prunes, and prunelles, two cents per pound; raisins and other dried grapes, two and one-half cents per pound; dates, one-half of one cent per pound; currants, Zante or other, two cents per pound; olives, green or prepared, in bottles, jars, or similar packages, twenty-five cents per gallon; in casks or otherwise than in bottles, jars, or similar packages, fifteen cents per gallon.

265. Grapes in barrels or other packages, twenty cents per cubic foot of capacity of barrels or packages.

266. Oranges, lemons, limes, grape fruit, shaddocks or pomelos, one cent per pound.

267. Orange peel or lemon peel, preserved, candied, or dried, and cocoanut meat or copra desiccated, shredded, cut, or similarly prepared, two cents per pound; citron or citron peel, preserved, candied, or dried, four cents per pound.

268. Pineapples, in barrels and other packages, seven cents per cubic foot of the capacity of barrels or packages: in bulk, seven dollars per thousand.

Nuts—

269. Almonds, not shelled, four cents per pound; clear almonds, shelled, six cents per pound.

270. Filberts and walnuts of all kinds, not shelled, three cents per pound; shelled, five cents per pound.

271. Peanuts or ground beans, unshelled, one-half of one cent per pound; shelled, one cent per pound.

272. Nuts of all kinds, shelled or unshelled, not specially provided for in this Act, one cent per pound.

MEAT PRODUCTS:

273. Bacon and hams, five cents per pound.

274. Fresh beef, veal, mutton, and pork, two cents per pound.

275. Meats of all kinds, prepared or preserved, not specially provided for in this Act, twenty-five per centum ad valorem.

276. Extract of meat, not specially provided for in this Act, thirty-five cents per pound; fluid extract of meat, fifteen cents per pound, but the dutiable weight of the extract of meat and of the fluid extract of meat shall not include the weight of the package in which the same is imported.

277. Lard, two cents per pound.

278. Poultry, live, three cents per pound; dressed, five cents per pound.

279. Tallow, three-fourths of one cent per pound; wool grease, including that known commercially as degras or brown wool grease, one-half of one cent per pound.

MISCELLANEOUS PRODUCTS:

280. Chicory-root, raw, dried, or undried, but unground, one cent per pound; chicory root, burnt or roasted, ground or granulated, or in rolls, or otherwise prepared, and not specially provided for in this Act, two and one-half cents per pound.

281. Chocolate and cocoa, prepared or manufactured, not specially provided for in this Act, valued at not over fifteen cents per pound, two and one-half cents per pound; valued above fifteen and not above twenty-four cents per pound, two and one-half cents per pound and ten per centum ad valorem; valued above twenty-four and not above thirty-five cents per pound, five cents per pound and ten per centum ad valorem; valued above thirty-five cents per pound, fifty per centum ad valorem. The weight and value of all coverings, other than plain wooden, shall be included in the dutiable weight and value of the foregoing merchandise; powdered cocoa, unsweetened, five cents per pound.

282. Cocoa-butter or cocoa-butterine, three and one-half cents per pound.

283. Dandelion-root and acorns prepared, and articles used as coffee, or as substitutes for coffee not specially provided for in this Act, two and one-half cents per pound.

284. Salt in bags, sacks, barrels, or other packages, twelve cents per one hundred pounds; in bulk, eight cents per one hundred pounds: *Provided*, That imported salt in bond may be used in curing fish taken by vessels licensed to engage in the fisheries, and in curing fish on the shores of the navigable waters of the United States, under such regulations as the Secretary of the Treasury shall prescribe; and upon proof that the salt has been used for either of the purposes stated in this proviso, the duties on the same shall be remitted: *Provided further*, That exporters of meats, whether packed or smoked, which have been cured in the United States with imported salt, shall, upon satisfactory proof, under such regulations as the Secretary of the Treasury shall prescribe, that such meats have been cured with imported salt, have refunded to them from the Treasury the duties paid on the salt so used in curing such exported meats, in amounts not less than one hundred dollars.

285. Starch, including all preparations, from whatever substance produced, fit for use as starch, one and one-half cents per pound.

286. Dextrine, burnt starch, gum substitute, or British gum, two cents per pound.

287. Spices: Mustard, ground or prepared, in bottles or otherwise, ten cents per pound; capsicum or red pepper, or cayenne pepper, two and one-half cents per pound; sage, one cent per pound; spices not specially provided for in this Act, three cents per pound.

288. Vinegar, seven and one-half cents per proof gallon. The standard proof for vinegar shall be taken to be that strength which requires thirty-five grains of bicarbonate of potash to neutralize one ounce troy of vinegar.

SCHEDULE H.—SPIRITS, WINES, AND OTHER BEVERAGES.

SPIRITS.

289. Brandy and other spirits manufactured or distilled from grain or other materials, and not specially provided for in this Act, two dollars and twenty-five cents per proof gallon.

290. Each and every gauge or wine gallon of measurement shall be counted as at least one proof gallon; and the standard for determining

the proof of brandy and other spirits or liquors of any kind imported shall be the same as that which is defined in the laws relating to internal revenue: *Provided,* That it shall be lawful for the Secretary of the Treasury, in his discretion, to authorize the ascertainment of the proof of wines, cordials, or other liquors, by distillation or otherwise, in cases where it is impracticable to ascertain such proof by the means prescribed by existing law or regulations: *And provided further,* That any brandy or other spirituous or distilled liquors imported in any sized cask, bottle, jug, or other package, of or from any country, dependency, or province under whose laws similar sized casks, bottles, jugs, or other packages of distilled spirits, wine, or other beverage put up or filled in the United States are denied entrance into such country, dependency, or province, shall be forfeited to the United States; and any brandy or other spirituous or distilled liquor imported in a cask of less capacity than ten gallons from any country shall be forfeited to the United States.

291. On all compounds or preparations of which distilled spirits are a component part of chief value, there shall be levied a duty not less than that imposed upon distilled spirits.

292. Cordials, liqueurs, arrack, absinthe, kirschwasser, ratafia, and other spirituous beverages or bitters of all kinds, containing spirits, and not specially provided for in this Act, two dollars and twenty-five cents per proof gallon.

293. No lower rate or amount of duty shall be levied, collected, and paid on brandy, spirits, and other spirituous beverages than that fixed by law for the description of first proof; but it shall be increased in proportion for any greater strength than the strength of first proof, and all imitations of brandy or spirits or wines imported by any names whatever shall be subject to the highest rate of duty provided for the genuine articles respectively intended to be represented, and in no case less than one dollar and fifty cents per gallon.

294. Bay rum or bay water, whether distilled or compounded, of first proof, and in proportion for any greater strength than first proof, one dollar and fifty cents per gallon.

WINES.

295. Champagne and all other sparkling wines, in bottles containing each not more than one quart and more than one pint, eight dollars per dozen; containing not more than one pint each and more than one-half pint, four dollars per dozen; containing one-half pint each or less, two dollars per dozen; in bottles or other vessels containing more than one quart each, in addition to eight dollars per dozen bottles, on the quantity in excess of one quart, at the rate of two dollars and fifty cents per gallon; but no separate or additional duty shall be levied on the bottles.

296. Still wines, including ginger wine or ginger cordial and vermuth, in casks or packages other than bottles or jugs, if containing fourteen per centum or less of absolute alcohol, forty cents per gallon; if containing more than fourteen per centum of absolute alcohol, fifty cents per gallon. In bottles or jugs, per case of one dozen bottles or jugs, containing each not more than one quart and more than one pint, or twenty-four bottles or jugs containing each not more than one pint, one dollar and sixty cents per case; and any excess beyond these quantities found in such bottles or jugs shall be subject to a duty of five cents per pint or fractional part thereof, but no separate or additional

duty shall be assessed on the bottles or jugs: *Provided*, That any wines, ginger cordial, or vermuth imported containing more than twenty-four per centum of alcohol shall be classed as spirits and pay duty accordingly: *And provided further*, That there shall be no constructive or other allowance for breakage, leakage, or damage on wines, liquors, cordials, or distilled spirits. Wines, cordials, brandy, and other spirituous liquors, including bitters of all kinds, and bay rum or bay water, imported in bottles or jugs, shall be packed in packages containing not less than one dozen bottles or jugs in each package, or duty shall be paid as if such package contained at least one dozen bottles or jugs, and in addition thereto, duty shall be collected on the bottles or jugs at the rates which would be chargeable thereon if imported empty. The percentage of alcohol in wines and fruit juices shall be determined in such manner as the Secretary of the Treasury shall by regulation prescribe.

297. Ale, porter, and beer, in bottles or jugs, forty cents per gallon, but no separate or additional duty shall be assessed on the bottles or jugs; otherwise than in bottles or jugs, twenty cents per gallon.

298. Malt extract, fluid, in casks, twenty cents per gallon; in bottles or jugs, forty cents per gallon; solid or condensed, forty per centum ad valorem.

299. Cherry juice and prune juice, or prune wine, and other fruit juices not specially provided for in this Act, containing no alcohol or not more than eighteen per centum of alcohol, sixty cents per gallon; if containing more than eighteen per centum of alcohol, sixty cents per gallon, and in addition thereto two dollars and seven cents per proof gallon on the alcohol contained therein.

300. Ginger ale, ginger beer, lemonade, soda water, and other similar beverages containing no alcohol in plain green or colored, molded or pressed, glass bottles, containing each not more than three-fourths of a pint, eighteen cents per dozen; containing more than three-fourths of a pint each and not more than one and one-half pints, twenty-eight cents per dozen; but no separate or additional duty shall be assessed on the bottles; if imported otherwise than in plain green or colored, molded or pressed, glass bottles, or in such bottles containing more than one and one-half pints each, fifty cents per gallon and in addition thereto, duty shall be collected on the bottles, or other coverings, at the rates which would be chargeable thereon if imported empty.

301. All mineral waters and all imitations of natural mineral waters, and all artificial mineral waters not specially provided for in this Act, in green or colored glass bottles, containing not more than one pint, twenty cents per dozen bottles. If containing more than one pint and not more than one quart, thirty cents per dozen bottles. But no separate duty shall be assessed upon the bottles. If imported otherwise than in plain green or colored glass bottles, or if imported in such bottles containing more than one quart, twenty-four cents per gallon, and in addition thereto duty shall be collected upon the bottles or other covering at the same rates that would be charged thereon if imported empty or separately.

SCHEDULE I.—COTTON MANUFACTURES.

302. Cotton thread and carded yarn, warps or warp yarn, in singles, whether on beams or in bundles, skeins or cops, or in any other form, except spool thread of cotton hereinafter provided for, not colored, bleached, dyed, or advanced beyond the condition of singles by group-

ing or twisting two or more single yarns together, three cents per pound on all numbers up to and including number fifteen, one-fifth of a cent per number per pound on all numbers exceeding number fifteen and up to and including number thirty, and one-fourth of a cent per number per pound on all numbers exceeding number thirty; colored, bleached, dyed, combed or advanced beyond the condition of singles by grouping or twisting two or more single yarns together, whether on beams, or in bundles, skeins or cops, or in any other form, except spool thread of cotton hereinafter provided for, six cents per pound on all numbers up to and including number twenty, and on all numbers exceeding number twenty and up to number eighty, one-fourth of one cent per number per pound; on number eighty and above, three-tenths of one cent per number per pound: cotton card laps, roping, sliver or roving, forty-five per centum ad valorem.

303. Spool thread of cotton, including crochet, darning, and embroidery cottons on spools or reels, containing on each spool or reel not exceeding one hundred yards of thread, six cents per dozen; exceeding one hundred yards on each spool or reel, for every additional hundred yards or fractional part thereof in excess of one hundred, six cents per dozen spools or reels; if otherwise than on spools or reels, one-half of one cent for each one hundred yards or fractional part thereof: *Provided*, That in no case shall the duty be assessed upon a less number of yards than is marked on the spools or reels.

304. Cotton cloth not bleached, dyed, colored, stained, painted, or printed, and not exceeding fifty threads to the square inch, counting the warp and filling, one cent per square yard; if bleached, one and one-fourth cents per square yard; if dyed, colored, stained, painted, or printed, two cents per square yard.

305. Cotton cloth, not bleached, dyed, colored, stained, painted, or printed. exceeding fifty and not exceeding one hundred threads to the square inch, counting the warp and filling, and not exceeding six square yards to the pound, one and one-fourth cents per square yard; exceeding six and not exceeding nine square yards to the pound, one and one-half cents per square yard; exceeding nine square yards to the pound, one and three-fourths cents per square yard; if bleached. and not exceeding six square yards to the pound, one and one-half cents per square yard; exceeding six and not exceeding nine square yards to the pound, one and three-fourths cents per square yard; exceeding nine square yards to the pound, two and one-fourth cents per square yard; if dyed, colored, stained, painted, or printed, and not exceeding six square yards to the pound, two and three-fourths cents per square yard; exceeding six and not exceeding nine square yards to the pound, three and one-fourth cents per square yard; exceeding nine square yards to the pound, three and one half cents per square yard: *Provided*, That on all cotton cloth not exceeding one hundred threads to the square inch, counting the warp and filling, not bleached, dyed, colored, stained, painted, or printed, valued at over seven cents per square yard, twenty-five per centum ad valorem; bleached, valued at over nine cents per square yard, twenty-five per centum ad valorem; and dyed, colored, stained, painted, or printed, valued at over twelve cents per square yard, there shall be levied, collected, and paid a duty of thirty per centum ad valorem.

306. Cotton cloth, not bleached, dyed, colored, stained, painted, or printed. exceeding one hundred and not exceeding one hundred and fifty threads to the square inch, counting the warp and filling, and not exceeding four square yards to the pound, one and one-half cents per

square yard; exceeding four and not exceeding six square yards to the pound, two cents per square yard; exceeding six and not exceeding eight square yards to the pound, two and one-half cents per square yard; exceeding eight square yards to the pound, two and three-fourths cents per square yard; if bleached, and not exceeding four square yards to the pound, two and one-half cents per square yard; exceeding four and not exceeding six square yards to the pound, three cents per square yard; exceeding six and not exceeding eight square yards to the pound, three and one-half cents per square yard; exceeding eight square yards to the pound, three and three-fourths cents per square yard; if dyed, colored, stained, painted, or printed, and not exceeding four square yards to the pound, three and one-half cents per square yard; exceeding six and not exceeding six square yards to the pound, three and three-fourths cents per square yard; exceeding six and not exceeding eight square yards to the pound, four and one-fourth cents per square yard; exceeding eight square yards to the pound, four and one-half cents per square yard: *Provided*, That on all cotton cloth exceeding one hundred and not exceeding one hundred and fifty threads to the square inch, counting the warp and filling, not bleached, dyed, colored, stained, painted, or printed, valued at over nine cents per square yard, thirty per centum ad valorem; bleached, valued at over eleven cents per square yard, thirty-five per centum ad valorem; dyed, colored, stained, painted, or printed, valued at over twelve and one-half cents per square yard, there shall be levied, collected, and paid a duty of thirty-five per centum ad valorem.

307. Cotton cloth not bleached, dyed, colored, stained, painted, or printed, exceeding one hundred and fifty and not exceeding two hundred threads to the square inch, counting the warp and filling, and not exceeding three and one-half square yards to the pound, two cents per square yard; exceeding three and one-half and not exceeding four and one-half square yards to the pound, two and three-fourths cents per square yard; exceeding four and one-half and not exceeding six square yards to the pound, three cents per square yard; exceeding six square yards to the pound, three and one-half cents per square yard; if bleached, and not exceeding three and one-half square yards to the pound, two and three-fourths cents per square yard; exceeding three and one-half and not exceeding four and one-half square yards to the pound, three and one-half cents per square yard; exceeding four and one-half and not exceeding six square yards to the pound, four cents per square yard; exceeding six square yards to the pound, four and one-fourth cents per square yard; if dyed, colored, stained, painted, or printed, and not exceeding three and one-half square yards to the pound, four and one-fourth cents per square yard; exceeding three and one-half and not exceeding four and one-half square yards to the pound, four and one-half cents per square yard; exceeding four and one-half and not exceeding six square yards to the pound, four and one-half cents per square yard; exceeding six square yards to the pound, five cents per square yard: *Provided*, That on all cotton cloth exceeding one hundred and fifty and not exceeding two hundred threads to the square inch, counting the warp and filling, not bleached, dyed, colored, stained, painted, or printed, valued at over ten cents per square yard, thirty-five per centum ad valorem; bleached, valued at over twelve cents per square yard, thirty-five per centum ad valorem; dyed, colored, stained, painted, or printed, valued at over twelve and one-half cents per square yard, there shall be levied, collected, and paid a duty of forty per centum ad valorem.

308. Cotton cloth not bleached, dyed, colored, stained, painted, or printed, exceeding two hundred and not exceeding three hundred threads to the square inch, counting the warp and filling, and not exceeding two and one-half square yards to the pound, three and one-half cents per square yard; exceeding two and one-half and not exceeding three and one-half square yards to the pound, four cents per square yard; exceeding three and one-half and not exceeding five square yards to the pound, four and one-half cents per square yard; exceeding five square yards to the pound, five cents per square yard; if bleached, and not exceeding two and one-half square yards to the pound, four and one-half cents per square yard; exceeding two and one-half and not exceeding three and one-half square yards to the pound, five cents per square yard; exceeding three and one-half and not exceeding five square yards to the pound, five and one-half cents per square yard; exceeding five square yards to the pound, six cents per square yard; if dyed, colored, stained, painted, or printed, and not exceeding three and one-half square yards to the pound, six and one-fourth cents per square yard; exceeding three and one-half square yards to the pound, seven cents per square yard: *Provided*, That on all such cotton cloths not bleached, dyed, colored, stained, painted, or printed, valued at over twelve and one-half cents per square yard: bleached, valued at over fifteen cents per square yard; and dyed, colored, stained, painted, or printed, valued at over seventeen and one-half cents per square yard, there shall be levied, collected, and paid a duty of forty per centum ad valorem.

309. Cotton cloth not bleached, dyed, colored, stained, painted, or printed, exceeding three hundred threads to the square inch, counting the warp and filling, and not exceeding two square yards to the pound, four cents per square yard; exceeding two and not exceeding three square yards to the pound, four and one-half cents per square yard; exceeding three and not exceeding four square yards to the pound, five cents per square yard; exceeding four square yards to the pound, five and one-half cents per square yard; if bleached and not exceeding two square yards to the pound, five cents per square yard; exceeding two and not exceeding three square yards to the pound, five and one-half cents per square yard; exceeding three and not exceeding four square yards to the pound, six cents per square yard; exceeding four square yards to the pound, six and one-half cents per square yard; if dyed, colored, stained, painted, or printed, and not exceeding three square yards to the pound, six and one-half cents per square yard; exceeding three square yards to the pound, eight cents per square yard: *Provided*, That on all such cotton cloths not bleached, dyed, colored, stained, painted, or printed, valued at over fourteen cents per square yard: bleached, valued at over sixteen cents per square yard; and dyed, colored, stained, painted, or printed, valued at over twenty cents per square yard, there shall be levied, collected, and paid a duty of forty per centum ad valorem.

310. The term cotton cloth, or cloth, wherever used in the paragraphs of this schedule, unless otherwise specially provided for, shall be held to include all woven fabrics of cotton in the piece or otherwise, whether figured, fancy, or plain, the warp and filling threads of which can be counted by unraveling or other practicable means.

311. Cloth, composed of cotton or other vegetable fiber and silk, whether known as silk-striped sleeve linings, silk stripes, or otherwise, of which cotton is the component material of chief value, eight cents per square yard and thirty per centum ad valorem: *Provided*, That no such cloth shall pay a less rate of duty than fifty per centum ad valorem. Cotton cloth, filled or coated, three cents per square yard and twenty per centum ad valorem.

312. Handkerchiefs or mufflers composed of cotton, whether in the piece or otherwise and whether finished or unfinished, if not hemmed, or hemmed only, shall pay the same rate of duty on the cloth contained therein as is imposed on cotton cloth of the same description, weight, and count of threads to the square inch; but such handkerchiefs or mufflers shall not pay a less rate of duty than forty-five per centum ad valorem. If such handkerchiefs or mufflers are hemstitched, or imitation hemstitched, or revered, or have drawn threads, they shall pay a duty of ten per centum ad valorem in addition to the duty hereinbefore prescribed, and in no case less than fifty-five per centum ad valorem; if such handkerchiefs or mufflers are embroidered in any manner, whether with an initial letter, monogram, or otherwise, by hand or machinery, or are tamboured, appliqued, or trimmed wholly or in part with lace or with tucking or insertion, they shall not pay a less rate of duty than sixty per centum ad valorem.

313. Cotton cloth in which other than the ordinary warp and filling threads have been introduced in the process of weaving to form a figure, whether known as lappets or otherwise, and whether unbleached, bleached, dyed, colored, stained, painted, or printed, shall pay, in addition to the duty herein provided for other cotton cloth of the same description, or condition, weight, and count of threads to the square inch, one cent per square yard if valued at not more than seven cents per square yard, and two cents per square yard if valued at more than seven cents per square yard.

314. Clothing, ready-made, and articles of wearing apparel of every description, including neck-ties or neckwear composed of cotton or other vegetable fiber, or of which cotton or other vegetable fiber is the component material of chief value, made up or manufactured, wholly or in part, by the tailor, seamstress, or manufacturer, and not otherwise provided for in this Act, fifty per centum ad valorem: *Provided*, That any outside garment provided for in this paragraph having india-rubber as a component material shall pay a duty of fifteen cents per pound and fifty per centum ad valorem.

315. Plushes, velvets, velveteens, corduroys, and all pile fabrics, cut or uncut; any of the foregoing composed of cotton or other vegetable fiber, not bleached, dyed, colored, stained, painted, or printed, nine cents per square yard and twenty-five per centum ad valorem; if bleached, dyed, colored, stained, painted, or printed, twelve cents per square yard and twenty-five per centum ad valorem: *Provided*, That corduroys composed of cotton or other vegetable fiber, weighing seven ounces or over per square yard, shall pay a duty of eighteen cents per square yard and twenty-five per centum ad valorem: *Provided further*, That manufactures or articles in any form including such as are commonly known as bias dress facings or skirt bindings, made or cut from plushes, velvets, velveteens, corduroys, or other pile fabrics composed of cotton or other vegetable fiber, shall be subject to the foregoing rates of duty and in addition thereto ten per centum ad valorem: *Provided further*, That none of the articles or fabrics provided for in this paragraph shall pay a less rate of duty than forty-seven and one-half per centum ad valorem.

316. Curtains, table covers, and all articles manufactured of cotton chenille or of which cotton chenille is the component material of chief value, fifty per centum ad valorem.

317. Stockings, hose and half-hose, made on knitting machines or frames, composed of cotton or other vegetable fiber, and not otherwise specially provided for in this Act, thirty per centum ad valorem.

318. Stockings, hose and half-hose, selvedged, fashioned, narrowed, or shaped wholly or in part by knitting machines or frames, or knit by hand, including such as are commercially known as seamless stockings, hose and half-hose, and clocked stockings, hose or half-hose, all of the above composed of cotton or other vegetable fiber, finished or unfinished, valued at not more than one dollar per dozen pairs, fifty cents per dozen pairs; valued at more than one dollar per dozen pairs, and not more than one dollar and fifty cents per dozen pairs, sixty cents per dozen pairs; valued at more than one dollar and fifty cents per dozen pairs, and not more than two dollars per dozen pairs, seventy cents per dozen pairs; valued at more than two dollars per dozen pairs, and not more than three dollars per dozen pairs, one dollar and twenty cents per dozen pairs; valued at more than three dollars per dozen pairs and not more than five dollars per dozen pairs, two dollars per dozen pairs; and in addition thereto, upon all the foregoing, fifteen per centum ad valorem; valued at more than five dollars per dozen pairs, fifty-five per centum ad valorem.

319. Shirts and drawers, pants, vests, union suits, combination suits, tights, sweaters, corset covers and all underwear of every description made wholly or in part on knitting machines or frames, or knit by hand, finished or unfinished, not including stockings, hose and half-hose, composed of cotton or other vegetable fiber, valued at not more than one dollar and fifty cents per dozen, sixty cents per dozen and fifteen per centum ad valorem; valued at more than one dollar and fifty cents per dozen and not more than three dollars per dozen, one dollar and ten cents per dozen, and in addition thereto fifteen per centum ad valorem; valued at more than three dollars per dozen and not more than five dollars per dozen, one dollar and fifty cents per dozen, and in addition thereto twenty-five per centum ad valorem; valued at more than five dollars per dozen and not more than seven dollars per dozen, one dollar and seventy-five cents per dozen, and in addition thereto thirty-five per centum ad valorem; valued at more than seven dollars per dozen and not more than fifteen dollars per dozen, two dollars and twenty-five cents per dozen, and in addition thereto thirty-five per centum ad valorem; valued above fifteen dollars per dozen, fifty per centum ad valorem.

320. Bandings, beltings, bindings, bone casings, cords, garters, lining for bicycle tires, ribbons, suspenders and braces, tapes, tubing, and webs or webbing, any of the foregoing articles made of cotton or other vegetable fiber, whether composed in part of india-rubber or otherwise, and not embroidered by hand or machinery, forty-five per centum ad valorem; spindle banding, woven, braided or twisted lamp, stove, or candle wicking made of cotton or other vegetable fiber, ten cents per pound and fifteen per centum ad valorem; loom harness or healds made of cotton or other vegetable fiber, or of which cotton or other vegetable fiber is the component material of chief value, fifty cents per pound and twenty-five per centum ad valorem; boot, shoe, and corset lacings made of cotton or other vegetable fiber, twenty-five cents per pound and fifteen per centum ad valorem; labels, for garments or other articles, composed of cotton or other vegetable fiber, fifty cents per pound and thirty per centum ad valorem.

321. Cotton table damask, forty per centum ad valorem; cotton duck, thirty-five per centum ad valorem.

322. All manufactures of cotton not specially provided for in this Act, forty-five per centum ad valorem.

SCHEDULE J.—FLAX, HEMP, AND JUTE, AND MANUFACTURES OF.

323. Flax straw, five dollars per ton.

324. Flax, not hackled or dressed, one cent per pound.

325. Flax, hackled, known as "dressed line," three cents per pound.

326. Tow of flax, twenty dollars per ton.

327. Hemp, and tow of hemp, twenty dollars per ton; hemp, hackled, known as "line of hemp," forty dollars per ton.

328. Single yarns made of jute, not finer than five lea or number, one cent per pound and ten per centum ad valorem; if finer than five lea or number, thirty-five per centum ad valorem.

329. Cables and cordage, composed of istle, Tampico fiber, manila, sisal grass or sunn, or a mixture of these or any of them, one cent per pound; cables and cordage made of hemp, tarred or untarred, two cents per pound.

330. Threads, twines, or cords, made from yarn not finer than five lea or number, composed of flax, hemp, or ramie, or of which these substances or either of them is the component material of chief value, thirteen cents per pound; if made from yarn finer than five lea or number, three-fourths of one cent per pound additional for each lea or number, or part of a lea or number, in excess of five.

331. Single yarns in the gray. made of flax, hemp, or ramie, or a mixture of any of them. not finer than eight lea or number, seven cents per pound; finer than eight lea or number and not finer than eighty lea or number, forty per centum ad valorem; single yarns, made of flax, hemp, or ramie, or a mixture of any of them, finer than eighty lea or number, fifteen per centum ad valorem.

332. Flax gill netting, nets, webs, and seines shall pay the same duty per pound as is imposed in this schedule upon the thread, twine, or cord of which they are made, and in addition thereto twenty-five per centum ad valorem.

333. Floor mattings, plain, fancy or figured, manufactured from straw, round or split, or other vegetable substances not otherwise provided for, including what are commonly known as Chinese, Japanese, and India straw mattings, valued at not exceeding ten cents per square yard, three cents per square yard; valued at exceeding ten cents per square yard, seven cents per square yard and twenty-five per centum ad valorem.

334. Carpets, carpeting, mats and rugs made of flax, hemp, jute, or other vegetable fiber (except cotton), valued at not exceeding fifteen cents per square yard, five cents per square yard and thirty-five per centum ad valorem; valued above fifteen cents per square yard, ten cents per square yard and thirty-five per centum ad valorem.

335. Hydraulic hose, made in whole or in part of flax, hemp, ramie, or jute, twenty cents per pound.

336. Tapes composed wholly or in part of flax, woven with or without metal threads, on reels, spools, or otherwise, and designed expressly for use in the manufacture of measuring tapes, forty per centum ad valorem.

337. Oilcloth for floors, stamped, painted, or printed, including linoleum or corticene, figured or plain, and all other oilcloth (except silk oilcloth) under twelve feet in width not specially provided for herein, eight cents per square yard and fifteen per centum ad valorem; oil

cloth for floors and linoleum or corticene, twelve feet and over in width, inlaid linoleum or corticene, and cork carpets, twenty cents per square yard and twenty per centum ad valorem; waterproof cloth, composed of cotton or other vegetable fiber, whether composed in part of india-rubber or otherwise, ten cents per square yard and twenty per centum ad valorem.

338. Shirt collars and cuffs, composed of cotton, forty-five cents per dozen pieces and fifteen per centum ad valorem: composed in whole or in part of linen, forty cents per dozen pieces and twenty per centum ad valorem.

339. Laces, lace window curtains, tidies, pillow shams, bed sets, insertings, flouncings, and other lace articles; handkerchiefs, napkins, wearing apparel, and other articles, made wholly or in part of lace, or in imitation of lace; nets or nettings, veils and veilings, etamines, vitrages, neck rufflings, ruchings, tuckings, flutings, and quillings; embroideries and all trimmings, including braids, edgings, insertings, flouncings, galloons, gorings, and bands; wearing apparel, handkerchiefs, and other articles or fabrics embroidered in any manner by hand or machinery, whether with a letter, monogram, or otherwise; tamboured or appliquéed articles, fabrics or wearing apparel; hemstitched or tucked flouncings or skirtings, and articles made wholly or in part of rufflings, tuckings, or ruchings; all of the foregoing, composed wholly or in chief value of flax, cotton, or other vegetable fiber, and not elsewhere specially provided for in this Act, whether composed in part of india rubber or otherwise, sixty per centum ad valorem: *Provided*, That no wearing apparel or other article or textile fabric, when embroidered by hand or machinery, shall pay duty at a less rate than that imposed in any schedule of this Act upon any embroideries of the materials of which such embroidery is composed.

340. Lace window curtains, pillow shams, and bed sets, finished or unfinished, made on the Nottingham lace-curtain machine or on the Nottingham warp machine, and composed of cotton or other vegetable fiber, when counting five points or spaces between the warp threads to the inch, one cent per square yard; when counting more than five such points or spaces to the inch, one-half of one cent per square yard in addition for each such point or space to the inch in excess of five; and in addition thereto, on all the foregoing articles in this paragraph, twenty per centum ad valorem: *Provided*, That none of the above-named articles shall pay a less rate of duty than fifty per centum ad valorem.

341. Plain woven fabrics of single jute yarns, by whatever name known, not exceeding sixty inches in width, weighing not less than six ounces per square yard and not exceeding thirty threads to the square inch, counting the warp and filling, five-eighths of one cent per pound and fifteen per centum ad valorem; if exceeding thirty and not exceeding fifty-five threads to the square inch, counting the warp and filling, seven-eighths of one cent per pound and fifteen per centum ad valorem.

342. All pile fabrics of which flax is the component material of chief value, sixty per centum ad valorem.

343. Bags or sacks made from plain woven fabrics, of single jute yarns, not dyed, colored, stained, painted, printed, or bleached, and not exceeding thirty threads to the square inch, counting the warp and filling, seven-eighths of one cent per pound and fifteen per centum ad valorem.

344. Bagging for cotton, gunny cloth, and similar fabrics, suitable for covering cotton, composed of single yarns made of jute, jute butts,

or hemp, not bleached, dyed, colored, stained, painted, or printed, not exceeding sixteen threads to the square inch, counting the warp and filling, and weighing not less than fifteen ounces per square yard, six-tenths of one cent per square yard.

345. Handkerchiefs composed of flax, hemp, or ramie, or of which these substances, or either of them, is the component material of chief value, whether in the piece or otherwise, and whether finished or unfinished, not hemmed or hemmed only, fifty per centum ad valorem; if hemstitched, or imitation hemstitched, or revered, or with drawn threads, but not embroidered or initialed, fitty-five per centum ad valorem.

346. Woven fabrics or articles not specially provided for in this Act, composed of flax, hemp, or ramie, or of which these substances or either of them is the component material of chief value, weighing four and one-half ounces or more per square yard, when containing not more than sixty threads to the square inch, counting the warp and filling, one and three-fourths cents per square yard; containing more than sixty and not more than one hundred and twenty threads to the square inch, two and three-fourths cents per square yard; containing more than one hundred and twenty and not more than one hundred and eighty threads to the square inch, six cents per square yard; containing more than one hundred and eighty threads to the square inch, nine cents per square yard, and in addition thereto, on all the foregoing, thirty per centum ad valorem: *Provided*, That none of the foregoing articles in this paragraph shall pay a less rate of duty than fifty per centum ad valorem. Woven fabrics of flax, hemp, or ramie, or of which these substances or either of them is the component material of chief value, including such as is known as shirting cloth, weighing less than four and one-half ounces per square yard and containing more than one hundred threads to the square inch, counting the warp and filling, thirty-five per centum ad valorem.

347. All manufactures of flax, hemp, ramie, or other vegetable fiber, or of which these substances, or either of them, is the component material of chief value, not specially provided for in this Act, forty-five per centum ad valorem.

Schedule K.—Wool and Manufactures of Wool.

348. All wools, hair of the camel, goat, alpaca, and other like animals shall be divided, for the purpose of fixing the duties to be charged thereon, into the three following classes:

349. Class one, that is to say, merino, mestiza, metz, or metis wools, or other wools of Merino blood, immediate or remote, Down clothing wools, and wools of like character with any of the preceding, including Bagdad wool, China lamb's wool, Castel Branco, Adrianople skin wool or butcher's wool, and such as have been heretofore usually imported into the United States from Buenos Ayres, New Zealand, Australia, Cape of Good Hope, Russia, Great Britain, Canada, Egypt, Morocco, and elsewhere, and all wools not hereinafter included in classes two and three.

350. Class two, that is to say, Leicester, Cotswold, Lincolnshire, Down combing wools, Canada long wools, or other like combing wools of English blood, and usually known by the terms herein used, and also hair of the camel, Angora goat, alpaca, and other like animals.

351. Class three, that is to say, Donskoi, native South American, Cordova, Valparaiso, native Smyrna, Russian camel's hair, and all such

wools of like character as have been heretofore usually imported into the United States from Turkey, Greece, Syria, and elsewhere, excepting improved wools hereinafter provided for.

352. The standard samples of all wools which are now or may be hereafter deposited in the principal custom-houses of the United States, under the authority of the Secretary of the Treasury, shall be the standards for the classification of wools under this Act, and the Secretary of the Treasury is authorized to renew these standards and to make such additions to them from time to time as may be required, and he shall cause to be deposited like standards in other custom-houses of the United States when they may be needed.

353. Whenever wools of class three shall have been improved by the admixture of Merino or English blood, from their present character as represented by the standard samples now or hereafter to be deposited in the principal custom-houses of the United States, such improved wools shall be classified for duty either as class one or as class two, as the case may be.

354. The duty on wools of the first class which shall be imported washed shall be twice the amount of the duty to which they would be subjected if imported unwashed; and the duty on wools of the first and second classes which shall be imported scoured shall be three times the duty to which they would be subjected if imported unwashed. The duty on wools of the third class, if imported in condition for use in carding or spinning into yarns, or which shall not contain more than eight per cent of dirt or other foreign substance, shall be three times the duty to which they would otherwise be subjected.

355. Unwashed wools shall be considered such as shall have been shorn from the sheep without any cleansing; that is, in their natural condition. Washed wools shall be considered such as have been washed with water only on the sheep's back, or on the skin. Wools of the first and second classes washed in any other manner than on the sheep's back or on the skin shall be considered as scoured wool.

356. The duty upon wool of the sheep or hair of the camel, Angora goat, alpaca, and other like animals, of class one and class two, which shall be imported in any other than ordinary condition, or which has been sorted or increased in value by the rejection of any part of the original fleece, shall be twice the duty to which it would be otherwise subject: *Provided*, That skirted wools as imported in eighteen hundred and ninety and prior thereto are hereby excepted. The duty upon wool of the sheep or hair of the camel, Angora goat, alpaca, and other like animals of any class which shall be changed in its character or condition for the purpose of evading the duty, or which shall be reduced in value by the admixture of dirt or any other foreign substance, shall be twice the duty to which it would be otherwise subject. When the duty assessed upon any wool equals three times or more that which would be assessed if said wool was imported unwashed, the duty shall not be doubled on account of the wool being sorted. If any bale or package of wool or hair specified in this Act invoiced or entered as of any specified class, or claimed by the importer to be dutiable as of any specified class, shall contain any wool or hair subject to a higher rate of duty than the class so specified, the whole bale or package shall be subject to the highest rate of duty chargeable on wool of the class subject to such higher rate of duty, and if any bale or package be claimed by the importer to be shoddy, mungo, flocks, wool, hair, or other material of any class specified in this Act, and such bale contain any admixture of any one or more of said materials, or of any other material, the whole

bale or package shall be subject to duty at the highest rate imposed upon any article in said bale or package.

357. The duty upon all wools and hair of the first class shall be eleven cents per pound, and upon all wools or hair of the second class twelve cents per pound.

358. On wools of the third class and on camel's hair of the third class the value whereof shall be twelve cents or less per pound, the duty shall be four cents per pound.

359. On wools of the third class, and on camel's hair of the third class, the value whereof shall exceed twelve cents per pound, the duty shall be seven cents per pound.

360. The duty on wools on the skin shall be one cent less per pound than is imposed in this schedule on other wools of the same class and condition, the quantity and value to be ascertained under such rules as the Secretary of the Treasury may prescribe.

361. Top waste, slubbing waste, roving waste, ring waste, and garnetted waste, thirty cents per pound.

362. Shoddy, twenty-five cents per pound; noils, wool extract, yarn waste, thread waste, and all other wastes composed wholly or in part of wool, and not specially provided for in this Act, twenty cents per pound.

363. Woolen rags, mungo, and flocks, ten cents per pound.

364. Wool and hair which have been advanced in any manner or by any process of manufacture beyond the washed or scoured condition, not specially provided for in this Act, shall be subject to the same duties as are imposed upon manufactures of wool not specially provided for in this Act.

365. On yarns made wholly or in part of wool, valued at not more than thirty cents per pound, the duty per pound shall be two and one-half times the duty imposed by this Act on one pound of unwashed wool of the first class; valued at more than thirty cents per pound, the duty per pound shall be three and one-half times the duty imposed by this Act on one pound of unwashed wool of the first class, and in addition thereto, upon all the foregoing, forty per centum ad valorem.

366. On cloths, knit fabrics, and all manufactures of every description made wholly or in part of wool, not specially provided for in this Act, valued at not more than forty cents per pound, the duty per pound shall be three times the duty imposed by this Act on a pound of unwashed wool of the first class; valued at above forty cents per pound and not above seventy cents per pound, the duty per pound shall be four times the duty imposed by this Act on one pound of unwashed wool of the first class, and in addition thereto, upon all the foregoing, fifty per centum ad valorem; valued at over seventy cents per pound, the duty per pound shall be four times the duty imposed by this Act on one pound of unwashed wool of the first class and fifty-five per centum ad valorem.

367. On blankets, and flannels for underwear composed wholly or in part of wool, valued at not more than forty cents per pound, the duty per pound shall be the same as the duty imposed by this Act on two pounds of unwashed wool of the first class, and in addition thereto thirty per centum ad valorem; valued at more than forty cents and not more than fifty cents per pound, the duty per pound shall be three times the duty imposed by this Act on one pound of unwashed wool of the first class, and in addition thereto thirty-five per centum ad valorem. On blankets composed wholly or in part of wool, valued at more than fifty cents per pound, the duty per pound shall be three times the duty

imposed by this Act on one pound of unwashed wool of the first class, and in addition thereto forty per centum ad valorem. Flannels composed wholly or in part of wool, valued at above fifty cents per pound, shall be classified and pay the same duty as women's and children's dress goods, coat linings, Italian cloths, and goods of similar character and description provided by this Act: *Provided*, That on blankets over three yards in length the same duties shall be paid as on cloths.

368. On women's and children's dress goods, coat linings, Italian cloths, and goods of similar description and character of which the warp consists wholly of cotton or other vegetable material with the remainder of the fabric composed wholly or in part of wool, valued at not exceeding fifteen cents per square yard, the duty shall be seven cents per square yard; valued at more than fifteen cents per square yard, the duty shall be eight cents per square yard; and in addition thereto on all the foregoing valued at not above seventy cents per pound, fifty per centum ad valorem; valued above seventy cents per pound, fifty-five per centum ad valorem: *Provided*, That on all the foregoing, weighing over four ounces per square yard, the duty shall be the same as imposed by this schedule on cloths.

369. On women's and children's dress goods, coat linings, Italian cloths, bunting, and goods of similar description or character composed wholly or in part of wool, and not specially provided for in this Act, the duty shall be eleven cents per square yard; and in addition thereto on all the foregoing valued at not above seventy cents per pound, fifty per centum ad valorem; valued above seventy cents per pound, fifty-five per centum ad valorem: *Provided*, That on all the foregoing, weighing over four ounces per square yard, the duty shall be the same as imposed by this schedule on cloths.

370. On clothing, ready-made, and articles of wearing apparel of every description, including shawls whether knitted or woven, and knitted articles of every description, made up or manufactured wholly or in part, felts not woven and not specially provided for in this Act, composed wholly or in part of wool, the duty per pound shall be four times the duty imposed by this Act on one pound of unwashed wool of the first class, and in addition thereto sixty per centum ad valorem.

371. Webbings, gorings, suspenders, braces, bandings, beltings, bindings, braids, galloons, edgings, insertings, flouncings, fringes, gimps, cords, cords and tassels, laces and other trimmings and articles made wholly or in part of lace, embroideries and articles embroidered by hand or machinery, head nets, netting, buttons or barrel buttons or buttons of other forms for tassels or ornaments, and manufactures of wool ornamented with beads or spangles of whatever material composed, any of the foregoing made of wool or of which wool is a component material, whether composed in part of india-rubber or otherwise, fifty cents per pound and sixty per centum ad valorem.

372. Aubusson, Axminster, moquette, and chenille carpets, figured or plain, and all carpets or carpeting of like character or description, sixty cents per square yard, and in addition thereto forty per centum ad valorem.

373. Saxony, Wilton, and Tournay velvet carpets, figured or plain, and all carpets or carpeting of like character or description, sixty cents per square yard, and in addition thereto forty per centum ad valorem.

374. Brussels carpets, figured or plain, and all carpets or carpeting of like character or description, forty-four cents per square yard, and in addition thereto forty per centum ad valorem.

375. Velvet and tapestry velvet carpets, figured or plain, printed on

the warp or otherwise, and all carpets or carpeting of like character or description, forty cents per square yard, and in addition thereto forty per centum ad valorem.

376. Tapestry Brussels carpets, figured or plain, and all carpets or carpeting of like character or description, printed on the warp or otherwise, twenty-eight cents per square yard, and in addition thereto forty per centum ad valorem.

377. Treble ingrain, three-ply, and all chain Venetian carpets, twenty-two cents per square yard, and in addition thereto forty per centum ad valorem.

378. Wool Dutch and two-ply ingrain carpets, eighteen cents per square yard, and in addition thereto forty per centum ad valorem.

379. Carpets of every description woven whole for rooms, and Oriental, Berlin, Aubusson, Axminster, and similar rugs, ten cents per square foot and in addition thereto, forty per centum ad valorem.

380. Druggets and bockings, printed, colored, or otherwise, twenty-two cents per square yard, and in addition thereto forty per centum ad valorem.

381. Carpets and carpeting of wool, flax, or cotton, or composed in part of either, not specially provided for in this Act, fifty per centum ad valorem.

382. Mats, rugs for floors, screens, covers, hassocks, bed sides, art squares, and other portions of carpets or carpeting made wholly or in part of wool, and not specially provided for in this Act, shall be subjected to the rate of duty herein imposed on carpets or carpetings of like character or description.

383. Whenever, in any schedule of this Act, the word "wool" is used in connection with a manufactured article of which it is a component material, it shall be held to include wool or hair of the sheep, camel, goat, alpaca or other animal, whether manufactured by the woolen, worsted, felt, or any other process.

SCHEDULE L.—SILKS AND SILK GOODS.

384. Silk partially manufactured from cocoons or from waste silk, and not further advanced or manufactured than carded or combed silk, forty cents per pound.

385. Thrown silk, not more advanced than singles, tram, organzine, sewing silk, twist, floss, and silk threads or yarns of every description, except spun silk, thirty per centum ad valorem; spun silk in skeins, cops, warps, or on beams, valued at not exceeding one dollar per pound, twenty cents per pound and fifteen per centum ad valorem; valued at over one dollar per pound and not exceeding one dollar and fifty cents per pound, thirty cents per pound and fifteen per centum ad valorem; valued at over one dollar and fifty cents per pound and not exceeding two dollars per pound, forty cents per pound and fifteen per centum ad valorem; valued at over two dollars per pound and not exceeding two dollars and fifty cents per pound, fifty cents per pound and fifteen per centum ad valorem; valued at over two dollars and fifty cents per pound, sixty cents per pound and fifteen per centum ad valorem; but in no case shall the foregoing articles pay a less rate of duty than thirty-five per centum ad valorem.

386. Velvets, velvet or plush ribbons, chenilles, or other pile fabrics, cut or uncut, composed of silk, or of which silk is the component material of chief value, not specially provided for in this Act, one dollar and fifty cents per pound and fifteen per centum ad valorem;

plushes, composed of silk, or of which silk is the component material of chief value, one dollar per pound and fifteen per centum ad valorem; but in no case shall the foregoing articles pay a less rate of duty than fifty per centum ad valorem.

387. Woven fabrics in the piece, not specially provided for in this Act, weighing not less than one and one-third ounces per square yard and not more than eight ounces per square yard, and containing not more than twenty per centum in weight of silk, if in the gum, fifty cents per pound, and if dyed in the piece, sixty cents per pound; if containing more than twenty per centum and not more than thirty per centum in weight of silk, if in the gum, sixty-five cents per pound, and if dyed in the piece, eighty cents per pound; if containing more than thirty per centum and not more than forty-five per centum in weight of silk, if in the gum, ninety cents per pound, and if dyed in the piece, one dollar and ten cents per pound; if dyed in the thread or yarn and containing not more than thirty per centum in weight of silk, if black (except selvedges), seventy-five cents per pound, and if other than black, ninety cents per pound; if containing more than thirty and not more than forty-five per centum in weight of silk, if black (except selvedges), one dollar and ten cents per pound, and if other than black, one dollar and thirty cents per pound; if containing more than forty-five per centum in weight of silk, or if composed wholly of silk, if dyed in the thread or yarn and weighted in the dyeing so as to exceed the original weight of the raw silk, if black (except selvedges), one dollar and fifty cents per pound, and if other than black, two dollars and twenty-five cents per pound; if dyed in the thread or yarn, and the weight is not increased by dyeing beyond the original weight of the raw silk, three dollars per pound; if in the gum, two dollars and fifty cents per pound; if boiled off, or dyed in the piece, or printed, three dollars per pound; if weighing less than one and one-third ounces and more than one-third of an ounce per square yard, if in the gum, or if dyed in the thread or yarn, two and one-half dollars per pound; if weighing less than one and one-third ounces and more than one-third of an ounce per square yard, if boiled off, three dollars per pound; if dyed or printed in the piece, three dollars and twenty-five cents per pound; if weighing not more than one-third of an ounce per square yard, four dollars and fifty cents per pound; but in no case shall any of the foregoing fabrics in this paragraph pay a less rate of duty than fifty per centum ad valorem.

388. Handkerchiefs or mufflers composed wholly or in part of silk, whether in the piece or otherwise, finished or unfinished, if not hemmed or hemmed only, shall pay the same rate of duty as is imposed on goods in the piece of the same description, weight, and condition as provided for in this schedule; but such handkerchiefs or mufflers shall not pay a less rate of duty than fifty per centum ad valorem; if such handkerchiefs or mufflers are hemstitched or imitation hemstitched, or revered or have drawn threads, or are embroidered in any manner, whether with an initial letter, monogram, or otherwise, by hand or machinery, or are tamboured, appliqued, or are made or trimmed wholly or in part with lace, or with tucking or insertion, they shall pay a duty of ten per centum ad valorem in addition to the duty hereinbefore prescribed, and in no case less than sixty per centum ad valorem.

389. Bandings, including hat bands, beltings, bindings, bone casings, braces, cords, cords and tassels, garters, gorings, suspenders, tubings, and webs and webbings, composed wholly or in part of silk, and whether composed in part of india-rubber or otherwise, if not embroidered in any manner by hand or machinery, fifty per centum ad valorem.

390. Laces, and articles made wholly or in part of lace, edgings, insertings, galloons, chiffon or other flouncings, nets or nettings and veilings, neck rufflings, ruchings, braids, fringes, trimmings, embroideries and articles embroidered by hand or machinery, or tamboured or appliqued, clothing ready made, and articles of wearing apparel of every description, including knit goods, made up or manufactured in whole or in part by the tailor, seamstress, or manufacturer; all of the above-named articles made of silk, or of which silk is the component material of chief value, not specially provided for in this Act, and silk goods ornamented with beads or spangles, of whatever material composed, sixty per centum ad valorem: *Provided*, That any wearing apparel or other articles provided for in this paragraph (except gloves) when composed in part of india-rubber, shall be subject to a duty of sixty per centum ad valorem.

391. All manufactures of silk, or of which silk is the component material of chief value, including such as have india-rubber as a component material, not specially provided for in this Act, and all Jacquard figured goods in the piece, made on looms, of which silk is the component material of chief value, dyed in the yarn, and containing two or more colors in the filling, fifty per centum ad valorem: *Provided*, That all manufactures, of which wool is a component material, shall be classified and assessed for duty as manufactures of wool.

392. In ascertaining the weight of silk under the provisions of this schedule, the weight shall be taken in the condition in which found in the goods, without deduction therefrom for any dye, coloring matter, or other foreign substance or material.

Schedule M.—Pulp, Papers, and Books.

Pulp and Paper:

393. Mechanically ground wood pulp, one-twelfth of one cent per pound, dry weight; chemical wood pulp, unbleached, one-sixth of one cent per pound, dry weight; bleached, one-fourth of one cent per pound, dry weight: *Provided*, That if any country or dependency shall impose an export duty on pulp wood exported to the United States, the amount of such export duty shall be added, as an additional duty, to the duties herein imposed upon wood pulp, when imported from such country or dependency.

394. Sheathing paper and roofing felt, ten per centum ad valorem.

395. Filter masse or filter stock, composed wholly or in part of wood pulp, wood flour, cotton or other vegetable fiber, one and one-half cents per pound and fifteen per centum ad valorem.

396. Printing paper, unsized, sized or glued, suitable for books and newspapers, valued at not above two cents per pound, three-tenths of one cent per pound; valued above two cents and not above two and one-half cents per pound, four-tenths of one cent per pound; valued above two and one-half cents per pound and not above three cents per pound, five-tenths of one cent per pound; valued above three cents and not above four cents per pound, six-tenths of one cent per pound; valued above four cents and not above five cents per pound, eight-tenths of one cent per pound; valued above five cents per pound, fifteen per centum ad valorem: *Provided*, That if any country or dependency shall impose an export duty upon pulp wood exported to the United States, there shall be imposed upon printing paper

when imported from such country or dependency, an additional duty of one-tenth of one cent per pound for each dollar of export duty per cord so imposed, and proportionately for fractions of a dollar of such export duty.

397. Papers commonly known as copying paper, stereotype paper, paper known as bibulous paper, tissue paper, pottery paper, and all similar papers, white, colored or printed, weighing not over six pounds to the ream of four hundred and eighty sheets, on a basis of twenty by thirty inches, and whether in reams or any other form, six cents per pound and fifteen per centum ad valorem; if weighing over six pounds and not over ten pounds to the ream, and letter copying books, whether wholly or partly manufactured, five cents per pound and fifteen per centum ad valorem; crepe paper and filtering paper, five cents per pound and fifteen per centum ad valorem.

398. Surface-coated papers not specially provided for in this Act, two and one-half cents per pound and fifteen per centum ad valorem; if printed, or wholly or partly covered with metal or its solutions, or with gelatin or flock, three cents per pound and twenty per centum ad valorem; parchment papers, two cents per pound and ten per centum ad valorem; plain basic photographic papers for albumenizing, sensitizing, or baryta coating, three cents per pound and ten per centum ad valorem; albumenized or sensitized paper or paper otherwise surface coated for photographic purposes, thirty per centum ad valorem.

MANUFACTURES OF PAPER:

399. Paper envelopes, plain, twenty per centum ad valorem; if bordered, embossed, printed, tinted, or decorated, thirty-five per centum ad valorem.

400. Lithographic prints from stone, zinc, aluminum or other material, bound or unbound (except cigar labels, flaps, and bands, lettered, or otherwise, music and illustrations when forming a part of a periodical or newspaper and accompanying the same, or if bound in or forming a part of printed books, not specially provided for in this Act), on paper or other material not exceeding eight one-thousandths of one inch in thickness, twenty cents per pound ; on paper or other material exceeding eight one-thousandths of one inch and not exceeding twenty one-thousandths of one inch in thickness, and exceeding thirty-five square inches, but not exceeding four hundred square inches cutting size in dimensions, eight cents per pound ; exceeding four hundred square inches cutting size in dimensions, thirty-five per centum ad valorem; prints exceeding eight one-thousandths of one inch and not exceeding twenty one-thousandths of one inch in thickness, and not exceeding thirty-five square inches cutting size in dimensions, five cents per pound; lithographic prints from stone, zinc, aluminum or other material, on cardboard or other material, exceeding twenty one-thousandths of one inch in thickness, six cents per pound; lithographic cigar labels, flaps and bands, lettered or blank, printed from stone, zinc, aluminum or other material, if printed in less than eight colors (bronze printing to be counted as two colors), but not including labels, flaps and bands printed in whole or in part in metal leaf, twenty cents

per pound. Labels, flaps and bands, if printed entirely in bronze printing, fifteen cents per pound; labels, flaps and bands printed in eight or more colors, but not including labels, flaps and bands printed in whole or in part in metal leaf, thirty cents per pound; labels, flaps and bands printed in whole or in part in metal leaf, fifty cents per pound. Books of paper or other material for children's use, containing illuminated lithographic prints, not exceeding in weight twenty-four ounces each, and all booklets and fashion magazines or periodicals printed in whole or in part by lithographic process or decorated by hand, eight cents per pound.

401. Writing, letter, note, hand-made, drawing, ledger, bond, record, tablet, and typewriter paper, weighing not less than ten pounds and not more than fifteen pounds to the ream, two cents per pound and ten per centum ad valorem; weighing more than fifteen pounds to the ream, three and one-half cents per pound and fifteen per centum ad valorem; but if any such paper is ruled, bordered, embossed, printed, or decorated in any manner, it shall pay ten per centum ad valorem in addition to the foregoing rates: *Provided*, That in computing the duty on such paper every one hundred and eighty thousand square inches shall be taken to be a ream.

402. Paper hangings and paper for screens or fireboards, and all other paper not specially provided for in this Act, twenty-five per centum ad valorem; all Jacquard designs of one line paper, or parts of such designs, finished or unfinished, thirty-five per centum ad valorem; all Jacquard designs cut on Jacquard cards, or parts of such designs, finished or unfinished, thirty-five per centum ad valorem.

Manufactures of Paper:

403. Books of all kinds, including blank books and pamphlets, and engravings bound or unbound, photographs, etchings, maps, charts, music in books or sheets, and printed matter, all the foregoing not specially provided for in this Act, twenty-five per centum ad valorem.

404. Photograph, autograph, and scrap albums, wholly or partly manufactured, thirty-five per centum ad valorem.

405. All fancy boxes made of paper, or of which paper is the component material of chief value, or if covered with surface-coated paper, forty-five per centum ad valorem.

406. Playing cards, in packs not exceeding fifty-four cards and at a like rate for any number in excess, ten cents per pack and twenty per centum ad valorem.

407. Manufactures of paper, or of which paper is the component material of chief value, not specially provided for in this Act, thirty-five per centum ad valorem.

Schedule N.—Sundries.

408. Beads of all kinds, not threaded or strung, thirty-five per centum ad valorem; fabrics, nets or nettings, laces, embroideries, galloons, wearing apparel, ornaments, trimmings and other articles not specially provided for in this Act, composed wholly or in part of beads or spangles made of glass or paste, gelatin, metal, or other material, but not composed in part of wool, sixty per centum ad valorem.

409. Braids, plaits, laces, and willow sheets or squares, composed wholly of straw, chip, grass, palm leaf, willow, osier, or rattan, suitable for making or ornamenting hats, bonnets, or hoods, not bleached, dyed, colored or stained, fifteen per centum ad valorem; if bleached, dyed, colored or stained, twenty per centum ad valorem; hats, bonnets, and hoods, composed of straw, chip, grass, palm leaf, willow, osier, or rattan, whether wholly or partly manufactured, but not trimmed, thirty-five per centum ad valorem; if trimmed, fifty per centum ad valorem. But the terms "grass" and "straw" shall be understood to mean these substances in their natural form and structure, and not the separated fiber thereof.

410. Brushes, brooms and feather dusters of all kinds, and hair pencils in quills or otherwise, forty per centum ad valorem.

411. Bristles, sorted, bunched or prepared, seven and one-half cents per pound.

BUTTONS AND BUTTON FORMS:

412. Trousers buckles made wholly or partly of iron or steel, or parts thereof, valued at not more than fifteen cents per hundred, five cents per hundred; valued at more than fifteen cents per hundred and not more than fifty cents per hundred, ten cents per hundred; valued at more than fifty cents per hundred, fifteen cents per hundred; and in addition thereto on each and all of the above buckles or parts of buckles, fifteen per centum ad valorem.

413. Button forms: Lastings, mohair, cloth, silk, or other manufactures of cloth, woven or made in patterns of such size, shape, or form, or cut in such manner as to be fit for buttons exclusively, ten per centum ad valorem.

414. Buttons or parts of buttons and button molds or blanks, finished or unfinished, shall pay duty at the following rates, the line button measure being one-fortieth of one inch, namely: Buttons known commercially as agate buttons, metal trousers buttons, (except steel), and nickel bar buttons, one-twelfth of one cent per line per gross; buttons of bone, and steel trousers buttons, one-fourth of one cent per line per gross; buttons of pearl or shell, one and one-half cents per line per gross; buttons of horn, vegetable ivory, glass, or metal, not specially provided for in this Act, three-fourths of one cent per line per gross, and in addition thereto, on all the foregoing articles in this paragraph, fifteen per centum ad valorem; shoe buttons made of paper, board, papier mache, pulp or other similar material, not specially provided for in this Act, valued at not exceeding three cents per gross, one cent per gross; buttons not specially provided for in this Act, and all collar or cuff buttons and studs, fifty per centum ad valorem.

415. Coal, bituminous, and all coals containing less than ninety-two per centum of fixed carbon, and shale, sixty-seven cents per ton of twenty-eight bushels, eighty pounds to the bushel; coal slack or culm, such as will pass through a half-inch screen, fifteen cents per ton of twenty-eight bushels, eighty pounds to the bushel: *Provided*, That on all coal imported into the United States, which is afterwards used for fuel on board vessels propelled by steam and engaged in trade with foreign countries, or in trade between the Atlantic and Pacific ports of the United States, and which are registered under the laws of the United States, a drawback shall be allowed equal to the duty imposed by law upon such coal, and shall be paid under such regulations as the

Secretary of the Treasury shall prescribe; coke, twenty per centum ad valorem.

416. Cork bark, cut into squares or cubes, eight cents per pound; manufactured corks over three-fourths of an inch in diameter measured at larger end, fifteen cents per pound; three-fourths of an inch and less in diameter, measured at larger end, twenty-five cents per pound; cork, artificial, or cork substitutes, manufactured from cork waste and not otherwise provided for, eight cents per pound.

417. Dice, draughts, chessmen, chess balls, and billiard, pool, and bagatelle balls, of ivory, bone, or other materials, fifty per centum ad valorem.

418. Dolls, doll heads, toy marbles of whatever materials composed, and all other toys not composed of rubber, china, porcelain, parian, bisque, earthen or stone ware, and not specially provided for in this Act, thirty-five per centum ad valorem.

419. Emery grains, and emery manufactured, ground, pulverized, or refined, one cent per pound; emery wheels, emery files, and manufactures of which emery is the component material of chief value, twenty-five per centum ad valorem.

EXPLOSIVE SUBSTANCES:

420. Firecrackers of all kinds, eight cents per pound, the weight to include all coverings, wrappings, and packing material.

421. Fulminates, fulminating powders, and like articles, not specially provided for in this Act, thirty per centum ad valorem.

422. Gunpowder, and all explosive substances used for mining, blasting, artillery, or sporting purposes, when valued at twenty cents or less per pound, four cents per pound; valued above twenty cents per pound, six cents per pound.

423. Matches, friction or lucifer, of all descriptions, per gross of one hundred and forty-four boxes, containing not more than one hundred matches per box, eight cents per gross; when imported otherwise than in boxes containing not more than one hundred matches each, one cent per one thousand matches.

424. Percussion caps, thirty per centum ad valorem; cartridges, thirty-five per centum ad valorem; blasting caps, two dollars and thirty-six cents per one thousand caps.

425. Feathers and downs of all kinds, including bird skins or parts thereof with the feathers on, crude or not dressed, colored, or otherwise advanced or manufactured in any manner, not specially provided for in this Act, fifteen per centum ad valorem; when dressed, colored, or otherwise advanced or manufactured in any manner, including quilts of down and other manufactures of down, and also dressed and finished birds suitable for millinery ornaments, and artificial or ornamental feathers, fruits, grains, leaves, flowers, and stems or parts thereof, of whatever material composed, not specially provided for in this Act, fifty per centum ad valorem.

426. Furs, dressed on the skin but not made up into articles, and furs not on the skin, prepared for hatters' use, including fur skins carroted, twenty per centum ad valorem.

427. Fans of all kinds, except common palm-leaf fans, fifty per centum ad valorem.

428. Gun wads of all descriptions, twenty per centum ad valorem.

429. Hair, human, if clean or drawn but not manufactured, twenty per centum ad valorem.

430. Hair, curled, suitable for beds or mattresses, ten per centum ad valorem.

431. Haircloth, known as "crinoline" cloth, ten cents per square yard; haircloth, known as "hair seating," and hair press cloth, twenty cents per square yard.

432. Hats, bonnets, or hoods, for men's, women's, boys', or children's wear, trimmed or untrimmed, including bodies, hoods, plateaux, forms, or shapes, for hats or bonnets, composed wholly or in chief value of fur of the rabbit, beaver, or other animals, valued at not more than five dollars per dozen, two dollars per dozen; valued at more than five dollars per dozen and not more than ten dollars per dozen, three dollars per dozen; valued at more than ten dollars per dozen and not more than twenty dollars per dozen, five dollars per dozen; valued at more than twenty dollars per dozen, seven dollars per dozen; and in addition thereto on all the foregoing, twenty per centum ad valorem.

433. Indurated fiber ware and manufactures of wood or other pulp, and not otherwise specially provided for, thirty-five per centum ad valorem.

JEWELRY AND PRECIOUS STONES:
434. Articles commonly known as jewelry, and parts thereof, finished or unfinished, not specially provided for in this Act, including precious stones set, pearls set or strung, and cameos in frames, sixty per centum ad valorem.
435. Diamonds and other precious stones advanced in condition or value from their natural state by cleaving, splitting, cutting, or other process, and not set, ten per centum ad valorem; imitations of diamonds or other precious stones, composed of glass or paste, not exceeding an inch in dimensions, not engraved, painted, or otherwise ornamented or decorated, and not mounted or set, twenty per centum ad valorem.
436. Pearls in their natural state, not strung or set, ten per centum ad valorem.

LEATHER, AND MANUFACTURES OF:
437. Hides of cattle, raw or uncured, whether dry, salted, or pickled, fifteen per centum ad valorem: *Provided*, That upon all leather exported, made from imported hides, there shall be allowed a drawback equal to the amount of duty paid on such hides, to be paid under such regulations as the Secretary of the Treasury may prescribe.
438. Band or belting leather, sole leather, dressed upper and all other leather, calfskins tanned or tanned and dressed, kangaroo, sheep and goat skins (including lamb and kid skins) dressed and finished, chamois and other skins and bookbinders' calfskins, all the foregoing not specially provided for in this Act, twenty per centum ad valorem; skins for morocco, tanned but unfinished, ten per centum ad valorem; patent, japanned, varnished or enameled leather, weighing not over ten pounds per dozen hides or skins, thirty cents per pound and twenty per centum ad valorem; if weighing over ten pounds and not over twenty-five pounds per dozen, thirty cents per pound and ten per centum ad valorem; if weighing over twenty-five pounds per dozen, twenty cents per pound and ten per centum ad valorem; pianoforte leather and pianoforte action leather, thirty-five per centum ad valorem; leather shoe laces, finished or unfinished, fifty cents per gross pairs and twenty per centum ad valorem; boots and shoes made of leather,

twenty-five per centum ad valorem: *Provided,* That leather cut into shoe uppers or vamps or other forms, suitable for conversion into manufactured articles, shall be classified as manufactures of leather and pay duty accordingly.

Gloves—

439. Gloves made wholly or in part of leather, whether wholly or partly manufactured, shall pay duty at the following rates, the lengths stated in each case being the extreme length when stretched to their full extent, namely:

440. Women's or children's "glace" finish, Schmaschen (of sheep origin), not over fourteen inches in length, one dollar and seventy-five cents per dozen pairs; over fourteen inches and not over seventeen inches in length, two dollars and twenty-five cents per dozen pairs; over seventeen inches in length, two dollars and seventy-five cents per dozen pairs; men's "glace" finish, Schmaschen (sheep), three dollars per dozen pairs.

441. Women's or children's "glace" finish, lamb or sheep, not over fourteen inches in length, two dollars and fifty cents per dozen pairs; over fourteen and not over seventeen inches in length, three dollars and fifty cents per dozen pairs; over seventeen inches in length, four dollars and fifty cents per dozen pairs; men's "glace" finish, lamb or sheep, four dollars per dozen pairs.

442. Women's or children's "glace" finish, goat, kid, or other leather than of sheep origin, not over fourteen inches in length, three dollars per dozen pairs; over fourteen and not over seventeen inches in length, three dollars and seventy-five cents per dozen pairs; over seventeen inches in length, four dollars and seventy-five cents per dozen pairs; men's "glace" finish, kid, goat, or other leather than of sheep origin, four dollars per dozen pairs.

443. Women's or children's, of sheep origin, with exterior grain surface removed, by whatever name known, not over seventeen inches in length, two dollars and fifty cents per dozen pairs; over seventeen inches in length, three dollars and fifty cents per dozen pairs; men's, of sheep origin, with exterior surface removed, by whatever name known, four dollars per dozen pairs.

444. Women's or children's kid, goat, or other leather than of sheep origin, with exterior grain surface removed, by whatever name known, not over fourteen inches in length, three dollars per dozen pairs; over fourteen inches and not over seventeen inches in length, three dollars and seventy-five cents per dozen pairs; over seventeen inches in length, four dollars and seventy-five cents per dozen pairs; men's, goat, kid, or other leather than of sheep origin, with exterior grain surface removed, by whatever name known, four dollars per dozen pairs.

445. In addition to the foregoing rates there shall be paid the following cumulative duties: On all leather gloves, when lined, one dollar per dozen pairs; on all pique or prix seam gloves, forty cents per dozen pairs; on all gloves stitched or embroidered, with more than three single strands or cords, forty cents per dozen pairs.

446. Glove tranks, with or without the usual accompanying pieces, shall pay seventy-five per centum of the duty provided for the gloves in the fabrication of which they are suitable.

447. Harness, saddles and saddlery, or parts of either, in sets or in parts, finished or unfinished, forty-five per centum ad valorem.

MISCELLANEOUS MANUFACTURES:

448. Manufactures of amber, asbestos, bladders, cork, catgut or whip gut or worm gut, or wax, or of which these substances or either of them is the component material of chief value, not specially provided for in this Act, twenty-five per centum ad valorem.

449. Manufactures of bone, chip, grass, horn, india-rubber, palm leaf, straw, weeds, or whalebone, or of which these substances or either of them is the component material of chief value, not specially provided for in this Act, thirty per centum ad valorem; but the terms "grass" and "straw" shall be understood to mean these substances in their natural form and structure, and not the separated fiber thereof.

450. Manufactures of leather, finished or unfinished, manufactures of fur, gelatin, gutta-percha, human hair, ivory, vegetable ivory, mother-of-pearl and shell, plaster of paris, papier mâché, and vulcanized india-rubber known as "hard rubber," or of which these substances or either of them is the component material of chief value, not specially provided for in this Act, and shells engraved, cut, ornamented, or otherwise manufactured, thirty-five per centum ad valorem.

451. Masks, composed of paper or pulp, thirty-five per centum ad valorem.

452. Matting made of cocoa fiber or rattan, six cents per square yard; mats made of cocoa fiber or rattan, four cents per square foot.

453. Musical instruments or parts thereof, pianoforte actions and parts thereof, strings for musical instruments not otherwise enumerated, cases for musical instruments, pitch pipes, tuning forks, tuning hammers, and metronomes; strings for musical instruments, composed wholly or in part of steel or other metal, all the foregoing, forty-five per centum ad valorem.

454. Paintings in oil or water colors, pastels, pen and ink drawings, and statuary, not specially provided for in this Act, twenty per centum ad valorem; but the term "statuary" as used in this Act shall be understood to include only such statuary as is cut, carved, or otherwise wrought by hand from a solid block or mass of marble, stone, or alabaster, or from metal, and as is the professional production of a statuary or sculptor only.

455. Peat moss, one dollar per ton.

456. Pencils of paper or wood filled with lead or other material, and pencils of lead, forty-five cents per gross and twenty-five per centum ad valorem; slate pencils, covered with wood, thirty-five per centum ad valorem; all other slate pencils, three cents per one hundred.

457. Pencil leads not in wood, ten per centum ad valorem.

458. Photographic dry plates or films, twenty-five per centum ad valorem.

459. Pipes and smokers' articles: Common tobacco pipes and pipe bowls made wholly of clay, valued at not more than forty cents per gross, fifteen cents per gross; other tobacco pipes and pipe bowls of clay, fifty cents per gross and twenty-five per centum ad valorem; other pipes and pipe bowls of whatever material composed, and all smokers' articles whatsoever, not specially provided for in this Act, including cigarette books, cigarette book covers, pouches for smoking or chewing tobacco, and cigarette paper in all forms, sixty per centum ad valorem.

460. Plows, tooth and disk harrows, harvesters, reapers, agricultural drills, and planters, mowers, horserakes, cultivators, threshing machines and cotton gins, twenty per centum ad valorem.

461. Plush, black, known commercially as hatters' plush, composed of silk, or of silk and cotton, such as is used exclusively for making men's hats, ten per centum ad valorem.

462. Umbrellas, parasols, and sun shades covered with material other than paper, fifty per centum ad valorem. Sticks for umbrellas, parasols, or sun shades, and walking canes, finished or unfinished, forty per centum ad valorem.

463. Waste, not specially provided for in this Act, ten per centum ad valorem.

FREE LIST.

SEC. 2. That on and after the passage of this Act, unless otherwise specially provided for in this Act, the following articles when imported shall be exempt from duty:

464. Acids: Arsenic or arsenious, benzoic, carbolic, fluoric, hydrochloric or muriatic, nitric, oxalic, phosphoric, phthalic, picric or nitropicric, prussic, silicic, and valerianic.

465. Aconite.

466. Acorns, raw, dried or undried, but unground.

467. Agates, unmanufactured.

468. Albumen, not specially provided for.

469. Alizarin, natural or artificial, and dyes derived from alizarin or from anthracin.

470. Amber, and amberoid unmanufactured, or crude gum.

471. Ambergris.

472. Aniline salts.

473. Any animal imported specially for breeding purposes shall be admitted free: *Provided*, That no such animal shall be admitted free unless pure bred of a recognized breed, and duly registered in the book of record established for that breed: *And provided further*, That certificate of such record and of the pedigree of such animal shall be produced and submitted to the customs officer, duly authenticated by the proper custodian of such book of record, together with the affidavit of the owner, agent, or importer that such animal is the identical animal described in said certificate of record and pedigree: *And provided further*, That the Secretary of Agriculture shall determine and certify to the Secretary of the Treasury what are recognized breeds and pure bred animals under the provisions of this paragraph. The Secretary of the Treasury may prescribe such additional regulations as may be required for the strict enforcement of this provision. Cattle, horses, sheep, or other domestic animals straying across the boundary line into any foreign country, or driven across such boundary line by the owner for temporary pasturage purposes only, together with their offspring, may be brought back to the United States within six months free of duty, under regulations to be prescribed by the Secretary of the Treasury.

474. Animals brought into the United States temporarily for a period not exceeding six months, for the purpose of exhibition or competition for prizes offered by any agricultural or racing association; but a bond shall be given in accordance with regulations prescribed by the Secretary of the Treasury; also teams of animals, including their harness and tackle and the wagons or other vehicles actually owned by persons

emigrating from foreign countries to the United States with their families, and in actual use for the purpose of such emigration under such regulations as the Secretary of the Treasury may prescribe; and wild animals intended for exhibition in zoological collections for scientific and educational purposes, and not for sale or profit.

475. Annatto, roucou, rocoa, or orleans, and all extracts of.

476. Antimony ore, crude sulphite of.

477. Apatite.

478. Arrowroot in its natural state and not manufactured.

479. Arsenic and sulphide of, or orpiment.

480. Arseniate of aniline.

481. Art educational stops, composed of glass and metal and valued at not more than six cents per gross.

482. Articles in a crude state used in dyeing or tanning not specially provided for in this Act.

483. Articles the growth, produce, and manufacture of the United States, when returned after having been exported, without having been advanced in value or improved in condition by any process of manufacture or other means; casks, barrels, carboys, bags, and other vessels of American manufacture exported filled with American products, or exported empty and returned filled with foreign products, including shooks and staves when returned as barrels or boxes; also quicksilver flasks or bottles, of either domestic or foreign manufacture, which shall have been actually exported from the United States; but proof of the identity of such articles shall be made, under general regulations to be prescribed by the Secretary of the Treasury, but the exemption of bags from duty shall apply only to such domestic bags as may be imported by the exporter thereof, and if any such articles are subject to internal tax at the time of exportation, such tax shall be proved to have been paid before exportation and not refunded: *Provided*, That this paragraph shall not apply to any article upon which an allowance of drawback has been made, the reimportation of which is hereby prohibited except upon payment of duties equal to the drawbacks allowed; or to any article manufactured in bonded warehouse and exported under any provision of law: *And provided further*, That when manufactured tobacco which has been exported without payment of internal-revenue tax shall be reimported it shall be retained in the custody of the collector of customs until internal-revenue stamps in payment of the legal duties shall be placed thereon.

484. Asbestos, unmanufactured.

485. Ashes, wood and lye of, and beet-root ashes.

486. Asafetida.

487. Balm of Gilead.

488. Barks, cinchona or other from which quinine may be extracted.

489. Baryta, carbonate of, or witherite.

490. Beeswax.

491. Binding twine: All binding twine manufactured from New Zealand hemp, istle or Tampico fiber, sisal grass, or sunn, or a mixture of any two or more of them, of single ply and measuring not exceeding six hundred feet to the pound: *Provided*, That articles mentioned in this paragraph if imported from a country which lays an import duty on like articles imported from the United States, shall be subject to a duty of one-half of one cent per pound.

492. Bells, broken, and bell metal broken and fit only to be remanufactured.

493. Birds, stuffed, not suitable for millinery ornaments.

494. Birds and land and water fowls.

495. Bismuth.

496. Bladders, and all integuments and intestines of animals and fish sounds, crude, dried or salted for preservation only, and unmanufactured, not specially provided for in this Act.

497. Blood, dried, not specially provided for.

498. Bolting cloths composed of silk, imported expressly for milling purposes, and so permanently marked as not to be available for any other use.

499. Bones, crude, or not burned, calcined, ground, steamed, or otherwise manufactured, and bone dust or animal carbon, and bone ash, fit only for fertilizing purposes.

500. Books, engravings, photographs, etchings, bound or unbound, maps and charts imported by authority or for the use of the United States or for the use of the Library of Congress.

501. Books, maps, music, engravings, photographs, etchings, bound or unbound, and charts, which shall have been printed more than twenty years at the date of importation, and all hydrographic charts, and publications issued for their subscribers or exchanges by scientific and literary associations or academies, or publications of individuals for gratuitous private circulation, and public documents issued by foreign Governments.

502. Books and pamphlets printed exclusively in languages other than English; also books and music, in raised print, used exclusively by the blind.

503. Books, maps, music, photographs, etchings, lithographic prints, and charts, specially imported, not more than two copies in any one invoice, in good faith, for the use or by order of any society or institution incorporated or established solely for religious, philosophical, educational, scientific, or literary purposes, or for the encouragement of the fine arts, or for the use or by order of any college, academy, school, or seminary of learning in the United States, or any State or public library, and not for sale, subject to such regulations as the Secretary of the Treasury shall prescribe.

504. Books, libraries, usual and reasonable furniture, and similar household effects of persons or families from foreign countries, all the foregoing if actually used abroad by them not less than one year, and not intended for any other person or persons, nor for sale.

505. Brass, old brass, clippings from brass or Dutch metal, all the foregoing, fit only for remanufacture.

506. Brazil paste.

507. Brazilian pebble, unwrought or unmanufactured.

508. Breccia, in block or slabs.

509. Bristles, crude, not sorted, bunched, or prepared.

510. Broom corn.

511. Bullion, gold or silver.

512. Burgundy pitch.

513. Cadmium.

514. Calamine.

515. Camphor, crude.

516. Castor or castoreum.

517. Cat gut, whip gut, or worm gut, unmanufactured.

518. Cerium.

519. Chalk, crude, not ground, precipitated, or otherwise manufactured.

520. Chromate of iron or chromic ore.

521. Civet, crude.

522. Clay: Common blue clay in casks suitable for the manufacture of crucibles.

523. Coal, anthracite, not specially provided for in this Act, and coal stores of American vessels, but none shall be unloaded.

524. Coal tar, crude, pitch of coal tar, and products of coal tar known as dead or creosote oil, benzol, toluol, naphthalin, xylol, phenol, cresol, tolnidine, xylidin, cumidin, binitrotoluol, binitrobenzol, benzidin, tolidin, dianisidin, naphtol, naphtylamiu, diphenylamiu, benzaldehyde, benzyl chloride, resorcin, nitro-benzol, and nitro-toluol; all the foregoing not medicinal and not colors or dyes.

525. Cobalt and cobalt ore.

526. Cocculus indicus.

527. Cochineal.

528. Cocoa, or cacao, crude, and fiber, leaves, and shells of.

529. Coffee.

530. Coins, gold, silver, and copper.

531. Coir, and coir yarn.

532. Copper in plates, bars, ingots, or pigs, and other forms, not manufactured or specially provided for in this Act.

533. Old copper, fit only for manufacture, clipping from new copper, and all composition metal of which copper is a component material of chief value not specially provided for in this Act.

534. Copper, regulus of, and black or coarse copper, and copper cement.

535. Coral, marine, uncut, and unmanufactured.

536. Cork wood, or cork bark, unmanufactured.

537. Cotton, and cotton waste or flocks.

538. Cryolite, or kryolith.

539. Cudbear.

540. Curling stones, or quoits, and curling-stone handles.

541. Curry, and curry powder.

542. Cutch.

543. Cuttlefish bone.

544. Dandelion roots, raw, dried, or undried, but unground.

545. Diamonds and other precious stones, rough, or uncut, and not advanced in condition or value from their natural state by cleaving, splitting, cutting, or other process, including miners', glaziers' and engravers' diamonds not set, and diamond dust or bort.

546. Divi-divi.

547. Dragon's blood.

548. Drugs, such as barks, beans, berries, balsams, buds, bulbs, and bulbous roots, excrescences, fruits, flowers, dried fibers, and dried insects, grains, gums, and gum resin, herbs, leaves, lichens, mosses, nuts, nutgalls, roots, and stems, spices, vegetables, seeds aromatic, and seeds of morbid growth, weeds, and woods used expressly for dyeing; any of the foregoing which are drugs and not edible and are in a crude state, and not advanced in value or condition by refining or grinding, or by other process, and not specially provided for in this Act.

549. Eggs of birds, fish, and insects: *Provided, however,* That this shall not be held to include the eggs of game birds or eggs of birds not used for food, the importation of which is prohibited except specimens for scientific collections, nor fish roe preserved for food purposes.

550. Emery ore.

551. Ergot.

552. Fans, common palm-leaf, plain and not ornamented or decorated

in any manner, and palm leaf in its natural state, not colored, dyed, or otherwise advanced or manufactured.

553. Felt, adhesive, for sheathing vessels.

554. Fibrin, in all forms.

555. Fish, fresh, frozen, or packed in ice, caught in the Great Lakes or other fresh waters by citizens of the United States.

556. Fish skins.

557. Flint, flints, and flint stones, unground.

558. Fossils.

559. Fruits or berries, green, ripe, or dried, and fruits in brine, not specially provided for in this Act.

560. Fruit plants, tropical and semitropical, for the purpose of propagation or cultivation.

561. Furs, undressed.

562. Fur skins of all kinds not dressed in any manner and not specially provided for in this Act.

563. Gambier.

564. Glass enamel, white, for watch and clock dials.

565. Glass plates or discs, rough-cut or unwrought, for use in the manufacture of optical instruments, spectacles, and eye glasses, and suitable only for such use: *Provided, however*, That such discs exceeding eight inches in diameter may be polished sufficiently to enable the character of the glass to be determined.

566. Grasses and fibers: Istle or Tampico fiber, jute, jute butts, manila, sisal grass, sunn, and all other textile grasses or fibrous vegetable substances, not dressed or manufactured in any manner, and not specially provided for in this Act.

567. Gold-beaters' molds and gold-beaters' skins.

568. Grease, and oils (excepting fish oils), such as are commonly used in soap making or in wire drawing, or for stuffing or dressing leather, and which are fit only for such uses, and not specially provided for in this Act.

569. Guano, manures, and all substances used only for manure.

570. Gutta percha, crude.

571. Hair of horse, cattle, and other animals, cleaned or uncleaned, drawn or undrawn, but unmanufactured, not specially provided for in this Act; and human hair, raw, uncleaned, and not drawn.

572. Hide cuttings, raw, with or without hair, and all other glue stock.

573. Hide rope.

574. Hones and whetstones.

575. Hoofs, unmanufactured.

576. Hop roots for cultivation.

577. Horns and parts of, unmanufactured, including horn strips and tips.

578. Ice.

579. India rubber, crude, and milk of, and old scrap or refuse India rubber which has been worn out by use and is fit only for remanufacture.

580. Indigo.

581. Iodine, crude.

582. Ipecac.

583. Iridium.

584. Ivory tusks in their natural state or cut vertically across the grain only, with the bark left intact, and vegetable ivory in its natural state.

585. Jalap.

586. Jet, unmanufactured.

587. Joss stick, or Joss light.
588. Junk, old.
589. Kelp.
590. Kieserite.
591. Kyanite, or cyanite, and kainite.
592. Lac dye, crude, seed, button, stick, and shell.
593. Lac spirits.
594. Lactarene.
595. Lava, unmanufactured.
596. Leeches.
597. Lemon juice, lime juice, and sour orange juice.
598. Licorice root, unground.
599. Lifeboats and life-saving apparatus specially imported by societies incorporated or established to encourage the saving of human life.
600. Lime, citrate of.
601. Lithographic stones, not engraved.
602. Litmus, prepared or not prepared.
603. Loadstones.
604. Madder and munjeet, or Indian madder, ground or prepared, and all extracts of.
605. Magnesite, crude or calcined, not purified.
606. Magnesium, not made up into articles.
607. Manganese, oxide and ore of.
608. Manna.
609. Manuscripts.
610. Marrow, crude.
611. Marshmallow or althea root, leaves or flowers, natural or unmanufactured.
612. Medals of gold, silver, or copper, and other metallic articles actually bestowed as trophies or prizes, and received and accepted as honorary distinctions.
613. Meerschaum, crude or unmanufactured.
614. Minerals, crude, or not advanced in value or condition by refining or grinding, or by other process of manufacture, not specially provided for in this Act.
615. Mineral salts obtained by evaporation from mineral waters, when accompanied by a duly authenticated certificate and satisfactory proof, showing that they are in no way artificially prepared, and are only the product of a designated mineral spring.
616. Models of inventions and of other improvements in the arts, including patterns for machinery, but no article shall be deemed a model or pattern which can be fitted for use otherwise.
617. Moss, seaweeds, and vegetable substances, crude or unmanufactured, not otherwise specially provided for in this Act.
618. Musk, crude, in natural pods.
619. Myrobolans.
620. Needles, hand sewing, and darning.
621. Newspapers and periodicals; but the term "periodicals" as herein used shall be understood to embrace only unbound or paper-covered publications, issued within six months of the time of entry, containing current literature of the day and issued regularly at stated periods, as weekly, monthly, or quarterly.
622. Nuts: Brazil nuts, cream nuts, palm nuts and palm-nut kernels; cocoanuts in the shell and broken cocoanut meat or copra, not shredded, desiccated, or prepared in any manner.
623. Nux vomica.

624. Oakum.

625. Oil cake.

626. Oils: Almond, amber, crude and rectified ambergris, anise or anise seed, aniline, aspic or spike lavender, bergamot, cajeput, caraway, cassia, cinnamon, cedrat, chamomile, citronella or lemon grass, civet, cocoanut, fennel, ichthyol, jasmine or jasimine, juglandium, juniper, lavender, lemon, limes, mace, neroli or orange flower, enfleurage grease, nut oil or oil of nuts not otherwise specially provided for in this Act, orange oil, olive oil for manufacturing or mechanical purposes fit only for such use and valued at not more than sixty cents per gallon, ottar of roses, palm, rosemary or anthoss, sesame or sesamum seed or bean, thyme, origanum red or white, valerian; and also spermaceti, whale, and other fish oils of American fisheries, and all fish and other products, of such fisheries; petroleum, crude or refined: *Provided*, That if there be imported into the United States crude petroleum, or the products of crude petroleum produced in any country which imposes a duty on petroleum or its products exported from the United States, there shall in such cases be levied, paid, and collected a duty upon said crude petroleum or its products so imported equal to the duty imposed by such country.

627. Orange and lemon peel, not preserved, candied, or dried.

628. Orchil, or orchil liquid.

629. Ores of gold, silver, copper, or nickel, and nickel matte: sweepings of gold and silver.

630. Osmium.

631. Palladium.

632. Paper stock, crude, of every description, including all grasses, fibers, rags (other than wool), waste, including jute waste, shavings, clippings, old paper, rope ends, waste rope, and waste bagging, including old gunny cloth and old gunny bags, fit only to be converted into paper.

633. Paraffin.

634. Parchment and vellum.

635. Pearl, mother of, and shells, not sawed, cut, polished or otherwise manufactured, or advanced in value from the natural state.

636. Personal effects, not merchandise, of citizens of the United States dying in foreign countries.

637. Pewter and britannia metal, old, and fit only to be remanufactured.

638. Philosophical and scientific apparatus, utensils, instruments, and preparations, including bottles and boxes containing the same, specially imported in good faith for the use and by order of any society or institution incorporated or established solely for religious, philosophical, educational, scientific, or literary purposes, or for the encouragement of the fine arts, or for the use or by order of any college, academy, school, or seminary of learning in the United States, or any State or public library, and not for sale, subject to such regulations as the Secretary of the Treasury shall prescribe.

639. Phosphates, crude.

640. Plants, trees, shrubs, roots, seed-cane, and seeds, imported by the Department of Agriculture or the United States Botanic Garden.

641. Platina, in ingots, bars, sheets, and wire.

642. Platinum, unmanufactured, and vases, retorts, and other apparatus, vessels, and parts thereof composed of platinum, for chemical uses.

643. Plumbago.

644. Potash, crude, or "black salts"; carbonate of potash, crude or refined; hydrate of, or caustic potash, not including refined in sticks or rolls; nitrate of potash or saltpeter, crude; sulphate of potash, crude or refined, and muriate of potash.

645. Professional books, implements, instruments, and tools of trade, occupation, or employment, in the actual possession at the time, of persons emigrating to the United States; but this exemption shall not be construed to include machinery or other articles imported for use in any manufacturing establishment, or for any other person or persons, or for sale, nor shall it be construed to include theatrical scenery, properties, and apparel; but such articles brought by proprietors or managers of theatrical exhibitions arriving from abroad, for temporary use by them in such exhibitions, and not for any other person, and not for sale, and which have been used by them abroad, shall be admitted free of duty under such regulations as the Secretary of the Treasury may prescribe; but bonds shall be given for the payment to the United States of such duties as may be imposed by law upon any and all such articles as shall not be exported within six months after such importation: *Provided*, That the Secretary of the Treasury may in his discretion extend such period for a further term of six months in case application shall be made therefor.

646. Pulu.

647. Quinia, sulphate of, and all alkaloids or salts of cinchona bark.

648. Rags, not otherwise specially provided for in this Act.

649. Regalia and gems, statuary, and specimens or casts of sculpture, where specially imported in good faith for the use and by order of any society incorporated or established solely for religious, philosophical, educational, scientific, or literary purposes, or for the encouragement of the fine arts, or for the use and by order of any college, academy, school, or seminary of learning in the United States, or any State or public library, and not for sale; but the term "regalia" as herein used shall be held to embrace only such insignia of rank or office or emblems as may be worn upon the person or borne in the hand during public exercises of the society or institution, and shall not include articles of furniture or fixtures, or of regular wearing apparel, nor personal property of individuals.

650. Rennets, raw or prepared.

651. Saffron and safflower, and extract of, and saffron cake.

652. Sago, crude.

653. Salacin.

654. Salep, or salop.

655. Sausages, bologna.

656. Seeds: Anise, caraway, cardamom, cauliflower, coriander, cotton, cummin, fennel, fenugreek, hemp, hoarhound, mangel-wurzel, mustard, rape, Saint John's bread or bean, sugar beet, sorghum or sugar cane for seed; bulbs and bulbous roots, not edible and not otherwise provided for; all flower and grass seeds; all the foregoing not specially provided for in this Act.

657. Sheep dip, not including compounds or preparations that can be used for other purposes.

658. Shotgun barrels, in single tubes, forged, rough bored.

659. Shrimps and other shell fish.

660. Silk, raw, or as reeled from the cocoon, but not doubled, twisted, or advanced in manufacture in any way.

661. Silk cocoons and silk waste.

662. Silkworm's eggs.

663. Skeletons and other preparations of anatomy.

664. Skins of all kinds, raw (except sheepskins with the wool on), and hides not specially provided for in this Act.

665. Soda, nitrate of, or cubic nitrate.

666. Specimens of natural history, botany, and mineralogy, when imported for scientific public collections, and not for sale.

667. Spices: Cassia, cassia vera, and cassia buds; cinnamon and chips of; cloves and clove stems; mace; nutmegs; pepper, black or white, and pimento; all the foregoing when unground; ginger root, unground and not preserved or candied.

668. Spunk.

669. Spurs and stilts used in the manufacture of earthen, porcelain, and stone ware.

670. Stamps; foreign postage or revenue stamps, canceled or uncanceled.

671. Stone and sand: Burrstone in blocks, rough or unmanufactured; cliff stone, unmanufactured; rotten stone, tripoli, and sand, crude or manufactured, not otherwise provided for in this Act.

672. Storax, or styrax.

673. Stroutia, oxide of, and protoxide of strontian, and strontianite, or mineral carbonate of strontia.

674. Sulphur, lac or precipitated, and sulphur or brimstone, crude, in bulk, sulphur ore as pyrites, or sulphuret of iron in its natural state, containing in excess of twenty-five per centum of sulphur, and sulphur not otherwise provided for.

675. Sulphuric acid which at the temperature of sixty degrees Fahrenheit does not exceed the specific gravity of one and three hundred and eighty thousandths, for use in manufacturing superphosphate of lime or artificial manures of any kind, or for any agricultural purposes: *Provided*, That upon all sulphuric acid imported from any country, whether independent or a dependency, which imposes a duty upon sulphuric acid imported into such country from the United States, there shall be levied and collected a duty of one-fourth of one cent per pound.

676. Tamarinds.

677. Tapioca, cassava or cassady.

678. Tar and pitch of wood.

679. Tea and tea plants.

680. Teeth, natural, or unmanufactured.

681. Terra alba, not made from gypsum or plaster rock.

682. Terra japonica.

683. Tin ore, cassiterite or black oxide of tin, and tin in bars, blocks, pigs, or grain or granulated.

684. Tobacco stems.

685. Tonquin, tonqua, or touka beans.

686. Turmeric.

687. Turpentine, Venice.

688. Turpentine, spirits of.

689. Turtles.

690. Types, old, and fit only to be remanufactured.

691. Uranium, oxide and salts of.

692. Vaccine virus.

693. Valonia.

694. Verdigris, or subacetate of copper.

695. Wax, vegetable or mineral.

696. Wafers, unleavened or not edible.

697. Wearing apparel, articles of personal adornment, toilet articles, and similar personal effects of persons arriving in the United States; but this exemption shall only include such articles as actually accompany and are in the use of, and as are necessary and appropriate for the wear and use of such persons, for the immediate purposes of the journey and present comfort and convenience, and shall not be held to apply to merchandise or articles intended for other persons or for sale: *Provided*, That in case of residents of the United States returning from abroad, all wearing apparel and other personal effects taken by them out of the United States to foreign countries shall be admitted free of duty, without regard to their value, upon their identity being established, under appropriate rules and regulations to be prescribed by the Secretary of the Treasury, but no more than one hundred dollars in value of articles purchased abroad by such residents of the United States shall be admitted free of duty upon their return.

698. Whalebone, unmanufactured.

699. Wood: Logs and round unmanufactured timber, including pulp-woods, firewood, handle-bolts, shingle-bolts, gun-blocks for gun-stocks rough-hewn or sawed or planed on one side, hop-poles, ship-timber and ship-planking; all the foregoing not specially provided for in this Act.

700. Woods: Cedar, lignum-vitæ, lancewood, ebony, box, granadilla, mahogany, rosewood, satinwood, and all forms of cabinet woods, in the log, rough, or hewn only; briar root or briar wood and similar wood unmanufactured, or not further advanced than cut into blocks suitable for the articles into which they are intended to be converted; bamboo, rattan, reeds unmanufactured, India malacca joints, and sticks of partridge, hair wood, pimento, orange, myrtle, and other woods not specially provided for in this Act, in the rough, or not further advanced than cut into lengths suitable for sticks for umbrellas, parasols, sunshades, whips, fishing rods, or walking-canes.

701. Works of art, drawings, engravings, photographic pictures, and philosophical and scientific apparatus brought by professional artists, lecturers, or scientists arriving from abroad for use by them temporarily for exhibition and in illustration, promotion, and encouragement of art, science, or industry in the United States, and not for sale, shall be admitted free of duty, under such regulations as the Secretary of the Treasury shall prescribe; but bonds shall be given for the payment to the United States of such duties as may be imposed by law upon any and all such articles as shall not be exported within six months after such importation: *Provided*, That the Secretary of the Treasury may, in his discretion, extend such period for a further term of six months in cases where applications therefor shall be made.

702. Works of art, collections in illustration of the progress of the arts, sciences, or manufactures, photographs, works in terra cotta, parian, pottery, or porcelain, antiquities and artistic copies thereof in metal or other material, imported in good faith for exhibition at a fixed place by any State or by any society or institution established for the encouragement of the arts, science, or education, or for a municipal corporation, and all like articles imported in good faith by any society or association, or for a municipal corporation for the purpose of erecting a public monument, and not intended for sale, nor for any other purpose than herein expressed; but bonds shall be given under such rules and regulations as the Secretary of the Treasury may prescribe, for the payment of lawful duties which may accrue should any of the articles aforesaid be sold, transferred, or used contrary to this provision, and such articles shall be subject, at any time, to examination and inspection by

the proper officers of the customs: *Provided,* That the privileges of this and the preceding section shall not be allowed to associations or corporations engaged in or connected with business of a private or commercial character.

703. Works of art, the production of American artists residing temporarily abroad, or other works of art, including pictorial paintings on glass, imported expressly for presentation to a national institution, or to any State or municipal corporation, or incorporated religious society, college, or other public institution, except stained or painted window-glass or stained or painted glass windows; but such exemption shall be subject to such regulations as the Secretary of the Treasury may prescribe.

704. Yams.

705. Zaffer.

SEC. 3. That for the purpose of equalizing the trade of the United States with foreign countries, and their colonies, producing and exporting to this country the following articles: Argols, or crude tartar, or wine lees, crude; brandies, or other spirits manufactured or distilled from grain or other materials; champagne and all other sparkling wines; still wines, and vermuth; paintings and statuary; or any of them, the President be, and he is hereby, authorized, as soon as may be after the passage of this Act, and from time to time thereafter, to enter into negotiations with the governments of those countries exporting to the United States the above-mentioned articles, or any of them, with a view to the arrangement of commercial agreements in which reciprocal and equivalent concessions may be secured in favor of the products and manufactures of the United States; and whenever the government of any country, or colony, producing and exporting to the United States the above-mentioned articles, or any of them, shall enter into a commercial agreement with the United States, or make concessions in favor of the products, or manufactures thereof, which, in the judgment of the President, shall be reciprocal and equivalent, he shall be, and he is hereby, authorized and empowered to suspend, during the time of such agreement or concession, by proclamation to that effect, the imposition and collection of the duties mentioned in this Act, on such article or articles so exported to the United States from such country or colony, and thereupon and thereafter the duties levied, collected, and paid upon such article or articles shall be as follows, namely:

Argols, or crude tartar, or wine lees, crude, five per centum ad valorem.

Brandies, or other spirits manufactured or distilled from grain or other materials, one dollar and seventy-five cents per proof gallon.

Champagne and all other sparkling wines, in bottles containing not more than one quart and more than one pint, six dollars per dozen; containing not more than one pint each and more than one-half pint, three dollars per dozen; containing one-half pint each or less, one dollar and fifty cents per dozen; in bottles or other vessels containing more than one quart each, in addition to six dollars per dozen bottles on the quantities in excess of one quart, at the rate of one dollar and ninety cents per gallon.

Still wines, and vermuth, in casks, thirty-five cents per gallon; in bottles or jugs, per case of one dozen bottles or jugs containing each not more than one quart and more than one pint, or twenty-four bottles or jugs containing each not more than one pint, one dollar and twenty-five cents per case, and any excess beyond these quantities found in such bottles or jugs shall be subject to a duty of four cents per pint or fractional part thereof, but no separate or additional duty shall be assessed upon the bottles or jugs.

Paintings in oil or water colors, pastels, pen and ink drawings, and statuary, fifteen per centum ad valorem.

The President shall have power, and it shall be his duty, whenever he shall be satisfied that any such agreement in this Section mentioned is not being fully executed by the Government with which it shall have been made, to revoke such suspension and notify such Government thereof.

And it is further provided that with a view to secure reciprocal trade with countries producing the following articles, whenever and so often as the President shall be satisfied that the Government of any country, or colony of such Government, producing and exporting directly or indirectly to the United States coffee, tea, and tonquin, tonqua, or tonka beans, and vanilla beans, or any of such articles, imposes duties or other exactions upon the agricultural, manufactured, or other products of the United States, which, in view of the introduction of such coffee, tea, and tonquin, tonqua, or tonka beans, and vanilla beans, into the United States, as in this Act hereinbefore provided for, he may deem to be reciprocally unequal and unreasonable, he shall have the power and it shall be his duty to suspend, by proclamation to that effect, the provisions of this Act relating to the free introduction of such coffee, tea, and tonquin, tonqua, or tonka beans, and vanilla beans, of the products of such country or colony, for such time as he shall deem just; and in such case and during such suspension duties shall be levied, collected, and paid upon coffee, tea, and tonquin, tonqua, or tonka beans, and vanilla beans, the products or exports, direct or indirect, from such designated country, as follows:

On coffee, three cents per pound.

On tea, ten cents per pound.

On tonquin, tonqua, or tonka beans, fifty cents per pound; vanilla beans, two dollars per pound; vanilla beans, commercially known as cuts, one dollar per pound.

SEC. 4. That whenever the President of the United States, by and with the advice and consent of the Senate, with a view to secure recip-rocal trade with foreign countries, shall, within the period of two years from and after the passage of this Act, enter into commercial treaty or treaties with any other country or countries concerning the admission into any such country or countries of the goods, wares, and merchan-dise of the United States and their use and disposition therein, deemed to be for the interests of the United States, and in such treaty or trea-ties, in consideration of the advantages accruing to the United States therefrom, shall provide for the reduction during a specified period, not exceeding five years, of the duties imposed by this Act, to the extent of not more than twenty per centum thereof, upon such goods, wares, or merchandise as may be designated therein of the country or coun-tries with which such treaty or treaties shall be made as in this section provided for; or shall provide for the transfer during such period from the dutiable list of this Act to the free list thereof of such goods, wares, and merchandise, being the natural products of such foreign country or countries and not of the United States; or shall provide for the retention upon the free list of this Act during a specified period, not exceeding five years, of such goods, wares, and merchandise now included in said free list as may be designated therein; and when any such treaty shall have been duly ratified by the Senate and approved by Congress, and public proclamation made accordingly, then and thereafter the duties which shall be collected by the United States upon any of the designated goods, wares, and merchandise from the foreign country with which such treaty has been made shall, during the period provided for, be the duties specified and provided for in such treaty, and none other.

SEC. 5. That whenever any country, dependency, or colony shall pay or bestow, directly or indirectly, any bounty or grant upon the exportation of any article or merchandise from such country, dependency, or colony, and such article or merchandise is dutiable under the provisions of this Act, then upon the importation of any such article or merchandise into the United States, whether the same shall be imported directly from the country of production or otherwise, and whether such article or merchandise is imported in the same condition as when exported from the country of production or has been changed in condition by remanufacture or otherwise, there shall be levied and paid, in all such cases, in addition to the duties otherwise imposed by this Act, an additional duty equal to the net amount of such bounty or grant, however the same be paid or bestowed. The net amount of all such bounties or grants shall be from time to time ascertained, determined, and declared by the Secretary of the Treasury, who shall make all needful regulations for the identification of such articles and merchandise and for the assessment and collection of such additional duties.

SEC. 6. That there shall be levied, collected, and paid on the importation of all raw or unmanufactured articles, not enumerated or provided for in this Act, a duty of ten per centum ad valorem, and on all articles manufactured, in whole or in part, not provided for in this Act, a duty of twenty per centum ad valorem.

SEC. 7. That each and every imported article, not enumerated in this Act, which is similar, either in material, quality, texture, or the use to which it may be applied, to any article enumerated in this Act as chargeable with duty, shall pay the same rate of duty which is levied on the enumerated article which it most resembles in any of the particulars before mentioned; and if any nonenumerated article equally resembles two or more enumerated articles on which different rates of duty are chargeable, there shall be levied on such nonenumerated article the same rate of duty as is chargeable on the article which it resembles paying the highest rate of duty; and on articles not enumerated, manufactured of two or more materials, the duty shall be assessed at the highest rate at which the same would be chargeable if composed wholly of the component material thereof of chief value; and the words "component material of chief value," wherever used in this Act, shall be held to mean that component material which shall exceed in value any other single component material of the article; and the value of each component material shall be determined by the ascertained value of such material in its condition as found in the article. If two or more rates of duty shall be applicable to any imported article, it shall pay duty at the highest of such rates.

SEC. 8. That all articles of foreign manufacture, such as are usually or ordinarily marked, stamped, branded, or labeled, and all packages containing such or other imported articles, shall, respectively, be plainly marked, stamped, branded, or labeled in legible English words in a conspicuous place, so as to indicate the country of their origin and the quantity of their contents; and until so marked, stamped, branded, or labeled they shall not be delivered to the importer. Should any article of imported merchandise be marked, stamped, branded, or labeled so as to indicate a quantity, number, or measurement in excess of the quantity, number, or measurement actually contained in such article, no delivery of the same shall be made to the importer until the mark, stamp, brand, or label, as the case may be, shall be changed so as to conform to the facts of the case.

SEC. 9. That section thirty-three hundred and forty-one of the Revised Statutes of the United States be, and hereby is, amended to read as follows:

"SEC. 3341. The Commissioner of Internal Revenue shall cause to be prepared, for the payment of such tax, suitable stamps denoting the amount of tax required to be paid on the hogsheads, barrels, and halves, thirds, quarters, sixths, and eighths of a barrel of such fermented liquors (and shall also cause to be prepared suitable permits for the purpose hereinafter mentioned), and shall furnish the same to the collectors of internal revenue, who shall each be required to keep on hand at all times a sufficient supply of permits and a supply of stamps equal in amount to two months' sales thereof, if there be any brewery or brewery warehouse in his district; and such stamps shall be sold, and permits granted and delivered by such collectors, only to the brewers of their district, respectively.

"Such collectors shall keep an account of the number of permits delivered and of the number and value of the stamps sold by them to each brewer."

SEC. 10. That section thirty-three hundred and ninety-four of the Revised Statutes of the United States, as amended, be, and the same is hereby, further amended, so as to read as follows:

"Upon cigars which shall be manufactured and sold, or removed for consumption or sale, there shall be assessed and collected the following taxes, to be paid by the manufacturer thereof: On cigars of all descriptions made of tobacco, or any substitute therefor, and weighing more than three pounds per thousand, three dollars per thousand; on cigars, made of tobacco, or any substitute therefor, and weighing not more than three pounds per thousand, one dollar per thousand; on cigarettes, made of tobacco, or any substitute therefor, and weighing more than three pounds per thousand, three dollars per thousand; on cigarettes, made of tobacco, or any substitute therefor, and weighing not more than three pounds per thousand, one dollar per thousand: *Provided*, That all rolls of tobacco, or any substitute therefor, wrapped with tobacco, shall be classed as cigars, and all rolls of tobacco, or any substitute therefor, wrapped in paper or any substance other than tobacco, shall be classed as cigarettes.

"And the Commissioner of Internal Revenue, with the approval of the Secretary of the Treasury, shall provide dies and adhesive stamps for cigars weighing not more than three pounds per thousand: *Provided*, That such stamps shall be in denominations of ten, twenty, fifty, and one hundred, and the laws and regulations governing the packing and removal for sale of cigarettes, and the affixing and canceling of the stamps on the packages thereof, shall apply to cigars weighing not more than three pounds per thousand.

"None of the packages of smoking tobacco and fine-cut chewing tobacco and cigarettes prescribed by law shall be permitted to have packed in, or attached to, or connected with, them, any article or thing whatsoever, other than the manufacturers' wrappers and labels, the internal revenue stamp and the tobacco or cigarettes, respectively, put up therein, on which tax is required to be paid under the internal revenue laws; nor shall there be affixed to, or branded, stamped, marked, written, or printed upon, said packages, or their contents, any promise or offer of, or any order or certificate for, any gift, prize, premium, payment, or reward."

SEC. 11. That no article of imported merchandise which shall copy or simulate the name or trade-mark of any domestic manufacture or manufacturer, or which shall bear a name or mark, which is calculated to induce the public to believe that the article is manufactured in the United States, shall be admitted to entry at any custom-house of the United States. And in order to aid the officers of the customs in enforcing this prohibition, any domestic manufacturer who has adopted trade-marks may require his name and residence and a description of his trade-marks to be recorded in books which shall be kept for that purpose in the Department of the Treasury, under such regulations as the Secretary of the Treasury shall prescribe, and may furnish to the Department facsimiles of such trade-marks; and thereupon the Secretary of the Treasury shall cause one or more copies of the same to be transmitted to each collector or other proper officer of the customs.

SEC. 12. That all materials of foreign production which may be necessary for the construction of vessels built in the United States for foreign account and ownership, or for the purpose of being employed in the foreign trade, including the trade between the Atlantic and Pacific ports of the United States, and all such materials necessary for the building of their machinery, and all articles necessary for their outfit and equipment, may be imported in bond under such regulations as the Secretary of the Treasury may prescribe; and upon proof that such materials have been used for such purposes no duties shall be paid thereon. But vessels receiving the benefit of this section shall not be allowed to engage in the coastwise trade of the United States more than two months in any one year except upon the payment to the United States of the duties of which a rebate is herein allowed: *Provided*, That vessels built in the United States for foreign account and ownership shall not be allowed to engage in the coastwise trade of the United States.

SEC. 13. That all articles of foreign production needed for the repair of American vessels engaged in foreign trade, including the trade between the Atlantic and Pacific ports of the United States, may be withdrawn from bonded warehouses free of duty, under such regulations as the Secretary of the Treasury may prescribe.

SEC. 14. That the sixteenth section of an Act entitled "An Act to remove certain burdens on the American merchant marine and encourage the American foreign carrying trade, and for other purposes," approved June twenty-sixth, eighteen hundred and eighty-four, be amended so as to read as follows:

"SEC. 16. That all articles of foreign or domestic production needed and actually withdrawn from bonded warehouses and bonded manufacturing warehouses for supplies (not including equipment) of vessels of the United States engaged in foreign trade, or in trade between the Atlantic and Pacific ports of the United States, may be so withdrawn from said bonded warehouses, free of duty or of internal-revenue tax, as the case may be, under such regulations as the Secretary of the Treasury may prescribe; but no such articles shall be landed at any port of the United States."

SEC. 15. That all articles manufactured in whole or in part of imported materials, or of materials subject to internal-revenue tax, and intended for exportation without being charged with duty, and without having an internal-revenue stamp affixed thereto, shall, under such regulations as the Secretary of the Treasury may prescribe, in order to be so manufactured and exported, be made and manufactured in bonded warehouses similar to those known and designated in Treasury Regulations as bonded warehouses, class six: *Provided*, That the manufacturer of such articles shall first give satisfactory bonds for the faithful observance of all the provisions of law and of such regulations as shall be prescribed by the Secretary of the Treasury: *Provided further*, That the manufacture of distilled spirits from grain, starch, molasses or sugar, including all dilutions or mixtures of them or either of them, shall not be permitted in such manufacturing warehouses.

Whenever goods manufactured in any bonded warehouse established under the provisions of the preceding paragraph shall be exported directly therefrom or shall be duly laden for transportation and immediate exportation under the supervision of the proper officer who shall be duly designated for that purpose, such goods shall be exempt from duty and from the requirements relating to revenue stamps.

Any materials used in the manufacture of such goods, and any packages, coverings, vessels, brands, and labels used in putting up the same may, under the regulations of the Secretary of the Treasury, be conveyed without the payment of revenue tax or duty into any bonded manufacturing warehouse, and imported goods may, under the aforesaid regulations, be transferred without the exaction of duty from any bonded warehouse into any bonded manufacturing warehouse; but this privilege shall not be held to apply to implements, machinery, or apparatus to be used in the construction or repair of any bonded manufacturing warehouse or for the prosecution of the business carried on therein.

No articles or materials received into such bonded manufacturing warehouse shall be withdrawn or removed therefrom except for direct shipment and exportation or for transportation and immediate exportation in bond under the supervision of the officer duly designated therefor by the collector of the port, who shall certify to such shipment and exportation, or ladening for transportation, as the case may be, describing the articles by their mark or otherwise, the quantity, the date of exportation, and the name of the vessel. All labor performed and services rendered under these provisions shall be under the supervision of a duly designated officer of the customs and at the expense of the manufacturer.

A careful account shall be kept by the collector of all merchandise delivered by him to any bonded manufacturing warehouse, and a sworn monthly return, verified by the customs officers in charge, shall be made by the manufacturers containing a detailed statement of all imported merchandise used by him in the manufacture of exported articles.

Before commencing business the proprietor of any manufacturing warehouse shall file with the Secretary of the Treasury a list of all the articles intended to be manufactured in such warehouse, and state the formula of manufacture and the names and quantities of the ingredients to be used therein.

Articles manufactured under these provisions may be withdrawn under such regulations as the Secretary of the Treasury may prescribe for transportation and delivery into any bonded warehouse at an exterior port for the sole purpose of immediate export therefrom.

The provisions of Revised Statutes thirty-four hundred and thirty-three shall, so far as may be practicable, apply to any bonded manufacturing warehouse established under this Act and to the merchandise conveyed therein.

SEC. 16. That all persons are prohibited from importing into the

United States from any foreign country any obscene book, pamphlet, paper, writing, advertisement, circular, print, picture, drawing, or other representation, figure, or image on or of paper or other material, or any cast, instrument, or other article of an immoral nature, or any drug or medicine, or any article whatever for the prevention of conception or for causing unlawful abortion, or any lottery ticket or any advertisement of any lottery. No such articles, whether imported separately or contained in packages with other goods entitled to entry, shall be admitted to entry; and all such articles shall be proceeded against, seized, and forfeited by due course of law. All such prohibited articles and the package in which they are contained in the course of importation shall be detained by the officer of customs, and proceedings taken against the same as hereinafter prescribed, unless it appears to the satisfaction of the collector of customs that the obscene articles contained in the package were inclosed therein without the knowledge or consent of the importer, owner, agent, or consignee: *Provided,* That the drugs hereinbefore mentioned, when imported in bulk and not put up for any of the purposes hereinbefore specified, are excepted from the operation of this section.

SEC. 17. That whoever, being an officer, agent, or employee of the Government of the United States, shall knowingly aid or abet any person engaged in any violation of any of the provisions of law prohibiting importing, advertising, dealing in, exhibiting, or sending or receiving by mail obscene or indecent publications or representations, or means for preventing conception or procuring abortion, or other articles of indecent or immoral use or tendency, shall be deemed guilty of a misdemeanor, and shall for every offense be punishable by a fine of not more than five thousand dollars, or by imprisonment at hard labor for not more than ten years, or both.

SEC. 18. That any judge of any district or circuit court of the United States, within the proper district, before whom complaint in writing of any violation of the two preceding sections is made, to the satisfaction of such judge, and founded on knowledge or belief, and if upon belief, setting forth the grounds of such belief, and supported by oath or affirmation of the complainant, may issue, conformably to the Constitution, a warrant directed to the marshal or any deputy marshal in the proper district, directing him to search for, seize, and take possession of any such article or thing mentioned in the two preceding sections, and to make due and immediate return thereof to the end that the same may be condemned and destroyed by proceedings, which shall be conducted in the same manner as other proceedings in the case of municipal seizure, and with the same right of appeal or writ of error.

SEC. 19. That machinery for repair may be imported into the United States without payment of duty, under bond, to be given in double the appraised value thereof, to be withdrawn and exported after said machinery shall have been repaired; and the Secretary of the Treasury is authorized and directed to prescribe such rules and regulations as may be necessary to protect the revenue against fraud and secure the identity and character of all such importations when again withdrawn and exported, restricting and limiting the export and withdrawal to the same port of entry where imported, and also limiting all bonds to a period of time of not more than six months from the date of the importation.

SEC. 20. That the produce of the forests of the State of Maine upon the Saint John River and its tributaries, owned by American citizens, and sawed or hewed in the Province of New Brunswick by American citizens, the same being otherwise unmanufactured in whole or in part, which is now admitted into the ports of the United States free of duty, shall continue to be so admitted, under such regulations as the Secretary of the Treasury shall from time to time prescribe.

SEC. 21. That the produce of the forests of the State of Maine upon the Saint Croix River and its tributaries owned by American citizens, and sawed or hewed in the Province of New Brunswick by American citizens, the same being otherwise unmanufactured in whole or in part, shall be admitted into the ports of the United States free of duty, under such regulations as the Secretary of the Treasury shall from time to time prescribe.

SEC. 22. That a discriminating duty of ten per centum ad valorem, in addition to the duties imposed by law, shall be levied, collected, and paid on all goods, wares, or merchandise which shall be imported in vessels not of the United States, or which being the production or manufacture of any foreign country not contiguous to the United States, shall come into the United States from such contiguous country; but this discriminating duty shall not apply to goods, wares, or merchandise which shall be imported in vessels not of the United States, entitled at the time of such importation by treaty or convention to be entered in the ports of the United States on payment of the same duties as shall then be payable on goods, wares, and merchandise imported in vessels of the United States, nor to such foreign products or manufactures as shall be imported from such contiguous countries in the usual course of strictly retail trade.

SEC. 23. That no goods, wares, or merchandise, unless in cases provided for by treaty, shall be imported into the United States from any foreign port or place, except in vessels of the United States, or in such foreign vessels as truly and wholly belong to the citizens or subjects of that country of which the goods are the growth, production, or manufacture, or from which such goods, wares, or merchandise can only be, or most usually are, first shipped for transportation. All goods, wares, or merchandise imported contrary to this section, and the vessel wherein the same shall be imported, together with her cargo, tackle, apparel, and furniture, shall be forfeited to the United States; and such goods, wares, or merchandise, ship, or vessel, and cargo shall be liable to be seized, prosecuted, and condemned in like manner, and under the same regulations, restrictions, and provisions as have been heretofore established for the recovery, collection, distribution, and remission of forfeitures to the United States by the several revenue laws.

SEC. 24. That the preceding section shall not apply to vessels or goods, wares, or merchandise imported in vessels of a foreign nation which does not maintain a similar regulation against vessels of the United States.

SEC. 25. That the importation of neat cattle and the hides of neat cattle from any foreign country into the United States is prohibited: *Provided*, That the operation of this section shall be suspended as to any foreign country or countries, or any parts of such country or countries, whenever the Secretary of the Treasury shall officially determine, and give public notice thereof that such importation will not tend to the introduction or spread of contagious or infectious diseases among the cattle of the United States; and the Secretary of the Treasury is hereby authorized and empowered, and it shall be his duty, to make all necessary orders and regulations to carry this section into effect, or to suspend the same as herein provided, and to send copies thereof to the proper officers in the United States, and to such officers or agents of the United States in foreign countries as he shall judge necessary.

SEC. 26. That any person convicted of a willful violation of any of the provisions of the preceding section shall be fined not exceeding five hundred dollars, or imprisoned not exceeding one year, or both, in the discretion of the court.

SEC. 27. That upon the reimportation of articles once exported, of the growth, product, or manufacture of the United States, upon which no internal tax has been assessed or paid, or upon which such tax has been paid and refunded by allowance or drawback, there shall be levied, collected, and paid a duty equal to the tax imposed by the internal-revenue laws upon such articles, except articles manufactured in bonded warehouses and exported pursuant to law, which shall be subject to the same rate of duty as if originally imported.

SEC. 28. That whenever any vessel laden with merchandise, in whole or in part subject to duty, has been sunk in any river, harbor, bay, or waters subject to the jurisdiction of the United States, and within its limits, for the period of two years, and is abandoned by the owner thereof, any person who may raise such vessel shall be permitted to bring any merchandise recovered therefrom into the port nearest to the place where such vessel was so raised free from the payment of any duty thereupon, but under such regulations as the Secretary of the Treasury may prescribe.

SEC. 29. That the works of manufacturers engaged in smelting or refining metals, or both smelting and refining, in the United States may be designated as bonded warehouses under such regulations as the Secretary of the Treasury may prescribe: *Provided*, That such manufacturers shall first give satisfactory bonds to the Secretary of the Treasury. Ores or metals in any crude form requiring smelting or refining to make them readily available in the arts, imported into the United States to be smelted or refined and intended to be exported in a refined but unmanufactured state, shall, under such rules as the Secretary of the Treasury may prescribe, and under the direction of the proper officer, be removed in original packages or in bulk from the vessel or other vehicle on which they have been imported, or from the bonded warehouse in which the same may be, into the bonded warehouse in which such smelting or refining, or both, may be carried on, for the purpose of being smelted or refined, or both, without payment of duties thereon, and may there be smelted or refined, together with other metals of home or foreign production: *Provided*, That each day a quantity of refined metal equal to ninety per centum of the amount of imported metal smelted or refined that day shall be set aside, and such metal so set aside shall not be taken from said works except for transportation to another bonded warehouse or for exportation, under the direction of the proper officer having charge thereof as aforesaid, whose certificate, describing the articles by their marks or otherwise, the quantity, the date of importation, and the name of vessel or other vehicle by which it was imported, with such additional particulars as may from time to time be required, shall be received by the collector of customs as sufficient evidence of the exportation of the metal, or it may be removed under such regulations as the Secretary of the Treasury may prescribe, upon entry and payment of duties, for domestic consumption, and the exportation of the ninety per centum of metals hereinbefore provided for shall entitle the ores and metals imported under the provisions of this section to admission without payment of the duties thereon: *Provided further*, That in respect to lead ores imported under the provisions of this section the refined metal set aside shall either be reexported or the regular duties paid thereon within six months from the date of the receipt of the ore. All labor performed and services rendered under these regulations shall be under the supervision of an officer of the customs, to be appointed by the Secretary of the Treasury, and at the expense of the manufacturer.

SEC. 30. That where imported materials on which duties have been paid are used in the manufacture of articles manufactured or produced in the United States, there shall be allowed on the exportation of such articles a drawback equal in amount to the duties paid on the materials used, less one per centum of such duties: *Provided*, That when the articles exported are made in part from domestic materials the imported materials, or the parts of the articles made from such materials, shall so appear in the completed articles that the quantity or measure thereof may be ascertained: *And provided further*, That the drawback on any article allowed under existing law shall be continued at the rate herein provided. That the imported materials used in the manufacture or production of articles entitled to drawback of customs duties when exported shall, in all cases where drawback of duties paid on such materials is claimed, be identified, the quantity of such materials used and the amount of duties paid thereon shall be ascertained, the facts of the manufacture or production of such articles in the United States and their exportation therefrom shall be determined, and the drawback due thereon shall be paid to the manufacturer, producer, or exporter, to the agent of either or to the person to whom such manufacturer, producer, exporter, or agent shall in writing order such drawback paid, under such regulations as the Secretary of the Treasury shall prescribe.

SEC. 31. That all goods, wares, articles, and merchandise manufactured wholly or in part in any foreign country by convict labor shall not be entitled to entry at any of the ports of the United States, and the importation thereof is hereby prohibited, and the Secretary of the Treasury is authorized and directed to prescribe such regulations as may be necessary for the enforcement of this provision.

SEC. 32. That sections seven and eleven of the Act entitled "An Act to simplify the laws in relation to the collection of the revenues," approved June tenth, eighteen hundred and ninety, be, and the same are hereby, amended so as to read as follows:

SEC. 7. That the owner, consignee, or agent of any imported merchandise which has been actually purchased may, at the time when he shall make and verify his written entry of such merchandise, but not afterwards, make such addition in the entry to the cost or value given in the invoice or pro forma invoice or statement in form of an invoice, which he shall produce with his entry, as in his opinion may raise the same to the actual market value or wholesale price of such merchandise at the time of exportation to the United States, in the principal markets of the country from which the same has been imported; but no such addition shall be made upon entry to the invoice value of any imported merchandise obtained otherwise than by actual purchase; and the collector within whose district any merchandise may be imported or entered, whether the same has been actually purchased or procured otherwise than by purchase, shall cause the actual market value or wholesale price of such merchandise to be appraised; and if the appraised value of any article of imported merchandise subject to an ad valorem duty or to a duty based upon or regulated in any manner by the value thereof shall exceed the value declared in the entry, there shall be levied, collected, and paid, in addition to the duties imposed by law on such merchandise, an additional duty of one per centum of the total appraised value thereof for each one per centum that such appraised value exceeds the value declared in the entry, but the additional duties shall only apply to the particular article or articles in each invoice that are so undervalued, and shall be limited to fifty per centum of the appraised value of such article or articles. Such additional duties shall not be construed to be penal, and shall not be remitted, nor payment thereof in any way avoided, except in cases arising from a manifest clerical error, nor shall they be refunded in case of exportation of the merchandise, or on any other account, nor shall they be subject to the benefit of drawback: *Provided*, That if the appraised value of any merchandise shall exceed the value declared in the entry by more than fifty per centum, except when arising from a manifest clerical error, such entry shall be held to be presumptively fraudulent, and the collector of customs shall seize such merchandise and proceed as in case of forfeiture for violation of the customs laws, and in any legal proceeding that may result from such seizure, the undervaluation as shown by the appraisal shall be presumptive evidence of fraud, and the burden of proof shall be on the claimant to rebut the same and forfeiture shall be adjudged unless he shall rebut such presumption of fraudulent intent by sufficient evidence. The forfeiture provided for in this section shall apply to the whole of the merchandise or the value thereof in the case or package containing the particular article or articles in each invoice which are undervalued: *Provided, further*, That all additional duties, penalties or forfeitures applicable to merchandise entered by a duly certified invoice, shall be alike applicable to merchandise entered by a pro forma invoice or statement in the form of an invoice, and no forfeiture or disability of any kind, incurred under the provisions of this section shall be remitted or mitigated by the Secretary of the Treasury. The duty shall not, however, be assessed in any case upon an amount less than the invoice or entered value.

SEC. 11. That, when the actual market value as defined by law, of any article of imported merchandise, wholly or partly manufactured and subject to an ad valorem duty, or to a duty based in whole or in part on value, can not be otherwise ascertained to the satisfaction of the appraising officer, such officer shall use all available means in his power to ascertain the cost of production of such merchandise at the time of exportation to the United States, and at the place of manufacture; such cost of production to include the cost of materials and of fabrication, all general expenses covering each and every outlay of whatsoever nature incident to such production, together with the expense of preparing and putting up such merchandise ready for shipment, and an addition of not less than eight nor more than fifty per centum upon the total cost as thus ascertained; and in no case shall such merchandise be appraised upon original appraisal or reappraisement at less than the total cost of production as thus ascertained. It shall be lawful for appraising officers, in determining the dutiable value of such merchandise, to take into consideration the wholesale price at which such or similar merchandise is sold or offered for sale in the United States, due allowance being made for estimated duties thereon, the cost of transportation, insurance, and other necessary expenses from the place of shipment to the United States, and a reasonable commission, if any has been paid, not exceeding six per centum.

SEC. 33. That on and after the day when this Act shall go into effect all goods, wares, and merchandise previously imported, for which no entry has been made, and all goods, wares, and merchandise previously entered without payment of duty and under bond for warehousing, transportation, or any other purpose, for which no permit of delivery to the importer or his agent has been issued, shall be subjected to the duties imposed by this Act and to no other duty, upon the entry or the withdrawal thereof: *Provided*, That when duties are based upon the weight of merchandise deposited in any public or private bonded warehouse, said duties shall be levied and collected upon the weight of such merchandise at the time of its entry.

SEC. 34. That sections one to twenty-four, both inclusive, of an Act entitled "An Act to reduce taxation, to provide revenue for the Government, and for other purposes," which became a law on the twenty-eighth day of August, eighteen hundred and ninety-four, and all acts and parts of acts inconsistent with the provisions of this Act are hereby repealed, said repeal to take effect on and after the passage of this Act, but the repeal of existing laws or modifications thereof embraced in this Act shall not affect any act done, or any right accruing or accrued, or any suit or proceeding had or commenced in any civil cause before the said repeal or modifications; but all rights and liabilities under said laws shall continue and may be enforced in the same manner as if said repeal or modifications had not been made. Any offenses committed and all penalties or forfeitures or liabilities incurred prior to the passage of this Act under any statute embraced in or changed, modified, or repealed by this Act may be prosecuted or punished in the same manner and with the same effect as if this Act had not been passed. All Acts of limitation, whether applicable to civil causes and proceedings or to the prosecution of offenses or for the recovery of penalties or forfeitures embraced in or modified, changed, or repealed by this Act shall not be affected thereby; and all suits, proceedings, or prosecutions, whether civil or criminal, for causes arising or acts done or committed prior to the passage of this Act may be commenced and prosecuted within the same time and with the same effect as if this Act had not been passed: *And provided further*, That nothing in this Act shall be construed to repeal the provisions of section three thousand and fifty-eight of the Revised Statutes as amended by the Act approved February twenty-third, eighteen hundred and eighty-seven, in respect to the abandonment of merchandise to underwriters or the salvors of property, and the ascertainment of duties thereon: *And provided further*, That nothing in this Act shall be construed to repeal or in any manner affect the sections numbered seventy-three, seventy-four, seventy-five, seventy-six, and seventy-seven of an Act entitled "An Act to reduce taxation, to provide revenue for the Government, and for other purposes," which became a law on the twenty-eighth day of August, eighteen hundred and ninety-four.

Approved, July 24, 1897.

INDEX TO TARIFF.[1]

JULY 24, 1897.

A.

[1] For articles specified in reciprocity sections 3 and 4, see page 219.

186

ARTICLES SPECIFIED IN RECIPROCITY SECTIONS 3 AND 4 OF TARIFF ACT OF JULY 24, 1897.

CUSTOMS ADMINISTRATIVE ACT OF JUNE 10, 1890, AS AMENDED BY ACT OF JULY 24, 1897.

Be it enacted by the Senate and House of Representatives of the United States of America in Congress assembled, That all merchandise imported into the United States shall, for the purpose of this act, be deemed and held to be the property of the person to whom the merchandise may be consigned; but the holder of any bill of lading consigned to order and indorsed by the consignor shall be deemed the consignee thereof; and in case of the abandonment of any merchandise to the underwriters the latter may be recognized as the consignee.

SEC. 2. That all invoices of imported merchandise shall be made out in the currency of the place or country from whence the importations shall be made or if purchased in the currency actually paid therefor, shall contain a correct description of such merchandise, and shall be made in triplicate or in quadruplicate in case of merchandise intended for immediate transportation without appraisement, and signed by the person owning or shipping the same, if the merchandise has been actually purchased, or by the manufacturer or owner thereof, if the same has been procured otherwise than by purchase, or by the duly authorized agent of such purchaser, manufacturer, or owner.

SEC. 3. That all such invoices shall, at or before the shipment of the merchandise, be produced to the consul, vice consul, or commercial agent of the United States of the consular district in which the merchandise was manufactured or purchased as the case may be, for export to the United States, and shall have indorsed thereon, when so produced, a declaration signed by the purchaser, manufacturer, owner, or agent, setting forth that the invoice is in all respects correct and true, and was made at the place from which the merchandise is to be exported to the United States; that it contains, if the merchandise was obtained by purchase, a true and full statement of the time when, the place where, the person from whom the same was purchased, and the actual cost thereof and of all charges thereon, as provided by this act; and that no discounts, bounties, or drawbacks are contained in the invoice .but such as have been actually allowed thereon; and when obtained in any other manner than by purchase, the actual market value or wholesale price thereof at the time of exportation to the United States in the principal markets of the country from whence exported; that such actual market value is the price at which the merchandise described in the invoice is freely offered for sale to all purchasers in said markets, and that it is the price which the manufacturer or owner making the declaration would have received, and was willing to receive, for such merchandise sold in the ordinary course of trade, in the usual wholesale quantities, and that it includes all charges thereon as provided by this act; and the actual quantity thereof; and that no different invoice of the merchandise mentioned in the invoice so produced has been or will be furnished to any one. If the merchandise was actually purchased, the declaration shall also contain a statement that the currency in which such invoice is made out is that which was actually paid for the merchandise by the purchaser.

223

SEC. 4. That, except in case of personal effects accompanying the passenger, no importation of any merchandise exceeding one hundred dollars in dutiable value shall be admitted to entry without the production of a duly-certified invoice thereof as required by law, or of an affidavit made by the owner, importer, or consignee, before the collector or his deputy, showing why it is impracticable to produce such invoice; and no entry shall be made in the absence of a certified invoice, upon affidavit as aforesaid, unless such affidavit be accompanied by a statement in the form of an invoice, or otherwise, showing the actual cost of such merchandise, if purchased, or if obtained otherwise than by purchase, the actual market value or wholesale price thereof at the time of exportation to the United States, in the principal markets of the country from which the same has been imported; which statement shall be verified by the oath of the owner, importer, consignee, or agent desiring to make entry of the merchandise, to be administered by the collector or his deputy, and it shall be lawful for the collector or his deputy to examine the deponent under oath touching the sources of his knowledge, information, or belief in the premises, and to require him to produce any letter, paper, or statement of account, in his possession, or under his control, which may assist the officers of customs in ascertaining the actual value of the importation or any part thereof; and in default of such production when so requested, such owner, importer, consignee, or agent shall be thereafter debarred from producing any such letter, paper, or statement for the purpose of avoiding any additional duty, penalty, or forfeiture incurred under this act, unless he shall show to the satisfaction of the court or the officers of the customs, as the case may be, that it was not in his power to produce the same when so demanded; and no merchandise shall be admitted to entry under the provisions of this section unless the collector shall be satisfied that the failure to produce a duly certified invoice is due to causes beyond the control of the owner, consignee, or agent thereof: *Provided*, That the Secretary of the Treasury may make regulations by which books, magazines, and other periodicals published and imported in successive parts, numbers, or volumes, and entitled to be imported free of duty, shall require but one declaration for the entire series. And when entry of merchandise exceeding one hundred dollars in value is made by a statement in the form of an invoice the collector shall require a bond for the production of a duly certified invoice.

SEC. 5. That whenever merchandise imported into the United States is entered by invoice, one of the following declarations, according to the nature of the case, shall be filed with the collector of the port, at the time of entry by the owner, importer, consignee, or agent; which declaration so filed shall be duly signed by the owner, importer, consignee, or agent, before the collector, or before a notary public or other officer duly authorized by law to administer oaths and take acknowledgments, who may be designated by the Secretary of the Treasury to receive such declarations and to certify to the identity of the persons making them, under regulations to be prescribed by the Secretary of the Treasury; and every officer so designated shall file with the collector of the port a copy of his official signature and seal: *Provided*, That if any of the invoices or bills of lading of any merchandise imported in any one vessel, which should otherwise be embraced in said entry, have not been received at the date of the entry, the declaration may state the fact, and thereupon such merchandise of which the invoices or bills of lading are not produced shall not be included in such entry, but may be entered subsequently.

DECLARATION OF CONSIGNEE, IMPORTER, OR AGENT.

I —— ——, do solemnly and truly declare that I am the consignee [importer or agent] of the merchandise described in the annexed entry and invoice; that the invoice and bill of lading now presented by me to the collector of —— —— are the true and only invoice and bill of lading by me received of all the goods, wares, and merchandise imported in the —— whereof —— —— is master, from —— ——, for account of any person whomsoever for whom I am authorized to enter the same; that the said invoice and bill of lading are in the state in which they were actually received by me, and that I do not know or believe in the existence of any other invoice or bill of lading of the said goods, wares, and merchandise; that the entry now delivered to the collector contains a just and true account of the said goods, wares, and merchandise, according to the said invoice and bill of lading; that nothing has been, on my part, nor to my knowledge on the part of any other person, concealed or suppressed, whereby the United States may be defrauded of any part of the duty lawfully due on the said goods, wares, and merchandise; that the said invoice and the declaration therein are in all respects true, and were made by the person by whom the same purports to have been made; and that if at any time hereafter I discover any error in the said invoice, or in the account now rendered of the said goods, wares, and merchandise, or receive any other invoice of the same, I will immediately make the same known to the collector of this district. And I do further solemnly and truly declare that to the best of my knowledge and belief [insert the name and residence of the owner or owners] is [or are] the owner (or owners) of the goods, wares, and merchandise mentioned in the annexed entry; that the invoice now produced by me exhibits the actual cost (if purchased) or the actual market value or wholesale price (if otherwise obtained) at the time of exportation to the United States in the principal markets of the country from whence imported of the said goods, wares, and merchandise, and includes and specifies the value of all cartons, cases, crates, boxes, sacks, and coverings of any kind, and all other costs, charges, and expenses incident to placing said goods, wares, and merchandise in condition, packed ready for shipment to the United States, and no other or different discount, bounty, or drawback but such as has been actually allowed on the same.

DECLARATION OF OWNER IN CASES WHERE MERCHANDISE HAS BEEN ACTUALLY PURCHASED.

I, —— —— do solemnly and truly declare that I am the owner of the merchandise described in the annexed entry and invoice; that the entry now delivered by me to the collector of —— contains a just and true account of all the goods, wares, and merchandise imported by or consigned to me, in the —— —— whereof —— —— is master, from ——; that the invoice and entry which I now produce contain a just and faithful account of the actual cost of the said goods, wares, and merchandise and include and specifies the value of all cartons, cases, crates, boxes, sacks, and coverings of any kind, and all other costs, charges, and expenses incident to placing said goods, wares, and merchandise in condition, packed ready for shipment to the United States, and no other discount, drawback, or bounty but such as has been actually allowed on the same; that I do not know nor believe in

3413——15

the existence of any invoice or bill of lading other than those now produced by me, and that they are in the state in which I actually received
them. And I further solemnly and truly declare that I have not in the
said entry or invoice concealed or suppressed anything whereby the
United States may be defrauded of any part of the duty lawfully due
on the said goods, wares, and merchandise; that to the best of my
knowledge and belief the said invoice and the declaration thereon are
in all respects true, and were made by the person by whom the same
purports to have been made; and that if at any time hereafter I discover any error in the said invoice or in the account now produced of
the said goods, wares, and merchandise, or receive any other invoice
of the same, I will immediately make the same known to the collector of
this district.

DECLARATION OF MANUFACTURER OR OWNER IN CASES WHERE
MERCHANDISE HAS NOT BEEN ACTUALLY PURCHASED.

I, ———— ————, do solemnly and truly declare that I am the owner
(or manufacturer) of the merchandise described in the annexed entry
and invoice; that the entry now delivered by me to the collector of ———
contains a just and true account of all the goods, wares, and merchandise
imported by or consigned to me in the ———, whereof ———— ———— is
master, from ————; that the said goods, wares, and merchandise were
not actually bought by me, or by my agent, in the ordinary mode of
bargain and sale, but that nevertheless the invoice which I now produce contains a just and faithful valuation of the same, at their actual
market value or wholesale price, at the time of exportation to the United
States, in the principal markets of the country from whence imported
for my account (or for account of myself or partners); that such actual
market value is the price at which the merchandise described in the
invoice is freely offered for sale to all purchasers in said markets, and
is the price which I would have received and was willing to receive for
such merchandise sold in the ordinary course of trade in the usual
wholesale quantities; that the said invoice contains also a just and
faithful account of all the cost of finishing said goods, wares, and merchandise to their present condition, and includes and specifies, the value
of all cartons, cases, crates, boxes, sacks, and coverings of any kind,
and all other costs and charges incident to placing said goods, wares,
and merchandise in condition packed ready for shipment to the United
States, and no other discount, drawback, or bounty but such as has
been actually allowed on the said goods, wares, and merchandise; that
the said invoice and the declaration thereon are in all respects true,
and were made by the person by whom the same purports to have been
made; that I do not know nor believe in the existence of any invoice
or bill of lading other than those now produced by me, and that they
are in the state in which I actually received them. And I do further
solemnly and truly declare that I have not in the said entry or invoice
concealed or suppressed anything whereby the United States may be
defrauded of any part of the duty lawfully due on the said goods, wares,
and merchandise; and that if at any time hereafter I discover any error
in the said invoice, or in the account now produced of the said goods,
wares, and merchandise, or receive any other invoice of the same, I will
immediately make the same known to the collector of this district.

SEC. 6. That any person who shall knowingly make any false statement in the declarations provided for in the preceding section, or shall
aid or procure the making of any such false statement as to any matter

material thereto, shall, on conviction thereof, be punished by a fine not exceeding five thousand dollars, or by imprisonment at hard labor not more than two years, or both, in the discretion of the court: *Provided*, That nothing in this section shall be construed to relieve imported merchandise from forfeiture by reason of such false statement or for any cause elsewhere provided by law.

SEC. 7. That the owner, consignee, or agent of any **Amended by Sec. 32 of the act of July 24, 1897.** imported merchandise which has been actually purchased may, at the time when he shall make and verify his written entry of such merchandise, but not afterwards, make such addition in the entry to the cost or value given in the invoice or pro forma invoice or statement in form of an invoice, which he shall produce with his entry, as in his opinion may raise the same to the actual market value or wholesale price of such merchandise at the time of exportation to the United States, in the principal markets of the country from which the same has been imported; but no such addition shall be made upon entry to the invoice value of any imported merchandise obtained otherwise than by actual purchase; and the collector within whose district any merchandise may be imported or entered, whether the same has been actually purchased or procured otherwise than by purchase, shall cause the actual market value or wholesale price of such merchandise to be appraised; and if the appraised value of any article of imported merchandise subject to an ad valorem duty or to a duty based upon or regulated in any manner by the value thereof shall exceed the value declared in the entry, there shall be levied, collected, and paid, in addition to the duties imposed by law on such merchandise, an additional duty of one per centum of the total appraised value thereof for each one per centum that such appraised value exceeds the value declared in the entry, but the additional duties shall only apply to the particular article or articles in each invoice that are so undervalued, and shall be limited to fifty per centum of the appraised value of such article or articles. Such additional duties shall not be construed to be penal, and shall not be remitted, nor payment thereof in any way avoided, except in cases arising from a manifest clerical error, nor shall they be refunded in case of exportation of the merchandise, or on any other account, nor shall they be subject to the benefit of drawback: *Provided*, That if the appraised value of any merchandise shall exceed the value declared in the entry by more than fifty per centum, except when arising from a manifest clerical error, such entry shall be held to be presumptively fraudulent, and the collector of customs shall seize such merchandise and proceed as in case of forfeiture for violation of the customs laws, and in any legal proceeding that may result from such seizure, the undervaluation as shown by the appraisal shall be presumptive evidence of fraud, and the burden of proof shall be on the claimant to rebut the same and forfeiture shall be adjudged unless he shall rebut such presumption of fraudulent intent by sufficient evidence. The forfeiture provided for in this section shall apply to the whole of the merchandise or the value thereof in the case or package containing the particular article or articles in each invoice which are undervalued: *Provided, further*, That all additional duties, penalties or forfeitures applicable to merchandise entered by a duly certified invoice, shall be alike applicable to merchandise entered by a pro forma invoice or statement in the form of an invoice, and no forfeiture or disability of any kind, incurred under the provisions of this section shall be remitted or mitigated by the Secretary of the Treasury. The duty shall not, however, be assessed in any case upon an amount less than the invoice or entered value.

Sec. 8. That when merchandise entered for customs duty has been consigned for sale by or on account of the manufacturer thereof, to a person, agent, partner, or consignee in the United States, such person, agent, partner, or consignee shall, at the time of the entry of such merchandise, present to the collector of customs at the port where such entry is made, as a part of such entry, and in addition to the certified invoice or statement in the form of an invoice required by law, a state- ment signed by such manufacturer, declaring the cost of production of such merchandise, such cost to include all the elements of cost as stated in section eleven of this act. When merchandise entered for customs duty has been consigned for sale by or on account of a person other than the manufacturer of such merchandise, to a person, agent, part- ner, or consignee in the United States, such person, agent, partner, or consignee shall at the time of the entry of such merchandise present to the collector of customs at the port where such entry is made, as a part of such entry, a statement signed by the consignor thereof, declar- ing that the merchandise was actually purchased by him or for his account, and showing the time when, the place where, and from whom he purchased the merchandise, and in detail the price he paid for the same: *Provided*, That the statements required by this section shall be made in triplicate, and shall bear the attestation of the consular officer of the United States resident within the consular district wherein the merchandise was manufactured, if consigned by the manufacturer or for his account, or from whence it was imported when consigned by a person other than the manufacturer, one copy thereof to be delivered to the person making the statement, one copy to be transmitted with the triplicate invoice of the merchandise to the collector of the port in the United States to which the merchandise is consigned, and the remaining copy to be filed in the consulate.

Sec. 9. That if any owner, importer, consignee, agent, or other per- son shall make or attempt to make any entry of imported merchandise by means of any fraudulent or false invoice, affidavit, letter, paper, or by means of any false statement, written or verbal, or by means of any false or fraudulent practice or appliance whatsoever, or shall be guilty of any willful act or omission by means whereof the United States shall be deprived of the lawful duties, or any portion thereof, accruing upon the merchandise, or any portion thereof, embraced or referred to in such invoice, affidavit, letter, paper, or statement, or affected by such act or omission, such merchandise, or the value thereof, to be recovered from the person making the entry, shall be forfeited, which forfeiture shall only apply to the whole of the merchandise or the value thereof in the case or package containing the particular article or articles of merchandise to which such fraud or false paper or statement relates; and such person shall, upon conviction, be fined for each offense a sum not exceeding five thousand dollars, or be imprisoned for a time not exceeding two years, or both, in the discretion of the court.

Sec. 10. That it shall be the duty of the appraisers of the United States, and every of them, and every person who shall act as such appraiser, or of the collector, as the case may be, by all reasonable ways and means in his or their power to ascertain, estimate, and appraise (any invoice or affidavit thereto or statement of cost, or of cost of production to the contrary notwithstanding) the actual market value and wholesale price of the merchandise at the time of exportation to the United States, in the principal markets of the country whence the

same has been imported, and the number of yards, parcels, or quantities, and actual market value or wholesale price of every of them, as
the case may require.

SEC. 11. That, when the actual market value as defined by law, of any article of imported merchandise,
wholly or partly manufactured and subject to an ad.
valorem duty, or to a duty based in whole or in part on
value, can not be otherwise ascertained to the satisfaction of the appraising officer, such officer shall use all available means in his power to
ascertain the cost of production of such merchandise at the time of
exportation to the United States, and at the place of manufacture; such
cost of production to include the cost of materials and of fabrication, all
general expenses covering each and every outlay of whatsoever nature
incident to such production, together with the expense of preparing
and putting up such merchandise ready for shipment, and an addition
of not less than eight nor more than fifty per centum upon the total
cost as thus ascertained; and in no case shall such merchandise be
appraised upon original appraisal or reappraisement at less than the
total cost of production as thus ascertained. It shall be lawful for
appraising officers, in determining the dutiable value of such merchandise, to take into consideration the wholesale price at which such or
similar merchandise is sold or offered for sale in the United States, due
allowance being made for estimated duties thereon, the cost of transportation, insurance, and other necessary expenses from the place of
shipment to the United States, and a reasonable commission, if any has
been paid, not exceeding six per centum.

*Amended by Sec.
32 of the act of
July 24, 1897.*

SEC. 12. That there shall be appointed by the President, by and with
the advice and consent of the Senate, nine general appraisers of merchandise, each of whom shall receive a salary of seven thousand dollars a year. Not more than five of such general appraisers shall be
appointed from the same political party. They shall not be engaged in
any other business, avocation, or employment, and may be removed from
office at any time by the President for inefficiency, neglect of duty, or
malfeasance in office. They shall be employed at such ports and within
such territorial limits, as the Secretary of the Treasury may from time
to time prescribe, and are hereby authorized to exercise the powers, and
duties devolved upon them by this act and to exercise, under the general direction of the Secretary of the Treasury, such other supervision
over appraisements and classifications, for duty, of imported merchandise as may be needful to secure lawful and uniform appraisements and
classifications at the several ports. Three of the general appraisers
shall be on duty as a board of general appraisers daily (except Sunday
and legal holidays) at the port of New York, during the business hours
prescribed by the Secretary of the Treasury, at which port a place for
samples shall be provided, under such rules and regulations as the
Secretary of the Treasury may from time to time prescribe, which shall
include rules as to the classes of articles to be deposited, the time of
their retention, and as to their disposition, which place of samples shall
be under the immediate control and direction of the board of general
appraisers on duty at said port.

SEC. 13. That the appraiser shall revise and correct the reports of
the assistant appraisers as he may judge proper, and the appraiser,
or, at ports where there is no appraiser, the person acting as such,
shall report to the collector his decision as to the value of the merchandise appraised. At ports where there is no appraiser, the certificate of the customs officer to whom is committed the estimating
and collection of duties, of the dutiable value of any merchandise
required to be appraised, shall be deemed and taken to be the ap-

praisement of such merchandise. If the collector shall deem the appraisement of any imported merchandise too low he may order a reappraisement, which shall be made by one of the general appraisers, or, if the importer, owner, agent, or consignee of such merchandise shall be dissatisfied with the appraisement thereof, and shall have complied with the requirements of law with respect to the entry and appraisement of merchandise, he may, within two days thereafter give notice to the collector, in writing, of such dissatisfaction, on the receipt of which the collector shall at once direct a reappraisement of such merchandise by one of the general appraisers. The decision of the appraiser or the person acting as such (in cases where no objection is made thereto, either by the collector or by the importer, owner, consignee, or agent), or of the general appraiser in cases of re-appraisement, shall be final and conclusive as to the dutiable value of such merchandise against all parties interested therein, unless the importer, owner, consignee, or agent of the merchandise shall be dissatisfied with such decision, and shall, within two days thereafter give notice to the collector in writing of such dissatisfaction, or unless the collector shall deem the appraisement of the merchandise too low, in either case the collector shall transmit the invoice and all the papers appertaining thereto to the board of three general appraisers, which shall be on duty at the port of New York, or to a board of three general appraisers who may be designated by the Secretary of the Treasury for such duty at that port or at any other port, which board shall examine and decide the case thus submitted, and their decision, or that of a majority of them, shall be final and conclusive as to the dutiable value of such merchandise against all parties interested therein, and the collector or the person acting as such shall ascertain, fix, and liquidate the rate and amount of duties to be paid on such merchandise, and the dutiable costs and charges thereon, according to law.

SEC. 14. That the decision of the collector as to the rate and amount of duties chargeable upon imported merchandise, including all dutiable costs and charges, and as to all fees and exactions of whatever character (except duties on tonnage), shall be final and conclusive against all persons interested therein, unless the owner, importer, consignee, or agent of such merchandise, or the person paying such fees, charges, and exactions other than duties, shall, within ten days after "but not before" such ascertainment and liquidation of duties, as well in cases of merchandise entered in bond as for consumption, or within ten days after the payment of such fees, charges, and exactions, if dissatisfied with such decision give notice in writing to the collector, setting forth therein distinctly and specifically, and in respect to each entry or payment, the reasons for his objections thereto, and if the merchandise is entered for consumption shall pay the full amount of the duties and charges ascertained to be due thereon. Upon such notice and payment the collector shall transmit the invoice and all the papers and exhibits connected therewith to the board of three general appraisers, which shall be on duty at the port of New York, or to a board of three general appraisers who may be designated by the Secretary of the Treasury for such duty at that port or at any other port, which board shall examine and decide the case thus submitted, and their decision, or that of a majority of them, shall be final and conclusive upon all persons interested therein, and the record shall be transmitted to the proper collector or person acting as such who shall liquidate the entry accordingly, except in cases where an application shall be filed in the circuit court within the time and in the manner provided for in section fifteen of this act.

SEC. 15. That if the owner, importer, consignee, or agent of any imported merchandise, or the collector, or the Secretary of the Treasury, shall be dissatisfied with the decision of the board of general appraisers, as provided for in section fourteen of this act, as to the construction of the law and the facts respecting the classification of such merchandise and the rate of duty imposed thereon under such classification, they or either of them, may, within thirty days next after such decision, and not afterwards, apply to the circuit court of the United States within the district in which the matter arises, for a review of the questions of law and fact involved in such decision. Such application shall be made by filing in the office of the clerk of said circuit court a concise statement of the errors of law and fact complained of, and a copy of such statement shall be served on the collector, or on the importer, owner, consignee, or agent, as the case may be. Thereupon the court shall order the board of appraisers to return to said circuit court the record and the evidence taken by them, together with a certified statement of the facts involved in the case, and their decisions thereon; and all the evidence taken by and before said appraisers shall be competent evidence before said circuit court; and within twenty days after the aforesaid return is made the court may, upon the application of the Secretary of the Treasury, the collector of the port, or the importer, owner, consignee, or agent, as the case may be, refer it to one of said general appraisers, as an officer of the court, to take and return to the court such further evidence as may be offered by the Secretary of the Treasury, collector, importer, owner, consignee, or agent, within sixty days thereafter, in such order and under such rules as the court may prescribe; and such further evidence with the aforesaid returns shall constitute the record upon which said circuit court shall give priority to and proceed to hear and determine the questions of law and fact involved in such decision, respecting the classification of such merchandise and the rate of duty imposed thereon under such classification, and the decision of such court shall be final, and the proper collector, or person acting as such, shall liquidate the entry accordingly, unless such court shall be of opinion that the question involved is of such importance as to require a review of such decision by the Supreme Court of the United States, in which case said circuit court, or the judge making the decision may, within thirty days thereafter, allow an appeal to said Supreme Court; but an appeal shall be allowed on the part of the United States whenever the Attorney-General shall apply for it within thirty days after the rendition of such decision. On such original application, and on any such appeal, security for damages and costs shall be given as in the case of other appeals in cases in which the United States is a party. Said Supreme Court shall have jurisdiction and power to review such decision, and shall give priority to such cases, and may affirm, modify, or reverse such decision of such circuit court, and remand the case with such orders as may seem to it proper in the premises, which shall be executed accordingly. All final judgments, when in favor of the importer, shall be satisfied' and paid by the Secretary of the Treasury from the permanent indefinite appropriation provided for in section twenty-three of this act. For the purposes of this section the circuit courts of the United States shall be deemed always open, and said circuit courts, respectively, may establish, and from time to time alter, rules and regulations not inconsistent herewith for the procedure in such cases as they shall deem proper.

SEC. 16. That the general appraisers, or any of them, are hereby authorized to administer oaths, and said general appraisers, the boards of general appraisers, the local appraisers or the collectors, as the case may be, may cite to appear before them, and examine upon oath any owner, importer, agent, consignee, or other person touching any matter or thing which they, or either of them, may deem material respecting any imported merchandise, in ascertaining the dutiable value or classification thereof; and they, or either of them, may require the production of any letters, accounts, or invoices relating to said merchandise, and may require such testimony to be reduced to writing, and when so taken it shall be filed in the office of the collector, and preserved for use or reference until the final decision of the collector or said board of appraisers shall be made respecting the valuation or classification of said merchandise, as the case may be.

SEC. 17. That if any person so cited to appear shall neglect or refuse to attend, or shall decline to answer, or shall refuse to answer in writing any interrogatories, and subscribe his name to his deposition, or to produce such papers, when so required by a general appraiser, or a board of general appraisers, or a local appraiser or a collector, he shall be liable to a penalty of one hundred dollars; and if such person be the owner, importer, or consignee, the appraisement which the general appraiser, or board of general appraisers, or local appraiser, or collector, where there is no appraiser, may make of the merchandise, shall be final and conclusive; and any person who shall willfully and corruptly swear falsely on an examination before any general appraiser, or board of general appraisers, or local appraiser, or collector, shall be deemed guilty of perjury; and if he is the owner, importer, or consignee, the merchandise shall be forfeited.

SEC. 18. That all decisions of the general appraisers and of the boards of general appraisers, respecting values and rates of duty, shall be preserved and filed, and shall be open to inspection under proper regulations to be prescribed by the Secretary of the Treasury. All decisions of the general appraisers shall be reported forthwith to the Secretary of the Treasury and to the board of general appraisers on duty at the port of New York, and the report to the board shall be accompanied, whenever practicable, by samples of the merchandise in question, and it shall be the duty of the said board, under the direction of the Secretary of the Treasury, to cause an abstract to be made and published of such decisions of the appraisers as they may deem important, and of the decisions of each of the general appraisers and boards of general appraisers, which abstract shall contain a general description of the merchandise in question, and of the value and rate of duty fixed in each case, with reference, whenever practicable, by number or other designation, to samples deposited in the place of samples at New York, and such abstract shall be issued from time to time, at least once in each week, for the information of customs officers and the public.

SEC. 19. That whenever imported merchandise is subject to an ad valorem rate of duty, or to a duty based upon or regulated in any manner by the value thereof, the duty shall be assessed upon the actual market value or wholesale price of such merchandise as bought and sold in usual wholesale quantities, at the time of exportation to the United States, in the principal markets of the country from whence imported, and in the condition in which such merchandise is there bought and sold for exportation to the United States, or consigned to the United States for sale, including the value of all cartons, cases, crates, boxes, sacks, and coverings of any kind, and all other costs, charges, and expenses incident to placing the merchandise in condition, packed ready for shipment to the United States, and if there be used for covering or holding imported merchandise, whether dutiable or free, any unusual article or form designed for use otherwise than in the bona fide transportation of such merchandise to the United States, additional duty shall be levied and collected upon such material or article at the rate to which the same would be subject if separately imported. That the words "value" or "actual market value" whenever used in this act or in any law relating to the appraisement of imported merchandise shall be construed to mean the actual market value or wholesale price as defined in this section.

SEC. 20. Any merchandise deposited in any public or private bonded warehouse may be withdrawn for consumption within three years from the date of original importation, on payment of the duties and charges to which it may be subject by law at the time of such withdrawal: *Provided*, That nothing herein shall affect or impair existing provisions of law in regard to the disposal of perishable or explosive articles.

SEC. 21. That in all suits or informations brought, where any seizure has been made pursuant to any act providing for or regulating the collection of duties on imports or tonnage, if the property is claimed by any person, the burden of proof shall lie upon such claimant: *Provided*, That probable cause is shown for such prosecution, to be judged of by the court.

SEC. 22. That all fees exacted and oaths administered by officers of the customs, except as provided in this act, under or by virtue of existing laws of the United States, upon the entry of imported goods and the passing thereof through the customs, and also upon all entries of domestic goods, wares, and merchandise for exportation, be, and the same are hereby, abolished; and in case of entry of merchandise for exportation, a declaration, in lieu of an oath, shall be filed, in such form and under such regulations as may be prescibed by the Secretary of the Treasury; and the penalties provided in the sixth section of this act for false statements in such declaration shall be applicable to declaratious made under this section: *Provided*, That where such fees, under existing laws, constitute, in whole or in part, the compensation of any officer, such officer shall receive, from and after the passage of this act, a fixed sum for each year equal to the amount which he would have been entitled to receive as fees for such services during said year.

SEC. 23. That no allowance for damage to goods, wares, and merchandise imported into the United States shall hereafter be made in the estimation and liquidation of duties thereon; but the importer thereof may, within ten days after entry, abandon to the United States all or any portion of goods, wares, and merchandise included in any invoice, and be relieved from the payment of the duties on the portion so abandoned: *Provided*, That the portion so abandoned shall amount to ten per centum or over of the total value or quantity of the invoice; and the property so abandoned shall be sold by public auction or otherwise disposed of for the account and credit of the United States under such regulations as the Secretary of the Treasury may prescribe.

SEC. 24. That whenever it shall be shown to the satisfaction of the Secretary of the Treasury that, in any case of unascertained or estimated duties, or payments made upon appeal, more money has been paid to or deposited with a collector of customs than, as has been ascertained by final liquidation thereof, the law required to be paid or deposited, the Secretary of the Treasury shall direct the Treasurer to refund and pay the same out of any money in the Treasury not otherwise appropriated. The necessary moneys therefor are hereby appropriated, and this appropriation shall be deemed a permanent indefinite appropriation; and the Secretary of the Treasury is hereby authorized to correct manifest clerical errors in any entry or liquidation, for or against the United States, at any time within one year of the date of such entry, but not afterwards: *Provided*, That the Secretary of the Treasury shall in his annual report to Congress, give a detailed statement of the various sums of money refunded under the provisions of this act or of any other act of Congress relating to the revenue, together with copies of the rulings under which repayments were made.

Sec. 25. That from and after the taking effect of this act no collector or other officer of the customs shall be in any way liable to any owner, importer, consignee, or agent of any merchandise, or any other person, for or on account of any rulings or decisions as to the classification of said merchandise or the duties charged thereon, or the collection of any dues, charges, or duties on or on account of said merchandise, or any other matter or thing as to which said owner, importer, consignee, or agent of such merchandise might, under this act, be entitled to appeal from the decision of said collector or other officer, or from any board of appraisers provided for in this act.

Sec. 26. That any person who shall give, or offer to give or promise to give any money or thing of value, directly or indirectly, to any officer or employee of the United States in consideration of or for any act or omission contrary to law in connection with or pertaining to the importation, appraisement, entry, examination, or inspection of goods, wares, or merchandise including herein any baggage, or of the liquidation of the entry thereof, or shall by threats or demands, or promises of any character attempt to improperly influence or control any such officer or employee of the United States as to the performance of his official duties shall, on conviction thereof, be fined not exceeding two thousand dollars, or be imprisoned at hard labor not more than one year, or both, in the discretion of the court; and evidence of such giving, or offering, or promising to give, satisfactory to the court in which such trial is had, shall be regarded as prima facie evidence that such giving or offering or promising was contrary to law, and shall put upon the accused the burden of proving that such act was innocent, and not done with an unlawful intention.

Sec. 27. That any officer or employee of the United States who shall, excepting for lawful duties or fees, solicit, demand, exact or receive from any person, directly or indirectly, any money or thing of value, in connection with or pertaining to the importation, appraisement, entry, examination, or inspection of goods, wares, or merchandise, including herein any baggage, or liquidation of the entry thereof, on conviction thereof, shall be fined not exceeding five thousand dollars, or be imprisoned at hard labor not more than two years, or both, in the discretion of the court. And evidence of such soliciting, demanding, exacting, or receiving, satisfactory to the court in which such trial is had, shall be regarded as prima facie evidence that such soliciting, demanding, exacting, or receiving was contrary to law, and shall put upon the accused the burden of proving that such act was innocent and not with an unlawful intention.

Sec. 28. That any baggage or personal effects arriving in the United States in transit to any foreign country may be delivered by the parties having it in charge to the collector of the proper district, to be by him retained, without the payment or exaction of any import duty, or to be forwarded by such collector to the collector of the port of departure and to be delivered to such parties on their departure for their foreign destination, under such rules and regulations as the Secretary of the Treasury may prescribe.

SEC. 29. That sections twenty-six hundred and eight, twenty-eight hundred and thirty-eight, twenty-eight hundred and thirty-nine, twenty-eight hundred and forty-one, twenty-eight hundred and forty-three, twenty-eight hundred and forty-five, twenty-eight hundred and fifty-three, twenty-eight hundred and fifty-four, twenty-eight hundred and fifty-six, twenty-eight hundred and fifty-eight, twenty-eight hundred and sixty, twenty-nine hundred, and twenty-nine hundred and two, twenty-nine hundred and five, twenty-nine hundred and seven, twenty-nine hundred and eight, twenty-nine hundred and nine, twenty-nine hundred and twenty-two, twenty-nine hundred and twenty-three, twenty-nine hundred and twenty-four, twenty-nine hundred and twenty-seven, twenty-nine hundred and twenty-nine, twenty-nine hundred and thirty, twenty-nine hundred and thirty-one, twenty-nine hundred and thirty-two, twenty-nine hundred and forty-three, twenty-nine hundred and forty-five, twenty-nine hundred and fifty-two, three thousand and eleven, three thousand and twelve, three thousand and twelve and one half, three thousand and thirteen, of the Revised Statutes of the United States, be, and the same are hereby, repealed, and sections nine, ten, eleven, twelve, fourteen, and sixteen of an act entitled "An act to amend the customs-revenue laws and to repeal moieties," approved June twenty-second, eighteen hundred and seventy-four, and sections seven, eight, and nine of the act entitled "An act to reduce internal-revenue taxation, and for other purposes," approved March third, eighteen hundred and eighty-three, and all other acts and parts of acts inconsistent with the provisions of this act, are hereby repealed, but the repeal of existing laws or modifications thereof embraced in this act shall not affect any act done, or any right accruing or accrued, or any suit or proceeding had or commenced in any civil cause before the said repeal or modifications; but all rights and liabilities under said laws shall continue and may be enforced in the same manner as if said repeal or modifications had not been made. Any offenses committed, and all penalties or forfeitures or liabilities incurred prior to the passage of this act under any statute embraced in or changed, modified, or repealed by this act may be prosecuted and punished in the same manner and with the same effect as if this act had not been passed. All acts of limitation, whether applicable to civil causes and proceedings or to the prosecution of offenses or for the recovery of penalties or forfeitures embraced in or modified, changed, or repealed by this act, shall not be affected thereby; and all suits, proceedings, or prosecutions, whether civil or criminal, for causes arising or acts done or committed prior to the passage of this act, may be commenced and prosecuted within the same time and with the same effect as if this act had not been passed. *And provided further*, That nothing in this act shall be construed to repeal the provisions of section three thousand and fifty-eight of the Revised Statutes as amended by the act approved February twenty-third, eighteen hundred and eighty-seven, in respect to the abandonment of merchandise to underwriters or the salvors of property, and the ascertainment of duties thereon.

SEC. 30. That this act shall take effect on the first day of August, eighteen hundred and ninety, except so much of section twelve as provides for the appointment of nine general appraisers, which shall take effect immediately.

Approved, June 10, 1890.

INDEX TO ACT OF JUNE 10, 1890.

237

Section.

O